THE FORTRESS

Center Point
Large Print

**This Large Print Book carries the
Seal of Approval of N.A.V.H.**

THE
FORTRESS

a love story

Danielle Trussoni

CENTER POINT LARGE PRINT
THORNDIKE, MAINE

This Center Point Large Print edition
is published in the year 2017 by arrangement with
Dey Street Books, an imprint of HarperCollins Publishers.

The text of this Large Print edition is unabridged.
In other aspects, this book may vary
from the original edition.
Printed in the United States of America
on permanent paper.
Set in 16-point Times New Roman type.

ISBN: 978-1-68324-266-6

Library of Congress Cataloging-in-Publication Data

Names: Trussoni, Danielle, author.
Title: The fortress : a love story / Danielle Trussoni.
Description: Large print edition. | Thorndike, Maine : Center Point Large
Print, 2016.
Identifiers: LCCN 2016049384 | ISBN 9781683242666
   (hardcover : alk. paper)
Subjects: LCSH: Trussoni, Danielle. | Authors, American—21st
century—Biography. | Large type books.
Classification: LCC PS3620.R93 Z46 2016 | DDC 813/.6 [B] —dc23
LC record available at https://lccn.loc.gov/2016049384

FOR ALEX AND NICO.

May all your castles rise from solid earth.

This is a true story. I have used the real names of major characters, and have changed the names of everyone else. My memory doesn't always follow a strictly linear timeline, and neither does this book. The dialogue and text messages have been reconstructed from memory. While I have confirmed the details of events with many of the people who experienced them with me, this is my story, and reflects my feelings and memories.

If you have built castles in the air, your work need not be lost; that is where they should be. Now put the foundations under them.

—HENRY DAVID THOREAU, *WALDEN*

Prologue

Tu aimerais danser? Would you like to dance? *Bien sûr*, the Frenchman says, and within seconds I'm making my way onto the dance floor with a scorching-hot monsieur. We push into the crush of people, pressing closer and closer under the blue and red lights. I step back, and he steps forward; I turn and find his hand ready to catch me. We've only just met, but we are dancing together, effortlessly, as if we've choreographed it all in advance. The music is pounding, and we are inside it, elevated by the crowd, by the rush of blood to the heart, by the sound pulsing around us. As we dance, he touches my arm, and my whole body goes electric. For the first time in forever, I want to reach out and hold someone, and that man is right here, inches from me, ready to pull me into his arms. I know I shouldn't be doing this. I am tempting fate, calling to the unknown, welcoming danger, courting it. Yet I move a little closer and then a little closer, until I am right there, in his arms. I can no longer tell the difference between walking to the edge of a cliff and jumping off. I just close my eyes and go for it.

When I open them, my husband is staring at us from the bar, his arms crossed over his chest, drill-sergeant style. A shiver of apprehension ripples through me. He doesn't like this dancing-with-a-Frenchman thing one bit.

"What's the matter?" the monsieur asks, leaning close to my ear.

"My husband," I reply.

He glances over toward the bar. "Do you need to go?"

"Probably," I say. "But I'd rather stay."

"Then you will just have to come back to Paris," he whispers, pressing his lips to my ear. "Without your husband."

Before I can respond, my husband is at my side. He grabs my arm and pulls me away from the Frenchman.

"What in the hell are you doing?"

"I'm dancing."

"We're leaving."

"I don't want to leave."

And I know, as soon as I say these words, that I mean them in every sense: I don't want to leave the club with my husband; I don't want to go back home with my husband; I don't want to spend the rest of my life struggling to believe a failed fairy tale. It is only now, at this moment, in this club with this man, that I know for sure that there is no going back. My life is about to change.

"Come on," my husband says, and turns away. I look back to the Frenchman, left standing on the dance floor, and wave. He smiles and lifts a finger into the air, as if checking the direction of the wind. I want to believe that this small gesture, this sign given in haste as I'm being hauled out of there, signals a turning point in my life. An ending. And a new beginning.

Enchantment

Before the club in Paris, and before the Frenchman, I was a woman in a fortress.

Or, more precisely, I lived with my husband and two children in La Commanderie, a medieval fortification at the center of the French village of Aubais, pronounced "obey," as in "love, honor and . . . Aubais." Built by the Knights Templar in the thirteenth century, the fortress stood high on a hilltop and could withstand attack from every angle. There were arrow slits in the walls and a perch from which to spy the enemy coming. The foundation was sunk deep into the rock of the village, rock that millions of years before had formed the Mediterranean seabed. Occasionally, when I examined the rock, I would find imprints of fossilized shells, ancient swirls of disintegrated calcium that created the bedrock of the entire region. The fortress rose from this long-gone sea like a stone Leviathan, strong and unsinkable. It was a defensive place, a place of barriers, one meant to resist catapults and battering rams. A place in which we could shut everything out, even the truth.

An ancient granite wall surrounded the fortress. Outside the wall the sun scorched the streets to a sizzle. Inside, a deep shadow fell over a courtyard, where my family ate lunch at a weathered wooden table. I picture us now, as we were then: My two children, Alex and Nico, our pug Fly Me to the Moon (Fly for short), and our three cats: Napoleon, Josephine, and ChouChou. I see me, a thirty-six-year-old woman in an oversize sundress and sunglasses, walking barefoot over hot flagstones, slipping between slats of sun and shade as I make my way past the cats, to my husband, Nikolai. Tall and dark and handsome, he wears a black top hat perched on his head. He bought the top hat in a junk store and wore it as a joke, but the joke became a habit and the habit an eccentricity, and so the hat stayed, giving him the air of a dark magician, one who could—with a flick of his wrist—coax a dove from the depths of nothingness.

Under our feet, deep below the hot flagstones, was a treasure-filled tunnel, or so we liked to imagine. According to legend, the Knights Templar had constructed a system of tunnels between La Commanderie and the fortified city of Aigues-Mortes, where St. Louis launched the Crusades. These passages allowed the Knights to move in stealth to defend the king, to hide valuables, and to transport goods for their voyages to the Holy Land, but anyone looking at a map would have serious doubts that such a tunnel actually existed. The swampy port of Aigues-Mortes is more than ten miles from Aubais, the terrain rocky. Even so, I liked to believe that there was some truth to the story and that deep below the fortress, carved into the compacted limestone, was a hidden space, a tunnel guarding Templar treasure.

La Commanderie was eight hundred years old and had many owners after the Knights Templar. One built an olive press on the property. Another created an Italianate courtyard with flagstones and a window-lined salon to border it. One used the garden as an arena for bullfights—or *les courses camarguaises*, as they say in the Languedoc—and I liked to imagine the matador and the bull moving around each other in the courtyard, attacking and hiding, one beast pursuing the other. When the Nazis requisitioned the property in the forties, they used it as the center of their operations in the region, a legacy that older villagers remembered. The fortress had seen olive oil and bullshit and swastikas. And then we arrived.

We hadn't been in the market for a dark, drafty, thirteenth-century fortress, but we walked through the door, took one look, and knew that La Commanderie had been waiting for us. The realities of buying and living in a historic compound in a tiny village in a foreign country didn't strike us as daunting. The fact that we were thousands of miles away from family and friends didn't dissuade us. The problems with the house itself—the oil-sucking monstrosity of a heater, the leaky roof, the mold-infested bathroom, the broken sewage pipe—seemed manageable. It was precisely the scale of the fortress—so outsize, so unrealistic—that made it ours.

The day we moved in, we pushed open the gate together. Over ten feet tall, the blue ironwork speckled with rust, it was so heavy that it took the two of us with our combined weight to move it. It swung open, creaking on old hinges, and suddenly we were not a couple on the verge of divorce. We were the owners of La Commanderie, a structure more powerful than us, a place so solid that it would—*it must*—be strong enough to save us. I remember looking at the thick walls of the fortress, at Alex and Nico in the courtyard, and thinking, *This is it. This is where we will finally be happy.*

The first time I saw Aubais was from behind a dusty windshield. Our car climbed a narrow, winding road, twisting and turning, and then suddenly it appeared: a medieval stronghold lifting into a perfect blue sky. One of my guidebooks claimed that the sun shone an average of three hundred days per year in the Midi, and it seemed to me then that this luxurious abundance of light had melted the edges of the village clear away—they declined softly from the center, leaving only the village château, its windows shuttered, at the top. Village houses crowded the streets below the château, yellowed and uneven as teeth in an ancient mouth. And at the very bottom of the hill roamed a herd of bulls, their horns long and sharp as daggers.

We found the village by looking online. I'd typed the words "South of France rentals" into a search engine and clicked on links, Web sites, and message boards. Also punched into the search engine were the words "beaches, mountains, vineyards, paradise." I'd strung these words together in a more or less random sequence, composing a surreal love poem to my fantasy home, and then thrown them out into the digital universe, asking the powers-that-be to send something special back. They sent me the village of Aubais.

As the car climbed up into the village center, I looked down at the surrounding countryside. Knotty black stumps of Syrah vines grew below, clipped back after the previous harvest. Now it was spring, and their leaves were beginning to sprout and twist, each new tendril spiraling up, seeking sun. A stream wrapped around the village, feeding water to a *laverie*, where villagers had once washed their clothes by hand. There was a *boulangerie* with fresh bread in the window, a *tabac* selling newspapers and cigarettes, and an *épicerie* filled with vegetables and spices. And through it all there floated a pervasive, almost eerie, sense of calm. When I rolled down the car window, I heard nothing but the hum of the engine. No sirens or screeching tires or garbage trucks or train clatter. Nothing. I grew up in rural Wisconsin, where the only sound (aside from the shouts of my sister and brother and me) was nature: birds singing in the trees, crickets chirping in the bushes, insects buzzing, bullfrogs croaking. I felt that I was home again.

As we parked, my eyes adjusted to take it all in: the angular sweep of clay roof tiles, the blue wooden shutters, the flinty peak of the church steeple. The village château was run-down, and while the romantic in me (which was about 90 percent of me at that juncture) liked to imagine a king and queen sitting on ramshackle thrones, in reality the building had been cut up into apartments owned by summer people. One day I would gaze through a window at the top of the château and see clear to the Mediterranean. In this vista there were white Camargue horses and, beyond this, the jagged rise of Pic Saint-Loup, craggy wine country known for its strong, delicious reds. *Garrigues* fields filled with lavender and rosemary and olive trees spread for as far as I could see. Beyond this, far from sight, were the remnants of Roman roads, limestone conduits grooved by the weight of ancient wheels that had once carried wine and soldiers to and from Rome. Two thousand years later, the tracks were overgrown with honeysuckle, blackberry bushes, buttercups. Olives, grapes, and flowers— such things thrived outside the village.

But in the village itself, all greenery died. The fields and streams were replaced by cool, lifeless limestone. A labyrinth of ancient passageways cut through the village—rue du Roc, rue Droite, rue de la Commanderie—forming a series of transits past the old marketplace, the statue honoring the dead of the First World War, a stone bridge overlooking the bulls. There were both a Catholic church and a Protestant church, and it was said that the village tolerated both religions, although Huguenots had not been allowed to bury their dead in the cemetery. Instead families dug into their cellars and gardens, leaving corpses in unblessed ground, causing all variety of ghosts and unquiet spirits to move through the old houses, through the winding streets, through the branches of the olive trees. We were a little like those ghosts: displaced outsiders searching for sacred ground.

For the first time in our marriage, we had the luxury to try. I'd just had a big professional success: My first novel was bought by a publisher in New York; then the movie rights sold. Offers for my second novel—which I hadn't even begun to write yet—were pouring in. At thirty-five years old, I had found success doing something I loved and, for the first time in my life, I wouldn't have to struggle to pay my bills. And yet when success arrived, it cracked the atmosphere of my life like a sonic boom, knocking me off balance. I didn't understand how to react. Struggle I understood. Scraping by, I knew what that felt like. But successful? That was a whole new game for a girl who had worked her way through college and was still paying off student loans. It's hard to imagine that the very thing I'd dreamed of could be so strange, so unmooring, but it was. I was wary of this success. I was fearful of it. I was worried that the same magic that had created good fortune would take it all away again. And then there was my marriage. Nikolai and I had been married eight years when we moved to France, and I doubted we would make nine. I blamed our rift on the endless hours we'd been working, the strain of being parents, and the lack of money. I blamed it on the fact that we hadn't taken time out for us and for our marriage. And so I proposed to use our windfall to move far away from every-thing—far from successes and troubles—to a beautiful, unreal place where we could protect our fragile love.

In the beginning there was nothing fragile about us. We met at a potluck in the fall of 2001, when I was a fiction-writing student at the Iowa Writers' Workshop. Nikolai was part of the International Writing Program at the University of Iowa, a three-month stint that had brought him to the United States from his native Sofia, Bulgaria.

"Let me help with that," he said, taking a platter of maki sushi from my hands so I could pick up Alex, my one-year-old son, who was tugging on my jeans. I swung Alex up onto my hip, balancing him as I set out wasabi and soy sauce with my free hand.

"You rolled these yourself?" Nikolai asked, impressed.

"I lived in Japan for three years," I said, giving Alex a piece of cucumber maki to chew on. "Sushi is easier than sandwiches."

"Japan?" he said. He had a soft accent and a way of speaking that was both definitive and careful. His hair was black and clipped short, his eyes large and green, his lips full and his skin olive. He was looking at me inquisitively, carefully, as if I were some exotic butterfly blown down from the sky. "Why Japan?"

I met his gaze and smiled. "Why *not* Japan?"

That was who I was then, a young woman ready to go anywhere and do anything, so long as it was new and exciting and far from home. I was trying life out, seeing what felt right, and my relationships with men weren't much different.

We met again at a party at my place a few weeks later. We stood at the stereo and chose music together—a mix of the Smiths and Depeche Mode and the Cure and Joy Division, bands we'd both listened to obsessively in high school. Over the course of the night, we talked and talked, telling stories about our lives, all the things we'd done before we knew each other.

I was a twenty-seven-year-old aspiring writer, mother of Alex, and maker of maki sushi. My parents had divorced when I was twelve, and I'd moved between my mother and father until I was eighteen. My grades were bad in high school, but I took classes at a local college to make up for it and was eventually accepted at the University of Wisconsin at Madison. I double-majored in history and literature and graduated summa cum laude and Phi Beta Kappa. After graduation I started traveling. I studied in London, spent time in France, and lived for nearly three years in Japan with my first husband, Sam, a man I'd met at a bar at age twenty-three and married before I knew what hit me. Alex was born in Japan, and I was accepted to Iowa's M.F.A. program the same month. Now, as the program was coming to an end, I found myself adrift, waiting for the next big thing to happen.

Nikolai grew up in Communist Sofia, where his childhood had been marked by food shortages and relatives in concentration camps. His parents encouraged him to play the piano as a means of escape, believing that a musician could travel beyond the Iron Curtain to perform all over the world, and so he played twelve hours a day from the age of five. Because he was talented and persistent, he won his first international competition at age nine. At eighteen, he left his music conservatory and moved to the United States, where he studied jazz composition. Three years later he packed his things and moved to India, where he became a Buddhist monk, studying at the Dalai Lama's Institute for Buddhist Dialectics in Dharamsala. After leaving the monkhood, he went back to Bulgaria, where he married, had a daughter, and wrote books about India. Now, at twenty-eight, he had left his wife and was listening to eighties New Wave bands in Iowa City with me.

I realized as we talked that we had a lot in common. Both of us had had unfulfilling first marriages. Both of us had one-year-old children we adored. We'd both lived in Asia—he in India, I in Japan. We both were interested in Buddhism, although his interest was far more serious than mine. And, of course, we were both writers, although he was more successful, having published two bestselling novels in Bulgaria. We were both extraordinary and wrecked, naïve and experienced, brilliant and stupid, our exceptional parts snapping together as seamlessly as the damaged ones.

When he put on the Cure's "Disintegration," I said, "I love this song. Although no one's going to dance. Too dark. Too slow."

"Come on, writers don't dance," he said, glancing at the apartment full of writing students. He was right—no one was dancing, not even a foot tap or a hip wiggle.

"I do," I said. "I love to dance."

"Really?"

"Of course," I said. "Don't you?"

He smiled a mysterious smile. *Maybe yes, maybe no.* "I'd rather play music than dance to it."

"Then you play and I'll dance."

"Deal," he said, sorting through the music and playing Depeche Mode's "Just Can't Get Enough."

But I didn't dance. I stayed by his side all night, unable to step away. There was something hypnotic about him, and I found myself gazing at him, transfixed. A scar jagged across his chin, a slash that appeared—in the dim light—to be an uneven cleft. I ran my finger over it, feeling the smoothness of the damaged skin. Later he would say that I'd chosen his weakest spot to touch him for the first time. But it wasn't weakness that I saw then. I saw a man with an aura of invincibility about him, a confidence in the way he spoke about seemingly impossible things, as if nothing could stand in his way. I saw a man who could help me leave behind the burden of an unhappy childhood, a weight I carried everywhere—into every room I walked and into every relationship I began.

He saw the same possibility in me. When we ran

into each other at the university library some days later, he told me that the day we'd met was the most important day of his life. "I will measure everything from that point in time," he said. "From the time before I met you and the time after. I loved you from the first second I saw you."

If I had been another woman, I might have been skeptical. He was visiting the United States for a short time and getting divorced, and so it was only natural that he would want to have a fling before going back home. But I wasn't another woman. I was a woman ready to be swept away. I was a woman ready for her story to begin. For me, as a writer, story was all that mattered. Rising action, dramatic complication, heroes and villains and dark plots. I believed I was the author of my life, that I controlled the narrative. But deep down I must have known it wasn't possible. Deep down I must have understood that my story had already been written.

Once upon a time, a woman met a sorcerer in the woods. High on horseback, he promised to take her far away, to a castle in the distance. Grasping his hand, she climbed onto his horse, and they rode into the tangled forest. She could feel her past fade as they went: the voice of her father, the face of her mother, the comfort of her friends. Her old life became as distant and diaphanous as a dream. Finally they arrived in a

26

strange land where the trees were pillars of salt and the seas were black as oil. A castle stood high on a hill. The castle, he said, had magic rooms, each one filled with treasure. Go, he said. It's my gift to you. But when she opened a door, dust clouded her sight. The rooms were dark and the magic thick. And yet she didn't turn back. She walked into the castle, opening the doors to every room, searching. Soon she had wandered too far to retrace her steps. When she opened a window, the real world glimmered on the horizon like a mirage.

"I've been looking for you my whole life," he said.

"You shouldn't say such pretty things if you don't mean them." I wanted him to know I was susceptible to fairy tales, that I was vulnerable to poetry and promises.

He picked up my hand and kissed it. "Everything is going to be okay now. I've found you. It's karma. It isn't even our choice. We've been waiting many lifetimes for this chance. We can't lose it."

If I'd had any resistance, it vanished at that moment. He squeezed my hand and led me through the library, past the endless stacks until we found a dark and deserted corner in the European history section. There were books about Catherine the Great, the Hapsburgs, the Napoleonic Wars, all the stories of treacherous kings and powerful queens I loved. I couldn't have known at the time that there, among the romances of history, my own story was beginning.

Nikolai pulled me close. He was six feet tall, broad-shouldered, strong-armed, smelling of expensive cologne. I held him tight, as if eliminating the space between us would create a singular being. Like two unstable atoms flung from opposite ends of the universe, we collided to form a new, whole, white-hot structure: us.

The Magician

I wasn't used to men like Nikolai, charming magicians who promised to make the impossible come true. When he came into my life, I was awestruck. I was spellbound. There are a hundred clichés I could conjure—entranced, hypnotized—and all of them applied to me. Nothing in my childhood, or all the years since I'd left home, had prepared me. There just weren't men like him in the Midwest, guys who spoke a handful of languages and could rip off a Chopin sonata and read sutras in Tibetan. He was so far out of my circle of reference, so foreign, so exotic, that I was utterly blinded.

But as with every romantic hero, there was a weak spot below the armor. As a child, Nikolai trained to play in the International Chopin Piano Competition in Poland. I'd never heard of the competition until I met him, but for young pianists this was the Wimbledon of contests, the most prestigious and famous forum for new musical talent. Contestants from all over the world applied to the Chopin Competition. Just qualifying to participate could make a musician's career. After winning in Italy at age nine, Nikolai had been considered a strong candidate, and he had trained relentlessly for years, memorizing Chopin sonatas and etudes, reading Chopin's letters, trying to find a way into the mind and music of his hero.

A date was announced for this preliminary competition, and Nikolai practiced night and day. When the audition came, he played his étude perfectly, and everyone in the audience—including teachers at the conservatory and other renowned musicians—declared that he'd been brilliant. After his performance he was surrounded by members of the audience and congratulated. The judges announced that he'd won and would be going to Poland. But then, in some dark twist that can happen only in a nightmare, the decision was overturned by a Communist official, the father of a girl who'd competed against Nikolai. He had given his entire childhood for this opportunity, and it went to a girl with less talent but better connections.

I once saw a videotape of Nikolai playing at the preliminary competition, the younger, awkward, and adorable teenage version of the man I loved, playing his heart out. In the video there was something hopeful and confident about him, something unspoiled. It was like watching a pristine forest minutes before a fire. Later I came to see this competition as a deep wound in his psyche, the underlying tragedy of his childhood from which he would never fully recover. After he was eliminated from the Chopin Competition, he was always looking for applause. In me he found someone who clapped until her hands bled.

Like so much else, our weaknesses were cut from the same cloth. While he needed applause, I needed someone to adore, a man to put on a pedestal, an artist to lift up and support. The men of my past were exactly this type: undiscovered geniuses I would take in. It began simply and with small gestures—making a man dinner or doing his laundry—and soon become larger acts of support, such as paying his rent or lending him money. Before long the boyfriend would be living with me and I would be covering his phone bill or his car payment. It happened through college and after college, but I was so unconscious of my actions, so wrapped up in feeling whatever I felt, that I didn't see a pattern. I couldn't have explained it then, but for me love meant proving myself—emotionally and financially—and laying these proofs of love at the feet of my beloved.

I remember once, when I was about thirteen, having dinner with my father in his small kitchen on the north side of La Crosse. He was railing about some woman who had hurt him—my mom or his first wife or an ex-girlfriend—going on and on about the parasitic, money-grabbing qualities of all womankind, the ones who took his cash and left him with nothing but kids to feed, when he turned to me, his eyes intense as those in a self-portrait by van Gogh, and said, "Don't you ever be like that, Danielle."

I can't say that this moment caused my inability to accept love with an open heart, but it remained with me, an apparition at the back of my mind, that I should never become a woman "like that."

Nikolai didn't have a piano, so I drove him to a music shop at the edge of Iowa City, where a polished black baby grand sat at the back of the showroom. He would sit, hit a few keys to warm up, and then launch into the piece, his fingers flying over the keyboard, his head held high, his patrician profile stiff and poised. It was Chopin's Prelude in B-flat minor, op. 28, no. 16, a racy, beautiful song, and he played the entire thing from memory, as if it had been burned into him by years of practice. I leaned against the piano, my reflection pale and watery in the black lacquer, awestruck by the beauty of his artistry, the complicated fingering, the speed and timing and confidence. That he could create such an explosion of beauty, something that took over my senses so completely, left me mesmerized.

I wasn't the only one. Eventually someone in the shop walked over, and then another person stopped by, then another, and soon there was a crowd around the piano, listening to Nikolai play. He was giving these people pleasure, something sublime in an ordinary day, and I was part of that gift. The last flourish of the prelude was punctuated by clapping, and Nikolai—so obviously used to applause—glowed with pleasure. He was the center of attention, the star performer taking a bow. He was the bright, hot center of the universe. I wanted to be near his light, to feel the warmth of him on my skin. I wanted to orbit him forever.

Our first months together coincided with a harsh midwestern winter, and so we spent most of our evenings inside by the fireplace. We would stack CDs by the stereo and play them one by one, filling the apartment with the sound of Thelonious Monk, Miles Davis, Bill Evans. Alex would play with his Thomas the Tank Engine train set, a huge, twisting wooden track that occupied the center of the living room, while Nikolai cooked something complicated from Bulgaria, stuffed peppers or roasted lamb or *musaka*. I would sip hot tea and watch my son, marveling at his beauty and strength. At two years old, Alex was a curly-haired blond dynamo of pure muscle and speed, who could jump up and run from one end of the playground to the other before I had a chance to get off the park bench. He was a fearless toddler, strong and fierce. When he'd run head-on into a pole and cut his eyebrow open, *I* was in tears, not Alex. Nikolai had held him as we drove to the ER, making funny faces to distract him from the pain. But Alex wasn't worried. Once on the surgery table, he fixed me with his huge brown eyes, as if to say, *Hey, calm down up there and let me get this over with.* Alex was exceptionally verbal for his age and spoke in full sentences at eight months. I'll never forget the eerie experi-ence of hearing a baby of less than a year say, "I would like more peas, Mama, please," as if he were ordering tea at the Ritz.

Every morning I drove Alex to day care at the Sprout House, a section of Alice's Rainbow Child Care Center in Iowa City. I helped him out of his snowsuit, kissed his cold red cheeks, and left him with the other two-year-olds to play with blocks or Play-Doh. Back home I would go to the desk in my bedroom and write, while Nikolai stationed himself in the living room, at the low coffee table, where he sat cross-legged on the floor as he finished his third novel, scheduled to be pub-lished in Bulgaria the following year. We spent the day working, meeting intermittently for lunch or coffee, and then, around four o'clock, I would pick up Alex, do the shopping, and our nightly ritual of Thomas the Tank Engine and complicated Bulgarian dinner would ensue.

It was a fairly mundane routine, but with Nikolai a part of it I felt that this was the way my life was meant to be lived. It was as if I'd been missing some essential nutrient for twenty-seven years and he made me healthy again.

Being with Nikolai felt essential, vital. It was like drinking water when you're dying of thirst, or getting a fix when you're addicted, or like looking into the eyes of your firstborn child and understanding, suddenly, the meaning of life. If you haven't experienced the wondrous surprise of it before, the simple joy of it, it might be hard to imagine. In fact, it had been hard for *me* to imagine until I met Nikolai. Some part of me felt that Nikolai was too good to be true. I would open my eyes and the dream would disappear.

And then one day that's exactly what happened. There was a problem with his visa status, and Nikolai would have to leave the country. He'd come to the International Writing Program on a J-1 visa as a guest of the State Department. Part of the fine print of the J-1, he told me, was that he needed to leave the United States before his visa expired—in his case six months—and return to his home country. He'd been in the United States for seven months, which was a violation of the visa, making him ineligible to renew it from within this country. He needed to either go home or face whatever penalties the newly created Department of Homeland Security had in store.

His anxiety about his visa was exacerbated by the fact that he had left his infant daughter, Rada, in Sofia with his soon-to-be ex-wife. His parents had hired a lawyer there in his absence, and they were giving Nikolai regular updates of the divorce proceedings by e-mail and Skype. Nikolai didn't like to talk about his relationship with his first wife, and when he did, he had nothing good to say about her. She'd been a model in Sofia, and he ridiculed her for what he perceived as super-ficiality and lack of intelligence. When I asked him why he'd married someone he so clearly despised, his answer was that he'd felt trapped: She became pregnant with their daughter and insisted he marry her. "There's no use in talking about her," he would say, and he uttered her full name just one time in my presence. For the remainder of our years together, he referred to her only by the first letter of her name: Z.

"I'm so happy here with you," he said, snuggling his nose into my neck one night as we lay in bed. We'd just made love and were lying under the covers talking, our limbs wrapped in the tangle of sheets. "I don't think I've ever imagined that someone like you could exist. You're perfect for me. You're not pretending to be someone you aren't. You're just yourself. You just love me."

It was true: I just loved him. I loved everything about him, from the way he cooked to the funny way he tapped his feet in his sleep to his habit of quoting Buddhist texts at strange moments to his fear of airplanes to his hypochondria to his adorable habit of looking in the mirror fifty times a day, as if to make sure he still existed. I loved his beautiful green-hazel eyes and his full lips and his long fingers. I loved his creativity, how he woke up every morning and went to his computer to write, how there was always another idea, another project, more and more and more to come. I loved his faith in me. Even though I had not published a thing, he believed that one day my writing would be widely read. He compared me to great writers, feeding my insecure soul. I loved that he promised to be good to Alex and to take care of him as if he were his own son. But most of all I loved that he made everything seem possible. With Nikolai the future was bigger and more exciting than I could ever have imagined.

"Promise me something," he said one morning over coffee.

"Anything," I said, meeting his eyes.

"Tell me you'll never leave me."

The problem with his visa had unsettled him. He was worried about being separated from me.

"I won't leave you," I said. "I won't leave. I'm here."

"I can't make it through this lifetime if you're not at my side. I've lost you before. I can feel it. We were separated from each other in a different life, and this is our chance to make up for it. This is our lifetime together. We can't waste it. Promise me."

"I promise," I said, wishing I could promise him more than one lifetime. I would give him five. I would give him a hundred. "I won't ever leave you."

After doing some reading on the U.S. Immigration and Naturalization Services Web site, Nikolai had decided that his best move would be to go back to Bulgaria, where he could change his visa status more easily. It was a simple bureaucratic matter, he said, one that could be quickly fixed in Sofia. But, he insisted, he wasn't leaving the United States without me, and I wasn't finished with my M.F.A. program until May.

"I'll stay here," he said. "I'd rather be illegal than to lose you."

"I don't want you to get in trouble."

"Why don't you come with me for the summer?" he said. "We'll go when your program is done. The weather will be perfect then, and we can go to the Black Sea. We could use a vacation. There are almost no tourists then."

"What about money?" I asked, feeling hesitant to bring it up. Nikolai was terrible with money. The International Writers Program had given him a stipend, but he'd spent nearly all of it on a laptop computer within a week of arriving. Until he met me, he, like many of the visiting writers, had survived mostly on free cocktails and hors d'oeuvres at literary events, potluck dinners, and the cookies left in the lobby of his hotel. Then he moved into my apartment, and I bought our food and whatever else he needed.

"They're holding my teaching job at Sofia University," he said. "I can start again as soon as I'm back."

"But what about all this?" I asked, gesturing to my things: my desk and my books and Alex's toys.

"Put it in storage for a few months," he said. "And pack Alex's toys. We'll replace what you can't fit in your suitcase. There are a thousand toy stores in Sofia. And playgrounds. And a zoo. And Rada can come over to play with Alex. He'll learn some Bulgarian. It will be good for you to spend more time with him for a few months."

It didn't take me long to decide. During the past years, I'd been so busy getting my master's degree that I hadn't had the option of spending whole weeks of uninterrupted time with Alex. If we went to Bulgaria, I would have an abundance of time and energy to lavish on my son, a luxury I hadn't imagined possible before. Equally important, I was with a man who had promised to raise Alex like his own child, who told me that it was time for me to stop worrying and live a little.

"Trust me," he said. "I'll take care of you."

I had never heard these words and believed them until now. And so I packed up everything I owned in the world, put it all in storage, and gave notice on my apartment. I bought plane tickets and prepared to follow my Prince Charming to the other side of the world.

Before we left, he would lie awake at night staring into space.

"You don't know how difficult this is for me," he once said. "I hate Bulgaria. I was a prisoner in my country until I was eighteen years old. It was like a gulag."

"A prisoner?" I echoed, propping myself up on my elbow. "A gulag?" His intensity—so dramatic and extreme and romantic—got my attention.

"No one could go in or out of Bulgaria during Communism. When I was nine, I was selected to play in a piano competition in Italy. My father and I had permission to go, but the Communists made my mom stay in Sofia, to ensure that we'd come back. I'd never been out of Bulgaria before, and seeing Italy was incredible, like a movie. It was the most beautiful place I'd ever seen. Suddenly I knew everything we were missing in Bulgaria—the food, the cars, the stores, everything. I was free there, really free. It changed me. I wanted to stay in Italy—we could have claimed political asylum, especially after I won the competition—but we couldn't leave my mom behind. And so we went back to our prison."

I took in this story, feeling the depth of his frustration, the incredible deprivation he must have felt, and the pain of going back to a country that had imprisoned him. I wanted to keep him from experiencing this pain again. I wanted to take his past and bury it in a shower of kisses. I wanted to give him a new life. I wanted to be his Italy.

"Being without a visa brings it all back for me," he said. "I can't help but feel like I'm on the train from Italy returning to Sofia."

"But it's not like that now," I said, stroking his hair and kissing him on the forehead. "The world has changed. You just have to renew your visa, and you can come back here. It's only a formality."

"Right," he said, but his face darkened. "But if I learned one thing from my childhood, it is that simple formalities can turn into bureaucratic nightmares. If Homeland Security wanted, they could arrest me. They could lock me up and deport me. Or hold me somewhere. Nobody knows what's happening out there now."

It was February of 2002, when the repercussions of 9/11 were still unknown. The recently passed Patriot Act could change everything for foreigners in the United States.

"I didn't realize that it could be so complicated," I said.

"That's because you're an American citizen.

You don't realize how privileged you are. You expect everything in life to work, and you're surprised when it doesn't. You haven't had your basic human rights stripped away like I have."

"You're right," I said. "I can't understand. I'm lucky to have you. My country would be lucky to have you, too."

"Do you mean that?" he said, his eyes intent on mine.

"Of course," I said. "I'm sure that with all your talents they'll give you citizenship in a second. I'll help you. I'll do anything you need."

"Then marry me," he said, gazing deeply into my eyes. "That's the best way."

Although we had known each other less than six months, I didn't hesitate. I loved him, and I wanted everything—good and bad, easy and difficult—with him. "Of course," I said, bursting with happiness. "I love you. I just want to be with you."

From that moment forward, we were co-creators of a fantasy, a dreamworld that became our shelter, protecting us from loneliness and disappointment and instability and failure, a structure capable of holding us apart from everyone and everything that could harm us. He extended his hand, and I, grasping it, went wherever he might take me.

Portcullis

During our first week in Aubais, I took the kids to the *boulangerie* to buy breakfast. At that time of day, the village was swarming with old women doing the daily shopping. Baskets in hand, they walked to the *boulangerie* to buy fresh bread. They stopped by the pharmacy to fill their prescriptions. They stopped by the *épicerie* for eggs. They passed by the *tabac* to buy a *Midi Libre* and—if they were not widowed, which I later learned most of them were—a pack of cigarettes for their husbands. Then they formed a tight circle on the corner and traded gossip, clucking their tongues and pursing their lips in disapproval of some new scandal, because in the village there was always some new scandal to keep the old women talking.

When I walked by, a wicker basket on my arm, the old women's voices fell quiet. My children trailed behind me, talking and laughing in what I would later think of as our "American voices," those loud and boisterous voices that we used back home. Our English was a magnet that drew the gaze of everyone we met, but we would have been conspicuous even without saying a word: Our clothes were bright and casual, our shoes—the kids' orange and pink Crocs and my flip-flops—so out of the realm of the village fashion code of neutral colors and sensible leather shoes that there was an air of the circus about us. There were tourists in the village every summer, and the locals were accustomed to seeing lost foreigners in July or August, but it was May. We were off-season.

Bonjour, madame, the old women said as we passed.

Bonjour, I replied, straightening my dress, self-conscious. How different these tough, stout women were from the women in Paris, with their trendy clothes and high heels, their scarves and leather bags. The village women were as gnarled and sturdy as roots, skin gone nutmeg from the sun—beautiful, earthy women. They looked at me a moment too long, their curiosity evident, before turning back into their tight circle.

Later, after living there for some time, I would recognize many of the villagers. There was the gendarme whom some of the villagers called "Robocop" because of his flat, inexpressive manner and his ability to deflect human inter-action with a single blank stare. *Bonjour*, I would say to Robocop when we walked past, and he would look into the distance with a profound emptiness, the kind of unknowing beatitude I associated with a holy man meditating in a cave. Then there was Pépé the wealthiest landowner in the village, a round, jolly man who owned the bulls in the field at the bottom of the hill and the only bar in town. Pépé spoke with an accent so strong, so inflected with the regional twang, that I never, even when my French had become good, understood him. Then there was Axel, who sold black truffles door-to-door. He would bring the truffles to our door, a scale under his arm to weigh out the hard black nuggets, each one encrusted with dirt like a diamond pried from a mine. He would take a blade from his pocket, slice into the edge of the truffle, exposing white veins swirling through the black matter like so many arteries in a brain, leaving the kitchen with a strong earthy scent. There were Lord and Lulu, an English couple who lived in a crumbling *maison de maître* near the château. Lord had come to Aubais to write his memoirs, a goal he pursued when he wasn't dancing and drinking and talking horses with the locals. In his gentleman's tweeds, he limped through the village, chatting in broken French with whoever would listen, and many people did: Lord was infamous in Aubais, celebrated as a true English Eccentric, a category of foreigner the French adore. Then there was Jett, who became one of my closest friends during my time in France, a hard-drinking, free-spirited, middle-aged Irish expatriate who made large abstract sculptures and did various odd jobs on the side to survive. A large woman with black hair and black eyes, she wore loose dresses and had an easiness in her movements that made her seem as if she'd been everywhere and done everything. We met Jett shortly after we arrived in the village, and she gave me all the basic information about France—the best markets, restaurants, doctors, wine, walks. Jett had lived in the area for over a decade and knew the secrets the locals guarded.

But during those first months in the village, we knew absolutely no one. We were free-floating, without friends, unable to communicate even the most basic information about ourselves. And yet somehow none of that mattered much to me. I was so caught up in the dream of our new life that I didn't care that we were outsiders. The church bells that chimed at the hour, the smell of baking bread in the morning, the geckos climbing the chalky limestone walls of the village houses, the old women gossiping in the street. I was exactly where I wanted to be: far, very far, from the real world.

The *boulangerie* shelves were stacked with fresh croissants, pain au chocolat, pain aux raisins, and ten kinds of bread—ficelles, baguettes, pain de campagne, pain au lin. There were marzipan confections, local wine, local jams, local every-thing. This wasn't the cult of "local" and "organic" that could be found in expensive American groceries—this was the real thing. Nothing had been packaged and shipped from China, because there was simply no need. It was all made there, near the village. This was the simple life, where choices were narrowed down to the essentials.

Alex stood before a glass case filled with pastries. He was small for nine, delicate-boned as bird, with thick hair that fell in curls over his large brown eyes. Putting my hand on his back, I gave him a weighty look, a look that said, *I know this sucks, but give it a shot.* Alex looked at me, doubtful. He didn't understand a word of French, and I didn't understand much myself, but I wanted him to try to communicate in some small way. I was throwing him in at the deep end. I was watching to see if he could swim.

Bonjour, said the woman behind the counter, deeply tanned with spiked, bleached-blond hair and a spate of earrings. She looked at me and then at my son, a flicker of interest crossing her features. She'd seen us before, or rather she'd seen people like us before: bright-eyed, confused foreigners desperate for direction.

Alex pointed to a pastry glistening with a sugar glaze, something that looked similar to the apple fritters we bought at bakeries back in the United States.

"*Chausson aux pommes?*" the woman asked.

"*Chausson aux pommes*," Alex replied, his tongue twisting around the new sounds.

Chausson aux pommes meant, I later learned, apple slipper, a pastry stocking stuffed with apples, cinnamon, and sugar. But at that moment I heard a mishmash of sounds whose closest aural equivalent was "Jones'n' for some."

Alex nodded, his eyes glistening. *Jones'n' for some.* That's exactly what he wanted, my American son, the biggest and the sweetest thing in the pastry shop.

The woman behind the counter reached for this treasure, and I raised my hand, stopping her. I squeezed Alex's arm and nudged him. A look of uncertainty filled his face. We'd discussed it earlier. He was going to speak French. He was going to use the phrase *j'aimerais*—I would like—or, at the very least, *s'il vous plaît.* He would be going to the village school in the fall, where there would be no English spoken at all. He needed to start somewhere. I decided to be tough on him: no French, no pastry.

Shifting her weight, the woman glanced from me to Alex, uncertain. Her look seemed to say, *What kind of people are these anyway, performing Pavlovian experiments on hungry children at nine in the morning?* Did she want to be part of this experimental educational moment? No, she did not.

"Go on," I said, touching Alex's shoulder.

"*J'aimerais . . . un*" Alex stammered, and pointed to the glass case, using the words we'd practiced that morning, taken from our French phrasebook. He was the type of child who could get straight A's without trying, who read novels in a single sitting, who memorized the fifty states and their capitals in fifteen minutes. He could speak three words of French if he tried.

"Try again," I said.

"*Je voudrais Jones'n' for some*," he said.

The woman raised an eyebrow at me—*That good enough for you, lady?*—and I smiled, satisfied, as she handed over Alex's breakfast. Nico looked on, taking everything in, smiling from ear to ear, sharing Alex's victory. At six, Nico was ready for anything. She ordered a *pain au chocolat* without hesitating, breaking out with "*Je voudrais* that one right there, the chocolate one!"

The rest of the order—two croissants, one for me and one for Nikolai, who had stayed back at the house—was conducted in a spirit of relief, with mangled sounds and quick, desperate gestures, an excruciating lexicon that I would cobble together to get me through moments of cultural and linguistic confusion. But for the moment I didn't care if I sounded like an idiot. I was thrilled to be there, happy that Alex and Nico had triumphed. Even the woman behind the counter was smiling.

I used the same piecemeal system to buy vegetables at a stand across the street. There was a plank table set up opposite the *tabac* with lettuce, red onions, *haricots verts*, melons the size of ostrich eggs. The table was loaded with tomatoes so fragrant I could smell them as I approached, grapes piled high in wooden wine crates, homemade confiture and tapenade. I bought three kinds of lettuce, a kilo of cherries, and basil. The old woman working the stand was preeminently practical, ignoring my awkward attempts at communication as she dropped items onto the scale, weighing them and sliding them into a paper sack in one sweeping gesture. She wrote down the weights and the prices and showed them to me, to be certain I understood.

With our haul of fruit, the kids and I followed the curvature of the road down, descending past the bulls and following the stream around the base of the hill. In the heat of the summer, the stream was a moat without depth, so shallow and clear that rocks snagged the surface. Alex and Nico wanted to watch the bulls, and so I walked to the *laverie* alone. Long and narrow, it straddled the stream. When it was in use, the water flowed in clean, filling stone basins, and swept out the other side, soiled. I walked into the cool, shadowy interior of the *laverie*, taking a reprieve from the heat.

Once a meeting place for women—perhaps even the old women who met every morning on the corner to gossip—the *laverie* was all but abandoned now, a picturesque relic of another era, when women spent hours washing their sheets and tablecloths and undergarments by hand, soaping their children's clothes with *savon* from Marseille before hanging them out to dry in the sun. It was a female space, a place where women blistered their hands and traded stories of sons dead to war, daughters lost to marriage, husbands gone off to work or to womanize. I was a person of modern appliances, and yet that space felt deeply comfortable to me. I peered over the edge, trying to see to the bottom of the basin. The water ran clear. I could see the glint of euro coins at the bottom, gleaming. Hoisting myself up, I climbed onto the edge, dug into my pocket for a coin, and dropped it in the water. *Make a wish.* I closed my eyes. There was one thing I wanted more than anything else: to find love in France.

I edged closer and closer to the water, daring gravity to take me.

Suddenly I was a little girl again, ready to jump into a deep country pond. I grew up in a wilderness of fields and forests. I would tie a bandanna around my head, tell myself that I was a warrior, and hike out beyond the cow fields into the hot, clover-heavy hills. I'd tromp through the woods looking for snakes, badgers, skunk, always seeking that sharp, poisonous thing that would transform the journey into an adventure. Victory was making it up to the top of the hill without stopping; victory was climbing into the trees without a scratch. My parents had bought the land cheap, built a house and paved a road, and I believed that the pure, unpeopled countryside was all mine. Our land seemed endless to me, a natural barrier of greenery, and while I loved getting lost in the wilderness, I was aware that I was only one step away from a rattler. When my parents divorced and our family split apart, all my premonitions were made plain: Eden cannot exist without the snake.

My mother owned a long, narrow cedar trunk that looked to me, when I was small, like a coffin. It sat at the end of her bed, piled with quilts. If the quilts were spread over a bed, I would see flowered panels carved into the wood of the trunk. A small copper lock, cool as a wasp, secured my mother's box from the destructive forces of curious children like me.

Eventually I found a way to open the trunk, but when I saw the contents, I couldn't understand why my mother had locked it up to begin with. It was filled with the most mundane things imaginable: a stack of white embroidered napkins; china cups and plates with silver at the edges; a cut-crystal candy bowl; an album that contained mementos of me, my sister, and my brother—locks of hair, scraps of baby blankets, inked baby footprints. The air was musty inside the trunk, and the contents bored me. I'd expected to find real treasures—bars of gold, a jeweled chalice, or at least a Barbie or two—hidden among the tissue paper. Disappointed, I closed the lid and left it alone.

The next time I paid attention to my mother's wooden trunk was an evening in December, many years later, when I was twenty years old and back home from college. It was dark outside, and snow had fallen in drifts over the driveway. My mother and I were wrapping Christmas presents together in her bedroom, and she opened the wooden trunk, looking for some special ribbon she'd tucked away. I recognized the smell of cedar and dust, scents I hadn't known how to name as a child. Now I could identify the climbing flowers—they were lilies— and I understood that the trunk didn't resemble a coffin at all. Looking inside as an adult, I saw that the contents had changed—instead of linens and china cups, there were stacks of report cards, my brother's high-school letter jacket, a trophy my sister had won playing basketball, a watercolor I'd painted in eleventh grade, every one of our school portraits from kindergarten through graduation preserved in slips of plastic. Every moment of glory her kids had experienced, she'd stashed away in the trunk.

"Where did you get this?" I asked her, running a finger over the varnished edge. "You've had it forever."

"Haven't I told you about my hope chest before?" she asked.

I must have made a strange face—the kind of face a young woman makes at her mother when the subject wavers toward certain subjects. "Hope chest?" I asked. "Hope for what?"

"You know," she said, her face turning slightly pink, as if she anticipated my criticism before it came. "Marriage. Kids. *Life.*"

I gave her a look that said, *You've got to be kidding.*

"Well, these kinds of things were much more common when I was young!" Mom said, ready to defend herself from me, something she had to do with some frequency. I was always looking to define myself against her, always searching for the ways that we were different, turning her into a mirror I could fracture, even if it cut us both in the smash-up.

Mom said, "I worked at the Elite candy shop making caramels on the weekends and saved up for it. After I'd bought it, I filled it with all the things I wanted to have when I was married— pretty sheets and tablecloths, that kind of thing. I bought the china dishes piece by piece—a cup here, a saucer there—until I had the entire set. It's a shame. The pattern was discontinued. If I break something, I can't replace it." She met my eye. "Don't look at me that way, young lady!"

"It's like you grew up in Victorian England," I

said, thinking myself free of my mother's pre-conceptions about what it meant to be a woman, free of the need to "hope" for anything, let alone a husband.

"It wasn't so long ago that girls did things like that," she replied, closing the lid of the hope chest softly. There was a hint of sadness in her voice, a subtle acknowledgment that the hopes of her younger self and the realities of love were two very different things. "If you were born in the fifties, you might have had a hope chest, too."

It wasn't until later that I understood that I did, in fact, have a hope chest of my own. Not of wood, not locked up and hidden under stacks of quilts, but a hope chest nonetheless, one filled with dreams about my life. I believed in romance and destiny. I believed in love at first sight. I believed that when I found the right person, time would stop and we would be suspended in a state of endless passion. There was no place in my hope chest for disappointment or failure. There was no place for imperfection or broken promises or compromise. And while my hope-chest ideas might have had all the trappings of a good romance, they didn't have the capacity to hold real love.

On long, hot August afternoons, the village closed down for a siesta. From two to four o'clock each day, the pharmacy and the *boulangerie* and the *tabac* locked their doors. The streets were silent, as if the whole village were holding its breath, waiting for the blazing sun to pass by. That first summer we lived in the village, my wired American self couldn't quite sync with the rhythm of the south of France. I would gather up my packages and walk to the post office after lunch, only to find the door locked. I'd look across the plaza at Le Bar de la Renaissance and find all the tables empty. Aubais was a ghost town, baking in the heat. With time, I understood that there was no sense in staying awake during the afternoon, and I began to take a nap after lunch, stripping down to panties and a tank top and crawling between the cool cotton sheets.

At first I would toss and turn, thinking of all the things I should be doing, making mental lists, the electricity in my mind unstoppable. I hadn't taken naps since I was five years old, and I remembered how desperately I'd fought against them back then. I'd always resisted the slow dissolve of my consciousness in the murky solution of dreams. I would lie in bed, close my eyes, and soon my mind would begin to drift.

I never slept peacefully. It felt as though I lay suspended between two worlds. If I dreamed, my mind filled with strange, amorphous terrors. Murder and torture and missing limbs. Iron maidens and Judas cradles and racks. I hadn't had dreams like these before, and I wondered if they were inspired by the books I was reading about the Knights Templar, and their gruesome end. I began to understand that these phantoms arose from the depths of the house, lifting through the stone floors, seeping into my mind like a noxious gas. I dreamed of rats scurrying through dark dungeons and children trapped in towers. I felt the Knights Templar crawling below me, scratching their way through secret tunnels. I dreamed of Nazis sleeping in the corridors and resistance fighters trapped in oubliettes bored into the rock. I dreamed of the previous owner's wife, who—I learned after we moved into La Commanderie—had died of cancer in the house. She was waiting for me at the bottom of the steep stone stairway, her arms open wide.

But one dream in particular haunted me, a recurrent dream in which a baby—not my child, but someone's child—had wandered onto the roof of La Commanderie and was walking timorously over the clay tiles toward the edge. As the child came closer and closer to the ledge, I tried to reach it, to save it, but the end was always the same: No matter how I tried, the baby fell. I was powerless. I could never stop its inexorable, gravity-bound end. I came to see the baby as my family, and the feeling of helplessness—the wrenching horror I felt as the baby stumbled toward its death—my fear of losing what I most loved.

I would wake in a panic, my heart racing, my body trembling, a scream balled in my throat like a wet sock. I was thankful to come back to the real world, to my world, where nothing terrible had happened, where there was nothing to be afraid of. Where harm was just a figment of the mind.

It wasn't long after we moved into La Commanderie that Nikolai started wearing all black—black jeans, black T-shirt, black socks, black shoes. He found a black top hat in a junk shop in Lunel and started wearing it around the courtyard. He was so monochromatic that sometimes when he sat in the courtyard playing chess, it seemed to me that he'd materialized from the shade of our *micocoulier*, the majestic hackberry tree that loomed overhead. In the summer it dropped a minefield of berries over the courtyard. Walking barefoot, I would pop purple juice over the hot flagstones, staining my feet wine-dark. In the fall it shed its dry, yellow leaves and Alex and Nico would rake them into a pile, covering Fly and watching him shake himself free.

Some nights we spent hours under the tree, sitting around the long wooden table with friends, eating, talking, drinking wine, arguing about whatever was in the news. The people we invited for dinner were never from Aubais, and rarely from the Midi. They were all foreigners like us:

expats from Australia or England or Belgium, Americans on holiday for a few weeks, French couples who had moved south from Paris for the weather. Several times a month, we formed a collective of happy outcasts gathered around a country feast, our wineglasses sweating in the heat, plates of sliced tomatoes and olives before us, the star-filled sky expanding overhead. The *micocoulier*'s branches spread at just the right angle to hang a plastic chandelier, and so we rigged one up, leaving a watery glow to fall gently from above, twinkling over the linen napkins, making patterns on the Provençal tablecloth. The food and wine and conversation acted as a fixing agent and some nights it felt like time had stopped. On those nights we lived in an eternal present. The cooling air, with its smell of wet chalk and rosemary, would never blow through to morning.

But alone in our courtyard, time barreled ahead. Shaded from the afternoon sun, we sat together, drinking glasses of Perrier with ice and lime. Bottled at the source in Vergèze just ten minutes from us, Perrier was the local water, and we drank it by the caseload. Every once in a while, Nikolai would wander into the house, where he would sit down at the Yamaha baby grand and play a piece of something that had been going through his head. The piano was my gift to him, bought with money from the sale of my novel, and

I was rewarded daily with short interludes of music. Nikolai played for a minute or two before returning to the chessboard. The music had cleared his mind. He was ready to make his next move.

When Nikolai played chess, everything else faded. He noticed nothing in the courtyard, not Fly as he terrorized the cats, not me pulling up a chair to sit by his side. In the dreamspace of the match, only the chess pieces existed, only the strategy. He could go on for hours, setting up openings and endings, mapping the middle game, sipping coffee as he planned his victories. He played speed chess on his phone when he needed to relax and live chess matches on the Internet on his laptop, locking himself away in his office for hours at a time only to emerge red-eyed, hungry, jumpy with adrenaline.

I didn't play chess, or any other game that involved abstract victories. For me, writing was a high-stakes game I waged every time I sat at my desk. I didn't feel triumph in complicated openings and endgames, but in the weight of just-written pages in my hands. I craved tangible rewards, quantifiable proof of my effort. This is how I was raised, the practical midwesterner who needed to hold the result of her labor, to capture it like a butterfly between plates of glass, lift it to the sunlight to marvel at the color of imagination made solid.

Glancing at Nikolai's chessboard, I saw a rook and a knight and a queen. I saw the bishop, and I saw the pawns. The cast was there, each character in position. I watched my husband pick up the black king and roll it between his fingers. He tipped the piece in his hand, considering his options, and then, with a decisive gesture, pinned the white queen. A look of surprise passed over his features, as if the move startled him, as if he hadn't predicted the elegance of the play. The white queen was trapped between the black king and a small but very significant pawn. Something in my mind grew alert as I watched him, as if the move were meant to warn me: *Beware, in the labyrinth it is easy to lose one's way.*

Enceinte

A number of surprises awaited me when we arrived in Sofia in May 2002.

First, I learned that Nikolai's visa situation was much more complicated than I had originally believed. It turned out that his J-1 visa was non-renewable, and he was required to spend two full years in Bulgaria before he could reenter the United States. Second, Nikolai's job teaching Tibetan at the University of Sofia paid about 250 leva per month, the equivalent of 125 U.S. dollars. And third, I was pregnant.

With these three pieces of information, the landscape of my visit to Bulgaria shifted. I had left home believing we would spend the summer in Eastern Europe, but it was now clear that we would be in Bulgaria for much longer than expected, two years minimum. His fears about being trapped in Bulgaria were realized: We were pinned.

"I can't believe this is happening," he said. He was furious about the visa restriction.

"But they must have told you about the restrictions when you got the visa," I said.

"I wouldn't have accepted the J-1 if I'd known I was agreeing to a prison term in Bulgaria," he insisted. "There must be a mistake. I'm sure they'll let me out of it if we go to the embassy and talk to them. You're an American citizen, after all. They'll take you seriously."

We did some reading online and discovered that we could get around the J-1's two-year requirement by asking for a visa waiver. "As an American citizen, you'll have more pull with them than I will," he said, a strain of bitterness in his voice. "Especially now that you're pregnant."

He put together a dossier of information about his visa, and we went down to the U.S. embassy together, where we spoke to a visa counselor about my pregnancy and our impending marriage. We'd decided that it would be better if I did the talking. Nikolai sat at my side, silent.

"I've just found out that I'm pregnant," I explained to the woman behind the desk. "And I'd like to have the baby in the States."

She looked at my navy blue American passport. "But you're free to go back," she said. "You have no restrictions."

Of course I knew I could go home if I wanted,\ but the prospect of being a pregnant and unemployed single mother with no health care was daunting, to say the least. I'd spent the last ten years trying be independent of my parents, and I couldn't imagine asking them to take me in now.

"But the baby's father is here," I pointed out. "He has to stay in Bulgaria for two years. Am I supposed to go back alone?"

"You can always return here after the baby is

born," she said sympathetically. "I'm afraid that is about all I can suggest."

She went on to explain that the two-year homestay requirement was strict, that Nikolai had agreed to it before he took the visa, and that we could apply for a waiver, but it was highly unlikely that one would be approved. "The only cases in which I've seen someone get past the two-year homestay requirement is in cases of extreme illness, when there's a verifiable need to be treated by doctors in the United States."

We left the embassy, walked out past the concrete blockades and the armed guards, and sat on a bench.

"How could you be so wrong about this?" I asked him, still trying to get my mind around it all. One minute we were going on vacation, the next we were relocating to Bulgaria.

"This isn't my fault—you know that, don't you?" he asked. "If I'd known, I would have come to the States on a tourist visa, or I would have applied for a DS-160 or an F-1."

Suddenly Nikolai was conversant in visa types and numbers and requirements. He hadn't seemed to know any of this back in Iowa City.

"What are we going to do?" I asked. I was beginning to feel the walls closing in, the drawbridge lifting, the portcullis clanking shut.

"We'll have to stay," he said, running his fingers through his thick hair.

"Stay? How? Do you honestly believe we can survive on one hundred and twenty-five dollars a month from your teaching? And what about Alex? He needs to go to preschool in the fall. And I need to apply for jobs back home. I can't spend *two years* here. This is totally crazy."

"They shouldn't be able to do this. It should be illegal."

"But *you* did this," I said. "You agreed to this requirement when you accepted your visa."

"I didn't know," he said. "If they told me, I didn't understand." He took my hand. "You believe me, don't you?"

I looked into his eyes for a long moment. "Of course," I said. "Of course I believe you." And I did believe, believed the way a convert believes in the untouchable, wholly unverifiable grace of the beyond. Love required blind faith, and despite the fact that I weighed what he said against the reality of what I saw, and it did not match up, I believed him.

He must have understood how bad it all looked, because he grasped me by the shoulders, gazed deep into my eyes, and said, "Please don't leave. Don't go back the United States without me. I hate it here. This is my worst nightmare. I don't know what I would do without you."

Seeing him in such distress was too much for me. "I'm not going to leave," I said, pulling him close. "I'm not going to leave when things get hard."

"I love you," he said. "As long as we're together, we'll be fine. Let me handle the money problem. I'll take care of everything."

We lived in one of his parents' apartments in Sofia, on the top floor of a building near the Russian embassy, in a part of town called Izgreva, an exclusive neighborhood with a sweeping view of the Vitosha mountains. During Communism only the highest of party officials, and those connected to them, had apartments in Izgreva. Our apartment had once belonged to Nikolai's paternal grandfather, Nester, who'd been a towering man of six feet five inches, a staunch Communist, and friend of Todor Zhivkov, the head of the Communist Party, whose life he had once saved.

Yana, Nikolai's beautiful, dark-haired mother, and Ivan, his brilliant father, were warm and generous people who welcomed Alex and me into their family without question. I liked Nikolai's parents right away. They were all the things that my parents weren't: overeducated professionals who loved music and art and literature and traveling, their dinner-table conversations filled with highbrow references, passionate discussions of philosophy and art and books. They were part of an elite, and they carried themselves that way.

I couldn't have come from more different circumstances. I had scratched my way out of my working-class background and, while I was educated and accomplished in my own right, I felt a gaping rift between Nikolai's past and my own. His parents had always expected that he would "amount to something." If it wasn't piano, it would be something else. There were no such expectations in my family. For me, going to college was an act of rebellion, a turning-away from what I had known. I had pushed myself to do more, to learn more, to feel more, and to see more because I knew that I had missed so many of the beautiful things people like Nikolai took for granted. I wanted to fit into his world. I wanted my son—and the baby we would soon have—to grow up in such an environment.

Nikolai's parents symbolized this future for me. Despite all the hardships they'd experienced—they'd lived through communism and lost their savings during a bank crash in the nineties—they had a joy for living I admired. Part of that joy revolved around taking care of their only son. When Nikolai was with his parents, I felt him glow with the same radiant confidence he'd displayed at the piano in Iowa City: He was the star performer, and his parents were always there, standing nearby, filled with pride. For them he could do no wrong.

My adoration was nearly as religious. Nikolai, Alex, and I spent the weeks of May exploring Bulgaria like tourists. We walked through the old center of Sofia, visiting the St. Alexander Nevsky Cathedral, the St. George Rotunda, and the antique markets, making our way through the dark, narrow, cobblestone streets behind Vitosha Boulevard to find lunch on a terrace. We took a day trip to Plovdiv with Yana and Ivan, climbing the stone steps of the ancient Roman amphitheater and having a long, traditional lunch of stuffed grape leaves, cabbage rolls, and the spicy lamb meatballs called *kufteta*. We took another day trip into the mountains, to the tenth-century Rila Monastery, and another to the Devil's Throat Cavern, a UNESCO world historical site that one day I would use as a setting in my first novel.

But there was another side of Sofia, one that I rarely saw. The poverty of Bulgaria in 2002 was grueling. Whole sections of the city were filled with the poor and unemployed, living in what Nikolai called panel buildings, Stalin-era prefab concrete apartment complexes that had once promised cheap mass housing. There were Gypsy camps—Nikolai always called the population of nomadic Roma living in Europe Gypsies—at the edge of the city. These makeshift villages had become the dumping ground for Sofia's refuse: There were wheelless Ladas, rusty bicycles, plastic bottles, broken toys, canvas tarps stretched between trees for shelter. I had never seen such poverty, and the juxtaposition of this suffering with my newly found happiness made the chasms between fortune and suffering all the more plain.

During these weeks I was blissfully happy. Nikolai did everything he could to make me comfortable in Sofia. He played Chopin on the upright piano at the apartment in Izgreva. He bought me flowers from the outdoor market and surprised me with sweet Bulgarian desserts from the *sladkarnitsa* down the street. He made complicated dishes on the old *pechka*, a Soviet-era stove that heated the whole kitchen. We re-created our Iowa City pattern in the apartment in Izgreva: I set up my laptop at a desk in the bedroom, and he took the back office, a room with a view of the stunning Vitosha mountains. It was spring, the trees green, the flowers in bloom, and Sofia seemed exotic and mysterious, an enchanted city from a legend. Two years in Bulgaria, I decided, wouldn't be so bad. I had taught English in Japan, and I could certainly do the same in Bulgaria. It would be hard, but we would make it. Maybe the visa problem had been a blessing in disguise.

The night Nikolai told his mother that I was pregnant, her eyes filled with tears of anxiety. In her heavily accented but grammatically perfect English, Yana said, "But think of how expensive this is going to be!"

Yana was right to worry. We didn't have money for a baby. My last check from the University of Iowa had gone to buying plane tickets to

Bulgaria, and my savings were about to run out. Nikolai, it became clear, had nothing of his own. His parents had been carrying him for years, since he'd returned from India, giving him money to support his first wife and daughter, giving him a place to live and an allowance and a car. Through their love, money, and time, they had helped Nikolai survive. Now he was asking them to take care of his newest problem: me.

I tried to decide what to do, go home to the United States and deal with the situation alone or stick it out in Bulgaria. The choices were like pathways, one looping back to the known world of my family, the other leading to the mysterious unknown. Later that night I pulled Alex onto my lap and held him. Whenever I didn't know what to do, I would sit with Alex and think. He was my compass, the strong magnetic force that steered me in the right direction. Being near him put my actions into perspective. The smell of his skin, the softness of his hair, his huge trusting eyes—I owed it to him to be sure that I was making the right choice. Would I put him at risk by staying in Bulgaria? Or would I be giving him a better life?

Meanwhile, Nikolai and his parents had intense discussions in the kitchen of our apartment, hours of talking and talking in Bulgarian. Nikolai seemed to be negotiating some kind of deal, although I couldn't understand a word of what they were saying. I never understood any of their monster family discussions, but throughout my time in Bulgaria I realized that this was how his family worked. When Nikolai had problems, they solved them together. His parents would rally around their son, take out their weapons, and fight whatever or whoever threatened his well-being. It was something I respected and admired, even when, ten years later, the enemy was me.

"Everything's going to be okay," Nikolai said when the conference was over. "My parents are going to help us."

"They're finding us jobs?"

"No," he said. "They understand that we're having trouble. With my visa and the baby coming, we need some extra help. They're going to support us until the baby comes."

This was a foreign concept for me. Money had always been a source of tension in my family. My parents told me I was on my own at eighteen, and I had gone off to college with the belief that I had no choice but to succeed. There was no one back home to save me if I failed.

"And they're okay with that?" I asked.

"They are now," he said. "I just told them that we're getting married."

Two weeks later Nikolai and I married in the windowless, lightless vault of the justice of the peace. Nobody was in attendance except his parents, who acted as witnesses, and, of course, the judge. There wasn't money for a new dress,

71

and so I wore a vintage purple shift from the sixties. I was six weeks pregnant, nauseous, and homesick, but in the one picture I have from that day I am smiling, a bouquet of white lilies in my hands. I understood not one word of the ceremony. The sound of the language was harsh and chill and elegant, somehow cruel. I tried to catch the sounds, but it was all utterly incomprehensible. Indeed, when it was my turn to say "I do," I stood silent, unaware that I was being asked a question at all. The judge asked again, and again I didn't respond. Finally I heard Nikolai whisper in my ear, "Now you say '*Da.*'" I looked at him for a long moment, to capture the flush of happiness in his face, the brightness in his eyes. He loved me. I could see it. There was no reason to be so unsure. There was no reason to doubt him.

"*Da*," I said, looking into Nikolai's eyes as I spoke my first word of Bulgarian. "*Da.*"

It was at the twelve-week prenatal exam that we learned we would be having a baby boy.

If anyone had asked me at the time, I would have said what all pregnant women say: *As long as it's healthy, I don't care about the sex.* But after the doctor told us the baby was a boy, I realized that I did care. I really cared. I had a whole list of girl names picked out and not one for a boy. When we went to a baby store, it was the pink section that drew me. I told myself I wanted the experience of raising a girl and a boy, of understanding the difference between having a daughter and having a son, but perhaps there was more to it than that. Although I wasn't aware of this at the time, I felt an irrational need to replace the daughter Nikolai had lost in his divorce.

Rada's mother remarried and, in a twist of irony, moved with her new husband to the United States. Nikolai had limited visitation rights, and we saw Rada rarely before she left, but we watched her grow up from a distance. Over the next decade, Rada would learn English, go to school in Connecticut, become a beautiful, whip-smart, and very American girl. Her life would be filled with opportunities she wouldn't have had in Bulgaria. Even so, we hadn't imagined, when we fell in love in Iowa City, how drastically our actions would change our children's lives. Rada would live with the consequences, as would Alex. No matter how happy I was with Nikolai, I understood that our choices had changed the lives of our children. Alex was far away from his father; Rada was far from hers.

In the skewed logic of my love for Nikolai, I believed that if I could give him another daughter, he wouldn't miss Rada so much. And so when I learned that we would have a son, I felt strangely unsettled, as if it were somehow incorrect. I developed a powerful resistance to the facts. The doctor said it was a boy, but in my mind the baby would be a girl.

"Doctors are not always accurate about these things, you know," I said as we drove through Sofia. "Especially at only twelve weeks. There's a chance he's wrong."

"He seemed pretty sure," Nikolai said.

"But I was positive it would be a girl," I said, disappointment in my voice.

"The baby will be beautiful," Nikolai said. "No matter what."

"Of course it will. I'm not making sense. I must be hormonal. As long as it's healthy, I don't care about the sex."

"You know, there's a Bulgarian superstition that says if you walk under a rainbow when pregnant, the sex of the baby will change."

"There's a superstition for everything here," I said, laughing. If your left hand itched, money was coming; if your right hand itched, you would be spending money. If a room was drafty, you would be sick. If an old woman looked at you funny, it was the evil eye. Just the other day, Yana had told me that if you put your purse on the ground, the money would disappear from inside. Not that it would be stolen, not that you'd get a hole in the bottom of the bag and the contents would fall out. The money would actually, materially disappear. *Poof.* Yana never, in all the years that I knew her, put her bag on the ground.

"I love that about your country," I said. "Everything is magic here."

Nikolai smiled. "Now we just need to find a rainbow."

Superstition created the texture of Nikolai's personality. The belief that he couldn't get his hair cut on Tuesdays (bad luck), or that leaving fingernail clippings in the bathroom sink was dangerous (they could be collected and used in a hex), or that drafts of wind caused sickness (carrying in spirits) and the evil eye could strike him at any moment, or that his ex-wife had hired Gypsies to cast curses and spells upon him—all of these superstitions formed his worldview. He told me that he had needed a blood transfusion after he was born and was at risk of dying until a Gypsy man had donated blood. The transfusion saved his life and connected him to the culture and magic of the Gypsies, at least in his own mind.

In the beginning these quirks were what made my husband interesting. They were artistic eccentricities, the strange but lovable oddities of his personality. I used them as proofs that he was an eccentric genius, the child-prodigy pianist, the chess wizard and the novelist. I didn't realize that these superstitions were prayers. They were his way of warding off demons.

But ill fortune wasn't so easy to keep at bay. One afternoon I was walking up the stairs of the apartment in Izgreva, Alex's hand in mine, and the wall of muscles in my abdomen locked up, hard and tight, as if a belt had been cinched. I stopped to catch my breath, letting go of Alex's hand and grasping the railing. Nikolai rushed to me and helped me sit down.

"What's happening?" he asked.

"Contraction," I said.

"Isn't it too soon for that?"

I tried to remember if I'd had contractions like that before, when I was pregnant with Alex. Of course I *did* have contractions like that, at the very end of my pregnancy, when Alex was about to be born.

"It's about four months too soon." I said, pulling myself up.

Alarmed, Nikolai called the obstetrician and made an emergency appointment. The doctor examined me and asked how often the contractions were happening. When I told him that I'd felt them for a few days but they were so gentle that I'd ignored them, he looked concerned. He folded his arms over his chest and spoke to Nikolai in Bulgarian, a language I found thick as honey, filled with gulps and slurs and swallows. The doctor shrugged as he spoke, as if there were nothing he could do.

"What's happening?" I asked, trying to stay calm.

"You're having regular contractions," Nikolai said.

"I know," I replied. "I can feel that. Does he know why?"

"No," Nikolai said. "You're dilated, which means that there's a chance the baby could be born early."

"How many weeks am I now?"

"Eighteen," Nikolai said.

"Is that enough for the baby to . . . ?"

Nikolai shook his head. "If he's born now, they won't be able to do much for him. At twenty-two weeks, there is more they can do. He wants to admit you to Maichin Dom."

Maichin Dom was the maternity hospital of Sofia, a huge Soviet concrete cube with darkened windows, old leather furniture, industrial art, and lightless hallways. Sofia's primary public facility for pregnant women, it had once been the only place in the city where babies were born. Nikolai was born there, and his daughter, Rada, was born there. Now the hospital was severely underfunded and understaffed, with whole floors closed down, hallways without lightbulbs in the fixtures, cracked windows, and insufficient medical equipment. There were private clinics popping up in Sofia, Nikolai told me, and these clinics might have nicer facilities, but they were unregulated. The best doctors in Bulgaria were still at Maichin Dom.

Nikolai checked me in, and a nurse led me to a room on the fifth floor. As we stepped out of the elevator, we saw a cluster of pregnant women standing together near an open window, smoking. The women were laughing and talking, making the most of whatever illness had brought them to Maichin Dom. There was a man with them, and as we passed by, I realized—from the stethoscope around his neck—that he was a doctor. A doctor having a smoke with his pregnant patients? I gave Nikolai a look of surprise, and he shrugged. "All Eastern Europeans smoke."

I had a room with a twin bed, bleached sheets, and one thin pillow. There was another bed, its occupant absent but signs of her remaining on her bedside table: a hairbrush, a bottle of perfume, and a cell phone.

"I'll go home and get some things," Nikolai said, seeing the state of the room. "What do you want?"

"Books. A notebook. And some of those Lindt hazelnut chocolate bars." I gestured to the thin wool blanket. "Maybe a heavier blanket?"

"Okay," he said, sighing heavily, clearly pained to be leaving me there. "I'll be bringing you food every day. If you need something else, I can bring it then."

"There isn't food served here?" I asked.

"There is," he said, wrinkling his nose. "But you won't want to eat it. It will be nettle soup and black bread every day."

"Can you bring Alex to visit?" I said. He was

staying with Yana and Ivan at their home in Bankya, a suburb of Sofia. "I want him to know that everything is fine."

"I'll see," Nikolai said. "I don't know if it's a good idea for him to see this place. We don't want to scare him."

I changed into my nightgown and tried to find the bathroom. It was down the hall, just past the smoking window, a two-stalled lavatory with an exposed bulb swinging from the ceiling. There was a concrete shower area at the far end of the room with a few rubber hoses poking from the walls. The toilets themselves had no seats—I couldn't tell if they had been broken and were never replaced or if there were never seats to begin with—and so I had to somehow balance my pregnant self over the toilet, holding my nightgown with one hand and the wall with the other, to pee. The first time I tried this acrobatic endeavor, I tipped sideways, sprinkling urine all over my legs. There was no toilet paper to be found—you needed to bring your own, apparently—and so I used my nightgown.

But more problematic than my inability to balance my belly-heavy self was the fact that squatting over a seatless toilet brought on contractions, and by the time I'd finished peeing and gone back to my room, I'd had two strong ones in a row. I didn't know how to tell the nurse that this was happening. There was no call button in my room, and even if there had been, she didn't speak English and I didn't speak Bulgarian. And so I slipped into my bed, pulled the starched sheets over my tight stomach, and tried to relax until Nikolai came back.

The reality of what was happening—that I was stuck in an understaffed, drafty, broken-toileted hospital in which I could not communicate with the doctors or nurses—was starting to hit me. How had I arrived here, at this strange place, sick, alone, my clothes smelling of pee? Only a few months before, I was in a comfortable rented house in the Midwest, Alex's wooden train track set up near the fireplace, jazz on the stereo, with a regular income and a toilet with a seat. I looked out the window at the hazy fall night, the lights of Sofia's concrete high-rise apartment buildings blinking in the distance, trying to imagine what would happen next.

I ran my hand over my stomach. I was five months pregnant, and the baby moved slowly, like a big fish, sending shivers through my body. Never had I felt so vulnerable. All the mechanisms I'd used in the past to save myself from trouble— my humor and my education and my charm— were useless now. I was far from home, sick, alone. As I felt the baby swimming in me, I made a promise to God or fate or whatever force ruled my life: *Get me out of this one, and I will be good forever.* I would be a good wife and mother.

I would be loyal and strong. No more complaints, no more requests. *If you help me get out of this Bulgarian hospital with my baby alive, I won't ask for help again.*

Nikolai came to the hospital with rice and kabobs, some Lindt hazelnut chocolate bars, and a case of Bankya mineral water. He'd filled a suitcase with extra clothes, some books, and a blanket. He handed me his favorite novel, *The Master and Margarita* by Mikhail Bulgakov, which I put on my nightstand.

"I'm having contractions again," I said, explaining to him about the toilet.

"Let me get the nurse," Nikolai replied, and he walked out.

Ten minutes later he'd tracked someone down. The nurse stood over my bed and put her cold hands on the tight basketball of my stomach, said something to Nikolai, and left again.

"She's getting you an IV drip," he said. "There's a muscle relaxant you need. Once you get that, they think the contractions will stop. You'll just have to lie still and relax."

"For how long?" I asked, meeting Nikolai's eye. "How long do I have to stay like this?"

"Until the baby is born."

My stay in Maichin Dom was long and dreary. For the first few days, my roommate—a pretty woman from the Mladost district—spoke to me in Bulgarian nonstop, telling me (I imagined) intimate details about her life, her hopes for her baby, and about her husband, who, I noted, did not come to visit. She didn't seem to mind the fact that I couldn't understand her. She offered me cigarettes, showed me pictures on her cell phone of her prepregnancy body, and introduced me to Bulgarian soap operas. After a week she gave birth to a baby girl and left the hospital, leaving the room to me and my endless hours of lying on my back looking out the window at the tarnished gray Sofia sky. I spent some of those hours reading, but the muscle relaxant made me drowsy, and so I would drift in and out of sleep many times each day. I carried a roll of toilet paper with me to the bathroom and learned to balance my uneven weight so that I didn't fall over. The concrete-block showers had no hot water, and so I washed myself slowly, part by part, in ice-cold splashes.

Nikolai came to my room every day to visit, bringing food and bottled water. Alex came once, bringing a Lego creation he'd made for me—a square of blue bricks with a bright yellow sun at the center. He was enrolled in day care and was learning to speak Bulgarian. Yana had cut his hair, and his long blond curls were gone. He looked older than his two years, more serious.

"You'll get better now, okay, Mama?" he said. "You're better, okay?"

I hugged him and told him I'd be better soon. I

could feel his body relax as I held him, and I knew that he must be worried and frightened.

I felt, on those lonely days in the hospital, profoundly disconnected from my own life. I lay in bed sodden with hormones and muscle relaxants, unable to process anything more complicated than the Bulgarian soap opera on TV. Part of it was culture shock to be sure, but the other part was the swiftness with which love had changed my life. Love for Nikolai had brought me so far from home, so far from my family and friends and culture, that I didn't recognize myself anymore. I had always believed love to be transformative, but this wasn't what I'd expected at all. I under-stood what Gregor Samsa must have known upon waking up a cock-roach: Metamorphosis is a fucking nightmare.

Eventually, after I'd spent weeks in the hospital, Nikolai persuaded my doctor to release me. If I had to lie in bed for four months, we argued, it would be much better to do it at home, where I could take a hot shower and eat well. The doctor approved my discharge, but only if we hired a private nurse to come to the apartment in Izgreva to give me shots of the muscle relaxant. I would still be in bed, and I would still be brain-dead, but at least I'd be in my own apartment.

Before I left the hospital, I was wheeled to an examination room. When I climbed up onto the table, I was relieved to find an English-speaking doctor, a woman who had studied medicine in Texas. "We'll just take a look in there," she said, her voice tinged with a southern accent. "To make sure everything is A-OK." Nikolai sat with me during the exam, holding my hand as the doctor squirted jelly onto my stomach and rolled the wand over the skin. "I hear you've had some troubles," she said, squinting at the monitor. "Well, everything looks good here. Your little girl seems very healthy."

"Little girl?" I said, looking from the doctor to Nikolai. "Did you say *girl?*"

"You don't know the sex?" she asked. "I'm sorry. You wanted it to be a surprise?"

"I had an ultrasound, and our doctor said it was a boy."

"Ah, well, he was mistaken. Look here," she said, turning the wand onto the baby. "This is very clearly a baby girl."

Somehow, without even knowing it, I had walked under a rainbow.

Back in Izgreva, Nikolai helped me up the five flights of stairs to the apartment, where Alex was waiting with Yana and Ivan. My son ran to me at top speed, throwing himself around my legs. In Maichin Dom I'd had little way of knowing how he was doing. He'd visited a few times, and Nikolai told me he was fine, but I hadn't spent a significant amount of time with Alex in weeks, and I felt unbalanced by the separation. I never wanted to be away from him for so long again, but he would be staying with Yana and Ivan until the baby's birth. I simply couldn't take care of Alex during the pregnancy. I had to stay in bed.

I bent over to hug my son, and Alex lunged into my arms, trying to crawl up over my stomach, deft and quick as a monkey. He was heavy, and the strain of holding him had an immediate effect: The contractions started again.

Seeing my distress, Nikolai pulled Alex out of my arms and set him on the floor. "Your mom can't carry you, sweetie," he said.

"But why?" Alex asked, looking confused and hurt. I understood his confusion. It didn't make sense that I couldn't pick him up and carry him. I had done so his whole life. It was unnatural and unjust.

"I can't pick up heavy things until your baby sister is born," I added, savoring the sound of the word "sister" as I said it. "It could hurt her. She could be born too soon."

"Am I a heavy thing?" he asked, looking at my stomach with consternation.

"Very heavy," I said. "I need you to help me for the next few months. You need to be a good boy for Yana and Ivan while I get better. Okay, monkey?"

Alex looked up at me, then wrapped himself gently around my legs, careful not to hurt me. "Okay, Mama," he said. "I will."

Later that night Nikolai sat at the edge of my bed. I was crying, missing Alex, wondering what I was doing there, stuck in bed, stuck in Bulgaria. One of the reasons I had come to Bulgaria to begin with—back when I'd believed we were on a summer vacation—had been to spend time with Alex. Now I couldn't even take care of him.

Taking my hand in his, Nikolai tried to comfort me. He told me that everything would be fine, that this would pass. The future was bright. The baby would arrive, we would move back to the States, and we would be famous writers. "Just wait," he said. "It is all ahead, waiting for us." Then he told me that he'd made a big decision: He was going to work exclusively in English from that point forward. While I'd been in Maichin Dom, he had begun writing his next book—his fourth—in English. He was switching languages.

As someone who found it a challenge to write in her native language, I thought the idea of writing in a second one seemed brave and ambitious. It was a wonderful idea, I told him. It was his chance to reach a bigger audience. His books were bestselling, but bestselling in Bulgaria, which is a little like saying you have a number-one hit song in Samoa. His audience was small, and very few Bulgarian writers were ever translated into English. If he wrote his books in English, the whole world would know what I knew already: that my husband was a genius.

Nikolai spent his days writing, while I was too overwhelmed by flesh and estrogen to put a single interesting sentence on paper. I was uneasy with my incapacitation, but I couldn't articulate how frustrated I felt. I didn't understand how to translate that mixture of pride in his work and jealousy that I wasn't working, too. I couldn't say that it seemed unfair, to have invested so much in my career only to find myself pregnant and bedridden. I couldn't actually admit, even to myself, that I felt resentful that my writing—my art and my vocation—was on hold while he was free to write a new book. I felt slighted, cheated somehow, but by whom? I'd *chosen* to have a baby. It was *my* uterus causing the trouble. This was *nature*. There was no one to blame.

I had been on the verge of delivering our daughter for months, and so the birth was quick. Nico was born in the middle of a cold January night at Maichin Dom. She came into the world with one sharp cry, a beautiful and pitch-perfect sound that sliced through the silent delivery room. After the birth I held Nico and looked into her eyes. Her face was puckered and pink, tiny and sedate. Nikolai snapped a picture and then took our daughter in his arms. As he rocked her softly, I could see that he was completely besotted. He looked at me, smiling with joy, and I knew that we were something extraordinary. With Alex and Nico, we were a family.

Moat

I was just getting used to our sleepy village when everything changed. At the beginning of August, protective iron gates began to appear on the streets, blocking the narrow, twisting roads at the center of Aubais. It was as if the village were preparing for a siege, the villagers slowly fortifying their stronghold.

On my daily visit to the *boulangerie*, where I'd perfected my order for *"Une baguette"* (feminine) and *"Un pain au chocolat"* (masculine), I noticed tables filled with new treasures: jars of local honey, *pâte d'amande* candies shaped like bananas and cherries, dried sausages made from bull's meat, bottles of the local wine and olive oil. There was hardly enough room to squeeze into the shop.

I bought our bread and asked, in my best French, "What is all this?"

"Zis," the blond-haired madame said, trying out her English, "zis is la Fête Votive!"

The Fête Votive d'Aubais, I would soon learn, was the highlight of the year for locals and tourists alike. It was a week of pure bacchanalia: wine, food, music, dancing, sex, and violence. The most famous event at the fête, and the reason for all the iron gates and protective fencing, was the daily running of the bulls, an event that occurred just before aperitif hour each day. Bull runs involved skill and danger, and many of the local boys waited all year to show off their prowess before the village.

On the first day of our very first fête, we walked to the main street and waited behind the gates, curious. Before us, with his twitching tail and sharp horns, stood an enormous, heaving black bull.

The villagers lined up along the main street, standing behind the protective iron gates, watching anxiously. A gun sounded, and a pack of white Camargue horses galloped up the street, running together like a single great wild beast, all legs and hooves. Charging after the horses was the bull, its horns long and sharp, its tail switching back and forth. A mob of teenage boys and young men in their twenties ran after the bull, trying to tackle and restrain it. One boy held the tail while another jumped on the neck while another grabbed the horns. Together they wrestled the beast to the pavement, absorbing the violent shocks of its twists and kicks. All the villagers screamed and cheered: Their boys had defeated the beast.

But sometimes they didn't defeat the bull. Sometimes the bull got the best of the boys. And these moments, when they happened, could be gruesome. I once saw a man dragged in one wild sweep from the pharmacy to the mayor's office. His shirt had ripped away, and his skin burned against the concrete, leaving his back raw and bloody. There were bull runs in many of the small villages surrounding Aubais—Calvisson, Aigues-Vives, Junas—and all of them had their share of injuries. One boy was gored by a horn; another boy was kicked in the chest, leaving a bruise the size of a wheel of blue cheese. But these were the risks they took to prove their strength and manhood. These injuries were the price of glory.

We met Lulu and her husband, Lord, at the festivities. "You *must* come and see tomorrow's bull run from our balcony!" Lulu said, pointing to a huge *maison de maître* on one of the main streets, just across from the château. Nikolai and I—knowing no one in the village and feeling adrift in the festivities—were grateful to accept the invitation.

"We have the very best view in the village, and we allow absolutely no one up there. But as this is your first fête and your children are so very darling, you must come!"

Lulu was a witty, articulate woman with red hair, myopic blue eyes, and an overbite that produced an extremely aristocratic lisp. Lord was half Lulu's size, thin as a rail, with elfin ears, twinkling eyes, and a long, bulbous nose. He'd been a jockey in his youth and still retained the disposition of a man ready to be thrown from a horse. With his tweeds and cap, he had all the markings of an English country gentleman and an obsession with examining the habits of the French as if labeling the anatomy of frogs in dissection.

"You see," Lord said the next day, holding open the carved wooden door of their *maison de maître* as we went inside, "the French would *never* have invited you to their home upon first meeting you," he said with an air of authority. "That is why I take such pleasure in having you here. I am *English,* and as such I invite perfect strangers—you, that is—to my home in the off chance you will be amusing."

Lord handed us glasses of chilled rosé and led us up a winding staircase to the third-floor balcony. The view was magnificent, fields and vineyards stretching in every direction. Below, the main street of Aubais was packed with villagers, ready for the bull run.

"Look at that!" Lulu exclaimed as all the sexy *jeunes hommes* of Aubais took off their shirts, preparing to run after that afternoon's bull. "What a view! Better than Chippendale's."

"I do like an au naturel look at the fête," Lord chimed in. "Wine?" he asked, holding up a bottle to refill our glasses.

"Do have more," Lulu said. "My advice: *Drink a lot.* It is the only way to feel even vaguely accepted by the villagers. They dislike foreigners. But don't worry: They hate Parisians more than they hate us!"

"Of course," Nikolai said, raising his glass for a refill, his charm turned all the way up. "Quite good, this local rosé!"

I shot Nikolai a look. Was it me, or had he picked up a British accent in the last five minutes? He was so adept at transforming his personality, at being a chameleon, that he could blend in almost anywhere. Some people might have thought this quality a defect, a kind of shiftiness, but I admired it. It was the writer in him, the novelist, picking up character.

"This is a fantastic painting," Nikolai said, standing with his arms across his chest, examining one of the oils on the wall. "First-rate. Reminds me of the Dutch."

"Are you keen on painting, Nikolai?" Lord asked, his eyes bright.

"Terribly," Nikolai responded. "Especially painters of that period."

If my weakness was blind romanticism, Nikolai's weakness was pretension. He wanted to be admired for his intelligence, his refine-ment, his obscure references to Schubert and Nietzsche. Lord was exactly the kind of person Nikolai could impress.

"Bravo, old chap," Lord said, slapping Nikolai on the back. "I don't care what they say: Eastern

Europeans are a jolly good addition to the European Union."

A gun went off, signaling that the bull run was about to begin and warning the townspeople to stay off the streets.

"It is so exciting," Lulu lisped, hanging over the balcony and waving to the boys below. "You can smell the sweat all the way up here."

"Here they come," Lord said.

Looking down the street, I saw the bull charging. In the distance, amid gusts of dust and rising shouts from the crowd, the white Camargue horses' hooves slammed the pavement, their riders—the village cowboys—steering the bull this way and that, angling to one side, then pushing it away from the spectators.

"You see what they're doing now, don't you?" Lord said, nodding at the horses. "They're slowing the bull down to give that poor kid a chance to gain his footing. Yes, that's right, it is all one coordinated ballet, a beautiful masterpiece. And it is only here, from our balcony, that you will see it so well."

I tried to see the masterpiece in the chaos, but all I could make out was a dustup of major proportions. Cowboys sat tall and strong on the horses, their hats perched on their heads, boots shiny in the afternoon sunlight. They were rough and beautiful and brutal.

"That big chap there," Lord continued, pointing

to a hulking boy. "He's going to get this one."

I peered over the iron railing, leaning into the hot, sticky, dust-filled air, watching as the beefy boy ran ahead of the pack, gaining on the bull, gaining, until, in one expert move, he leaped up, blocking its path. He grabbed the horns in his hands and, with a tremendous twist of his arms, screwed the head down to the ground, pinning it there. The bull kicked, but there were more men behind who, seeing that it was in a weak position, piled on, jumping on the beast's back and yanking its tail and pushing it down, down until that great wild thing buckled to the ground. The population of Aubais erupted into a great cheer. *The hero has slain the minotaur! The monster is banished for another year!*

"What will that guy do now that he's got him?" I asked, swirling the cold rosé in my glass and taking a long sip. It was crisp and fruity, like a burst of iced cherries on the tongue. "Tie him up?"

"My dear," Lord said, clucking at me, "this is not one of your American rodeos."

"You're right," I said, turning back to Lord. "This isn't at all like an American rodeo."

"No?" he asked, his eyebrow raised.

"Not at all," I said, finishing my glass of wine. "It is so much better."

Lord beamed with pleasure, his smile stretching from elfin ear to elfin ear. "Magnificently said, my dear," he said, as if I'd passed some sort of test. "Simply magnificent."

Later, after the run, when the bull was led back to the pasture, the crowd gathered at the festival grounds by the mayor's office. Under a mass of tents, chickens were roasted and sausages grilled and served with salad and cheese. One side of the parking lot was set up with children's rides and the other with a stage, where a band would play later that night. Alex and Nico ran off to shoot balloons with BB guns. After losing a few times, they consoled themselves with enormous cones of cotton candy, pink *barbe à papa* bigger than their heads.

Nikolai and I sat at a picnic table, taking it all in, watching the laughter and jokes, listening to the incomprehensible French. I was beginning to feel the weight of our decision to move to a small village. I couldn't understand anything going on around me. I knew almost no one. I had no idea why people loved watching bulls run in the street and maul their boys. We were outsiders, strangers, people unaccustomed to the rites of the Fête d'Aubais. And yet I was strangely happy. We were doing this thing, however crazy it might be, together. I reached out for his hand, and he took mine. We exchanged a glance that said, *We did it.* I went to the tent and bought two more glasses of wine, feeling it best to follow Lord and Lulu's suggestion: We should drink until the locals accepted us, or at least until we felt accepted. And then we would drink some more.

Soon the band arrived and started to play covers of American pop songs from the eighties, and the combination of something familiar with something foreign—songs of my childhood sung with a French accent—made me even happier. The makeshift dance floor was packed. Lulu and Lord danced; the woman from the *boulangerie* danced; Nico and a pack of village girls danced. I wanted to dance with Nikolai in this strange place, hold his hand under the impossible abundance of stars, to face my new life with laughter and an open heart. I finished my wine and grabbed Nikolai by the hand, pulling him toward the dance floor.

"Come on!" I said, smiling, hoping to entice him.

Nikolai shook his head. *No way.*

"What's wrong?" I opened my arms to Nikolai: *Take me! I'm yours.* "It will be fun."

"I don't dance," he replied.

"So what?" I said. "Nobody cares here. Everyone is so sloshed they won't even remember you tomorrow."

Nikolai gave me a dark look that said no matter how much wine was consumed, he would go nowhere near that dance floor.

"But why not?" I asked, realizing that I sounded like Nico when she wanted candy. I was pleading. "Just one dance."

"Dancing is for idiots."

"Then be an idiot with me," I said, and what I meant was this: Let's let go of our disappointments and our problems and dance until we believe, just for a moment, that we're in love again.

I visited France for the first time when I was sixteen. I had never been outside of Wisconsin, let alone the United States, and my high school had organized a trip to Paris. To me, France was as abstract as the moon, but I knew I wanted to go *somewhere, anywhere,* and France seemed as good enough a place as any. I begged and pleaded and lobbied my mom, and she, seeing that this was something I really wanted, paid for my ticket.

In Paris I was dressed like any American teenage girl: jean shorts, Converse tennis shoes, Red Hot Chili Peppers T-shirt. I wore a black leather motorcycle jacket and black nail polish and too much eyeliner. I noticed right away how different the American girls were from the natives: French girls wore simple, elegant clothes, light makeup, and they were stick-thin. They seemed to have an aura of melancholy and restraint about them, as if they'd been trained like geisha. We, on the other hand, were loud and fun and brimming with energy, our presence filling the boulevard Saint-Germain to bursting.

I walked the streets of Paris for the first time

feeling as if someone had dropped me into a movie. We went to the Tour Eiffel, the Louvre, and all the other places tourists go. One afternoon I stood on the Pont Neuf, looking into the gray Seine, the *bateaux-mouches* swooshing by, and for the first time I understood the incomprehensible bigness of the world, the vastness of it. Girlhood was just the beginning, the starting line. There was more, much more, waiting for me.

At some point during my week in Paris, I went to Shakespeare and Co. I'd read about the bookstore in my guidebook, but I hadn't imagined that it would be quite so wonderful. I stayed for hours and bought so many books that there was no room for clothes in my suitcase. When one of the chaperones of our group asked me why I would buy English books in France, I shrugged, but the truth was that I had felt the possibility of my future there. In those books, and in that store, I found the promise of who I could be. I bought the books because I wanted to carry that promise home with me.

Back in Wisconsin, I'd tried to slip into my old life and continue as if I were the same person. I closed my bedroom door and looked at my belongings—the Doc Martens and the Cure posters on my walls—but nothing seemed to be mine anymore. Something had shifted. I wanted something else, something far away. I didn't become a Francophile, and I didn't throw myself into learning French, but I was altered. It's possible that this change would have happened had I visited Barcelona or Rome. It's entirely possible that when my marriage seemed hopeless and I searched for that perfect place to restore it, I could have chosen Spain or Italy. But what I'd felt in Paris at sixteen had always stayed with me, buried under layers and layers of experience yet there nonetheless, waiting.

There were no whisperings in the long hallways of La Commanderie and no eerie reflections in the glass panes of the French doors. She just appeared in the kitchen late one night as I was making a pot of tea. The house was dark, my children asleep, Nikolai locked away in his office playing online chess. I'd put the kettle on the stove and was waiting for the water to boil when I found myself gazing into her clear blue eyes. She was dressed in old-fashioned clothes—a full blue crinoline skirt and a white blouse with buttons climbing to her chin—and seemed to be about my age, mid-thirties, perhaps a little older. Her hair was braided and piled on her head, giving the impression that her pale face was set in a band of gold. She looked at me with tenderness, as if she understood some-thing that I couldn't quite grasp. A secret. A lesson. Some truth I had only just begun to understand.

I turned my gaze slightly, as if blinking against a bright light, and the woman disappeared.

I stared at the empty space for a moment before turning back to the tea. I filled the pot with chamomile flowers and poured the boiling water. I noticed, as I grasped the kettle, that my hand was steady. My heart wasn't thumping in my chest, and my breathing wasn't irregular. I wasn't frightened, and I didn't doubt what I had seen. A phantom had stood before me, so close that I could have touched her, and I wasn't unsettled in the least. Instead I felt a sweet, reassuring calm. I couldn't think of her as a ghost—she seemed too real, too good, for that. Whatever she was, something in my mind had opened to allow for the existence of this strange presence in my house and to accept it. I couldn't explain what had happened, but I felt that this woman had come to offer me comfort.

I sorely needed it. In the months since we'd moved into La Commanderie, I felt more and more estranged from my husband. While I'd hoped that our move to Aubais would bring us closer, we'd fallen even deeper into a state of mutual isolation. We marked off territories in the house and made our separate spaces, spending most of our time on different floors—he had the first floor (or *rez-de-chaussée*, as the French called it), and I had the second. One of the previous owners had installed a small kitchen on the second floor, and I found myself more comfortable there than in the larger one downstairs. Nikolai, who had never liked to go to sleep before midnight, stayed in his office all night, working or playing online chess or listening to music or studying French, arriving in our bed at four or five in the morning and sinking into a dead sleep. There was no official declaration of our separation. We simply drifted to where we were most comfortable—far away from each other.

As if to secure his solitude, Nikolai begun installing locks on doors throughout the house as soon as we moved in—a lock between the hallway and the salon, another lock on his office door, another lock between the downstairs kitchen and a sitting room, two bolt locks on the back door leading to the rue Droite, and a chain lock on the Paris-Lyon door between the stairwell and the second floor. The Paris-Lyon door had been custom-made for a train, clearly the route between Paris and Lyon, and its weathered oak panels held a huge Art Nouveau frosted-glass vitrine etched with bursting flowers. The words "Paris-Lyon" were inscribed into the glass. One of the many previous owners had installed the door, and it now separated the upstairs bedrooms from a deep stairwell that opened onto the first floor.

I disliked the locks as soon as they were installed. I would hear the clicking and turning of a key in its mechanism many times a day as Nikolai moved through the interior of our home. When I asked him why he did this, he shrugged, as if his reasons were obvious. He later told me the locks were for our safety, that there had been stories of Gypsies breaking into houses all through the south of France. The locks kept thieves out. The locks kept us safe.

He was right—there *were* stories of Gypsies ransacking homes in the area—but it was too safe for me. Hating the sensation of being caged up, I would sometimes walk though the house and open the doors after he locked them, propping them wide with heavy stones from the garden. To the outside ear, my ritual must have sounded like a postmodern symphony, all arrhythmic metal clicks and wooden percussion, but to me it was an act of resistance against an ever-narrowing world. My efforts didn't have much effect—the doors would be relocked the next time he passed through them—and so I began to take the keys and hide them, throwing the keyless doors open so that anyone—kids, dogs, cats, Gypsies, anyone at all—could pass unimpeded.

The night I saw the woman in our kitchen, I stopped at the door of Nikolai's office. The doors in La Commanderie were huge, fashioned of thick wood. His door was locked, of course, and so I knocked lightly until he let me in. His office was warm and comfortable, with a leather couch, stacks of books, and the soft glow of a desk lamp, but I always felt like a stranger going to see him, as if I were not his wife but a neighbor dropping in for a chat. *You know this man,* I would remind myself. *He's your husband, he's the father of your daughter, he's the man raising your son, you've been married to this guy for nearly ten years.*

He didn't join me on the couch but returned behind his desk, slid his Bose headphones around his neck, and waited. It was late, and I was usually in bed by midnight. I could see him mentally scrolling through the reasons I might have come: *Kids? No, they were long asleep. Fly? Fed and walked. Sex? No, we hadn't touched each other in months.*

I'd come for reassurance. I wanted to tell him what had happened in the kitchen and for him to tell me that I wasn't going out of my mind. The ghost hadn't upset me when I saw her but, nonetheless, I was spooked. If anyone could help me make sense of what I had seen, it would be him. During his years in India, he'd come to view the world as a system that worked on the principles of spiritual transfers, of reincarnation and karma, mind over matter. He'd shown me how to burn incense at the altar he'd installed upstairs, and he'd taught me to say the correct Tibetan mantras to build positive karma. He'd told me stories of seeing spirits in India and Bulgaria. He believed in what he'd seen. But I'd never seen a ghost before. I'd never even entertained the possibility that such things existed.

I leaned back on the couch and took a sip of my tea. After a moment of working up my courage, I said, "Something weird happened in the kitchen."

This got his attention. "Downstairs?"

"By the old wall," I said.

He thought for a moment. "Near the trapdoor?"

"Right over the trapdoor, actually," I replied.

I hadn't even considered the trapdoor. Not long after we moved in, we discovered a square carved into the floor of the kitchen and immediately connected it with the stories of secret passageways below the fortress. One afternoon we'd cracked open the floor, cutting away the white marble, and found a narrow trapdoor, just big enough for a grown person to squeeze through. We hoisted up the wooden door and peered into the darkness. There was a chamber below. One of the men from the village, whom we'd invited over for the floor-cracking, inspected it and declared that it was a concrete *cuve*, or vat, for storing olive oil. The chamber below the house was filled with nothing more than fungal, deoxygenated air.

"I saw something, actually some*one,* a person."

"Was it a woman?" he asked. "A woman in blue?"

I sat up, feeling a prickling sensation in my spine. How had he known I'd seen a woman? And how did he know she'd been wearing blue?

"How did you know?"

He removed his headphones, set them on his desk, and said, "Because I've seen her, too."

Battlements

The Christmas after Nico was born, Sam asked me to bring Alex back to the States for a visit. I readily agreed. Alex hadn't seen his father for over a year, and the trip was long overdue. Yet, there was more to my eagerness to leave Sofia than that. With six months of his J-1 homestay requirement left, Nikolai couldn't leave the country. I would be going alone.

I couldn't wait. There were a thousand small reasons for this: I wanted to eat American food; to see a dozen movies in English; to buy something, anything, from an American bookstore and read it cover to cover; to listen to NPR, letting the sweet sound of my language wash over me. And then there were the larger, more profound reasons. In the past months, ever since Nico was born, we had been in a state of conflict. I realized, as the plane took off into the sky, lifting over the snowy peaks of the Vitosha mountains and turning over the endless blocks of concrete apartment complexes, that I was relieved to get away. It was my fault.

The problems started after we brought Nico home from the hospital. There were all sorts of superstitions surrounding the birth of a child. There was a belief that a baby's soul was weak and easily harmed, and so a newborn should be kept inside the home for at least forty days, to avoid its being hexed. Guests and visitors were kept away during these forty days, so that they didn't accidentally (or intentionally) curse the child. If anyone except the parents complimented the baby, that person should say *"Pu! Pu! Pu!"* so as not to curse the baby.

I didn't believe in any of these superstitions. I had taken Alex out walking the week after his birth, believing that fresh air would be good for him. But Nikolai did believe, or believed enough to follow these dictums, and so we stayed inside for the first months of Nico's life, taking her out only rarely and only when no one was around. It was winter, and cold, and so I didn't object.

For the first month, I stayed with Nico night and day, sleeping on a twin bed near her crib, to be close at hand when she woke. I would feed her, change her, and put her back to sleep the way my mom had taught me: quick, without talking or playing or singing, so that the baby would understand that she must sleep through the night. One morning I found Nikolai standing in the doorway, watching. When I asked him what was going on, he told me that Z had excluded him from the nursery after Rada was born and that he wanted to be a part of Nico's nightly routine. His first wife had believed in the strict division of traditional gender roles: that a man should work and provide money while a woman had control of the house. It had been a parenting power struggle, and Z had won. Now, with Nico, he wanted to be part of the action.

That sounded like heaven to me. I didn't believe in the traditional division of gender roles at all. The combination of breast-feeding, exhaustion, and postpartum hormonal fluctuations made me feel like a carnival mirror image of myself: Distorted and slow and hazy. I was thrilled to have Nikolai's help. In fact, I expected it. But, it turned out, we had vastly different ideas about how to care for Nico. We had disagreements about how she should be bathed and changed and put to sleep. He wanted to make her sleeping schedule, and he wanted to decide when she could go out for a walk and when and how she should be fed. When I tried to explain my way of doing things or impose rules of my own, he brought in his parents, who defended his choices.

Things got particularly heated about breast-feeding. Nikolai told me he wanted to feed our daughter, and while he was equipped to provide her with care in every way, he didn't actually have breasts. The solution: formula. Nico was over two months old, hungry all the time, and needed a lot of milk. We consulted a doctor and was told it was fine for a baby to have a mixture of breast milk and formula, so there was no reason not to add formula. And honestly, I hated breast-feeding. My breasts were always sore, and Nico wanted more milk than I could produce. I couldn't leave the apartment for more than a few hours at a time without leaking, and I had all sorts of dietary restrictions. I felt like a cow, pumping milk and bottling it, and I didn't feel like being intimate with my husband with stinging, leaky, cracked nipples. And so we agreed that Nico would transition to formula. We would begin slowly, introducing just a little formula into her diet while continuing with breast milk for a few more weeks.

It was Nico's midnight feeding, and I was groggy with sleep when I found her in Nikolai's arms, a bottle of formula in her mouth. I stared at them, my husband and my child, trying to put it all together. We had just agreed to wait. Yet here he was feeding the baby a bottle.

"Hey, what's going on?" I said, squinting in the darkness.

"Go back to bed," he whispered. "I've got this."

"You've got what?"

"Shhhh!" he said. "You'll wake her up."

"But we agreed that—"

Nikolai gave me a look: *Stop overreacting.* He put his hand on my back and gently ushered me out into the hall.

"Go back to bed," he whispered. Then, he closed the door.

From that day on, Nico had formula instead of breast milk. She was a healthy girl and was absolutely fine without breast milk. But the problem wasn't really about breast-feeding versus not breast-feeding. I'd been more than ready to switch over. The problem was that we had agreed to wait, and he'd gone ahead anyway, ignoring what we'd decided. He had closed the door on the discussion. He'd said one thing and done the opposite. And I stewed, silently, adding this slight to a growing stockpile of slights, storing them up. The formula-versus-breast-milk conflict hurt us, and our marriage, more than it hurt our child.

Thus the dynamic that would define our relationship as parents was set: Nikolai told me what I wanted to hear and then did exactly as he pleased. This kind of thing happened with many small, daily decisions and with bigger ones as well, such as the naming of our daughter. Months before Nico had been born, even before we knew the sex of our child, Nikolai and I had made a deal. If the baby was a boy, he would have Nikolai's family name. If the baby turned out to be a girl, she would have mine. I had made the same bargain with Sam before Alex was born, and Alex had Sam's family name. I felt strongly about this system. I didn't particularly like hyphenated names, where the father and mother stick their names together so that both parties will be equally represented, but I wanted my identity as a parent to be recognized. I didn't believe it was right that the father's name was always passed down. It seemed outdated and out of step with the modern world, where mothers were equal to fathers in every way. Nikolai agreed with me. His parents listened to our agreement and did not object, chalking it up to my American need to upend tradition. It seemed fair enough, this deal. Fifty-fifty odds. After we learned that our child would be a girl, we agreed that she would be called Nico Sidonie Trussoni. The name Nico was inspired by the female singer of the Velvet Underground, and simultaneously had an echo of her father's name. Her last name was to be my family name. The middle name was French, a reference to the given name of the writer Colette. I loved our daughter's name, and I thought Nikolai did, too.

The registration of a baby's birth at the U.S embassy in Sofia had to be completed soon after the child was born, and so Nikolai did all the paperwork right away. But when the Certificate of a U.S. Citizen Born Abroad came back in the mail some weeks later, Nico's name was different from the one we had agreed upon. Printed on the birth certificate was the name Nico, then Nikolai's family name and my family name. The middle name had been left out entirely. He had in essence inserted his name alongside mine, giving her two family names. The name was all wrong, an awkward mistake. I wanted to think that it was an accident and that he had in a moment of distraction written the wrong words on the registration. It couldn't be possible that he'd done it intentionally. That would mean that our deal had been turned on its head: Instead of valuing my identity as an equal, he had purposely devalued it.

Then it happened again, this time with Nico's vaccinations. Bulgarian children were required to have a BCG tuberculosis vaccination, a shot that leaves a knotty scar on the upper left arm. I objected to the inoculation: It isn't required in the States, and Nico, as a U.S. citizen, didn't need it. Nikolai and I talked it over, and he agreed with me: Nico stayed home and wasn't exposed to other kids, so she wasn't at risk of getting TB. She had all of the other vaccinations and would receive the rest on the recommended schedule. And besides, the two-year requirement to stay in Bulgaria would be over in just a few months. We were going home soon. There was no need to subject our daughter to something that would leave a scar. But when she came home from her next visit to the pediatrician—Nikolai and Yana had taken her, while I stayed home with Alex— she had a bandage on her arm and swelling all the way to her shoulder. He had gone ahead with the vaccination, despite what we had agreed.

"Did we decide against that?" Nikolai asked. "I thought we came around to the idea in the end. Well, it's too late now."

When I tried to talk to him about these incidents, he said he'd acted in my interest (feeding Nico formula instead of breast milk), or he'd forgotten what we'd agreed upon (Nico's name), or he'd misunderstood (the vaccination). He acted as if it were all perfectly normal behavior to say one thing to me and do the exact opposite. But it wasn't normal behavior. We had different ideas about how to parent, yes, but there was something else, a deeper problem, that I was only beginning to fully understand. The birth of our child allowed me to see a side of my husband I hadn't known before.

There'd been other warnings. One day, not long after Nikolai and I had moved in together in Iowa City, he saw a red suitcase in my closet and asked what was inside. The suitcase was where I kept my journals, about fifty or so notebooks filled with stories and poems, bits of this and that I'd glued onto the pages: a note from my first boyfriend, a rejection letter from the *New Yorker* magazine, a receipt from the coffee shop where I'd written my first awkward short story. The pages were filled with disfigured self-portraits, twisted and half-real reflections of me at sixteen, at eighteen, at twenty. Much of what was inside these notebooks was badly written and embar-rassing, but I felt too attached to the efforts—the deformed beauty of my ungainly sixteen-year-old handwriting—to throw them out. As a result I'd lugged these notebooks with me from apartment to apartment for years. I never opened the red suitcase but slipped it into the closet of whatever apartment I was renting.

I had unlatched the brass clasps of the red suitcase and shown Nikolai the rows of neatly arrayed notebooks. He picked one up and began to open the cover. I eased it from his fingers and replaced it in the suitcase, snapping the clasps closed.

"They're private," I'd said, and although nothing in the notebooks was exactly a secret, the collection of them together created my own bible of sacred texts.

"I can't read them?" he asked, hurt.

"Nobody has ever read them but me," I said. "And I want to keep it that way."

A week or so later, I came home from class to find him sitting cross-legged in the middle of the living room, stacks of my notebooks spread at his side. There was a cup of tea steaming on the floor next to him, and as he looked up, he gave me a big goofy smile, an awkward *I didn't expect you back* this *soon* grin. The suitcase was open at his side. I was so surprised I could hardly speak. "What are you doing?"

"Reading," he replied as he closed the journal and set it aside, as if he had been glancing through the *New York Times* style section.

"But I asked you not to read these," I said, taking the journal and hugging it to my chest. A subtle shift had developed in my perception of him, a wavering of my confidence, the first doubt.

"Did you say that?" he said, a look of consternation crossing his features.

"Yes," I responded, but part of me didn't want to acknowledge that I had said it. A hopeful part of me wished that there'd been a mistake, that I actually hadn't told him, that he had not broken my trust.

"Well, maybe you did," he admitted. "But you didn't actually mean it, did you? You want to share everything with me. So there are no secrets between us."

He took a long sip of his tea, still smiling, and I realized that he didn't think he'd done anything wrong. But for me it was an enormous surprise, this invasion of privacy, this lack of respect and the absence of remorse. I tried to rationalize Nikolai's betrayal of trust. I thought maybe he didn't understand me when I'd told him it was private. Maybe it was a cultural misunderstanding, and he assumed I wasn't serious when I'd made the red suitcase off-limits. I took my journals and replaced them in the red suitcase, and I stashed it away again. But somewhere, at the back of my mind, a loud buzzer was going off. This buzzer, I later realized, is called instinct. My instincts were telling me something important about this charming, handsome, brilliant man, but I didn't listen. I knew, deep down, at a visceral level, that something wasn't right. It was the first of my many errors about love: I thought the heart more prescient than the gut.

When I landed in Chicago with Alex, Sam met me at the airport. I turned on my phone and found it filled with voice messages from the previous nine hours. Nikolai had texted or called about every fifteen minutes. The content of the messages wasn't memorable, or at least I don't remember it. What I remember is the quantity. There were dozens of texts, a deluge of messages pouring forth from my phone.

Later, when I checked my e-mail, I found the first of his many love letters to me. His Christmas letters, as I came to think of them, were beautiful and tender, but most of all they convinced me that despite our growing problems, Nikolai loved me. The letters were filled with references to his writing and our life together. I saw how funny he was, how smart, but also how needy he could get, how badly he craved my attention. In every letter he made it clear that he was struggling without me. At one point, he said that he couldn't write unless I was nearby, and that his days felt empty. I didn't feel that way at all. We had become symbiotic, he and I, and while losing myself in him had once made me feel strong and hopeful, now it felt good to have some space. I needed room to breathe.

There was one passage in particular in these letters that was seared into my memory, just a few sentences about the pain he'd felt when I left Sofia. It was the first and only time he would be honest with me about the emotional baggage he carried around with him. When he was with me, he wrote, he forgot the scars of his past. When I was gone, all the pain came rushing back to him. I was an anesthetic, a drug that numbed him. He wrote that he wanted to forget the scars but couldn't unless I was there. Later I would ask him what he meant by this passage, but he wouldn't explain in any real depth. When I tried to go deeper into his past, he shut down. I wondered if this pain came from his time as a pianist or if there was some deeper secret, something he was too ashamed to tell me. I would reread these letters years later, looking for ways to reach him. I would find his voice, his humor, his intelligence, and his need for me. His letters gave me a way back to the man who, over time, had become a stranger.

I'd waited for months to see pages from Nikolai's first book in English, and when he finally gave them to me, I read them all in one sitting. The book was brilliant, with all his customary humor and energy, his stream-of-consciousness sentences, and his wild and funny characters. I was sure that he was ready for the next step, and so I suggested that he apply to M.F.A. programs in the States.

"It will be great," I said. "Getting an M.F.A. will help you perfect your English, and you can also teach one day, if you want."

"But I've written two bestsellers," he objected. "I'm overqualified."

"I know," I said. "This is a way to get your foot in the door."

"My academic history isn't good enough," he said. "I never graduated from high school."

"You didn't?" I said, taking this in, one more surprise in a year of surprises. "You told me you went to college in Boston."

"I did."

"So how did you get into college if you dropped out of high school?"

"They let me in after hearing a tape of my music," he said. "They waived all the requirements and gave me a full scholarship."

"Wow," I said, impressed. I had to admit— why finish high school if you get that kind of treatment?

"And then I dropped out of college," he added, as if it were the most natural thing in the world to throw away a free ride at one of Boston's more prestigious universities. "And went to India."

This I knew. He'd told me that he'd left in the last semester of college for Dharamsala, to study Tibetan Buddhism. And still, I was amazed that he'd been so rash, so ready to give up on his degree. I had struggled through my undergraduate years, taking loans and working full-time while going to school, graduating with thirty-five thousand dollars in student-loan debt. Nikolai had been given a free education, and he'd just walked away from all of it.

"Creative-writing programs don't care much about transcripts," I said. "They tend to focus on the writing itself."

"Will they hold India against me?" he wondered, warming up to the idea. "I can say it was good material for my writing."

"It *was* good material," I said. "Don't worry. You're talented. You'll get into a program. I'm sure of it."

This was a particularly American belief, that with hard work and talent one will inevitably succeed, and Nikolai eyed me with suspicion when I said it. I knew he was thinking of the Chopin Competition, where it had been connections, not talent, that paved the way to victory. I could feel how difficult it was for him, to put his work out for judgment, to be vulnerable. I wanted to help him get past that fear. I wanted to help him trust the world again. I wanted his future to be brilliant.

There was more at stake than just finding a good writing program. If Nikolai wanted to live in the United States, he would need a job. He couldn't arrive on American soil unemployed and directionless. As it was, Nikolai was qualified for very little. He had no work history, no degree, and no clear plan as a writer. He wrote beautiful books in Bulgarian and played Chopin that could make me cry, but these skills weren't easy to translate professionally. His parents had raised him to be a hothouse flower, one protected behind glass, but he couldn't survive like that away from home. If he could get into a graduate program, he would be on a path toward sustaining himself. If he had a degree, he would find his way. I was sure of it.

Never before had I been so practical-minded. Usually I was the artistic one, my head in the clouds over some new project. But after a year and a half in Bulgaria, I understood what it meant to be really poor. While my parents had never had money for luxuries, we'd always had enough food and clothes and cheap entertainment. But Nikolai and I lived—like so many other people in Eastern Europe—on very little. Yana gave us 250 leva, the equivalent of about $125, each Friday, and we supported a family of four on it. This worked out to about $18 a day, or $4.50 a day per person.

We developed a program to make our leva last through the week. On Friday night, when we were flush, we might go to a movie, spending 20 leva on tickets and paying a babysitter to stay with Alex and Nico. For the rest of the week, we scrimped. We bought cheap vegetables from the market—potatoes and leeks and cucumbers and tomatoes—and rationed them. Nico's formula was expensive, and so Yana sometimes dropped off a container midweek, along with cute baby clothes, but we didn't have money to buy clothes or shoes for Alex. We didn't go for a drink in the bars in the center of Sofia, and we didn't have lunch at the pizza place near Alex's day care. By the time Friday came around again, we were scraping for change to go have a coffee at the neighborhood café, where a cappuccino was 2 leva. I would sip my coffee, grateful to be out of the apartment, happy that we would soon be leaving Bulgaria.

Before long, the two-year homestay requirement ended, and we were free to go home. Nikolai had been accepted to Brown University's M.F.A. program, and so we moved to the East Side of Providence, Rhode Island, filling a two-bedroom Cape with all the furniture, books, and toys we'd left in Iowa City three years before. After we'd settled in, we chose a day care for Nico and enrolled Alex in the neighborhood public school. We made new friends, went to dinner parties and book readings. We threw ourselves into our writing projects, hoping we would find success.

We were on our way. My first book, a memoir about my relationship with my father, was going to be published. It had sold to a publisher in New York City in 2004, just months after my thirtieth birthday, when Nico was less than a year old. For the first time in my life, I would be published, a goal I'd worked toward since I was a freshman in college. I found profound happiness in this achievement: My work—and my self, which was so deeply bound up in my work—was being taken seriously for the first time. My writing had been rejected in the past—a five-hundred-page novel I'd written as a graduate student had been turned down by over twenty publishers in 2002—and these rejections had pushed me to write another book, to try another approach, to keep rewriting and experimenting. Now, finally, it had paid off. The advance had allowed us to buy airline tickets back to the United States from Bulgaria and put a down payment on a used Toyota RAV4. The advance had put us back on track from (what I considered at the time) our detour in Bulgaria. Now our real life could begin.

Nikolai began classes at Brown. The M.F.A. program was small and consisted of a collection of young, talented, and primarily "experimental" writers. One student in his program wrote a story in Morse code, for example, and flicked the lights of the classroom on and off to "read" it. Nikolai came home after that particular class and demonstrated the short story to the kids, flicking the lights on and off until we were all laughing. Eccentricity was accepted at Brown's M.F.A. program. In fact, Nikolai told me, eccentric was the norm, and he felt he belonged there. His work was unusual, experimental, and this program gave him a community in the United States. It also gave him some professional clout: He got an agent after he began his master's at Brown, and he sold his first book in English—a memoir about his time in India as a Buddhist monk—a year later.

Now we were both memoirists, two people who used our own lives to create story, people who fashioned characters from living and breathing human beings. We both understood the moral risks of writing about people we'd known and loved. We didn't want to hurt anyone we wrote about, but we also wanted to represent our own experiences, the way we lived and felt them. In between the objective and the subjective, we needed to find truth and make that truth our own.

I had been trying to write about my father for many years before my memoir was accepted for publication. My dad knew I was writing the book, and had allowed me to interview him, but I didn't ask his permission, and I didn't share drafts with him. I gave him a copy of the final book, and he read it in one long sitting. He told me he was proud of me, but I knew that my book was surely not the book he would have written about him-self. It was my book, with my perspective of our relationship. He understood that. He knew I had told our story from my limited, emotionally colored, and singular point of view.

It couldn't have been otherwise. I had adored my father as a child, but this love had not always been good for me. He was a charming, damaged man, who never fully came to terms with his own destructiveness. As a kid I'd loved him despite—and even because of—his flaws, glorifying his wild and reckless behavior, elevating him to a legend in my heart. No one was quite as charming, quite as crazy, as my dad. But when I became an adult, this adoration ended. I left home. I formed my own opinions. I wanted to be free of him.

Writing about our relationship helped me find this freedom. Readers of the book always asked me if it was cathartic to write, and it was, I suppose, a release from the past. Yet the real magic came not from getting feelings out but from the turning inward, the examining of myself and my past, in relation to my father. I saw us both more clearly, more truly, than before. Re-creating the past required an imaginative possession of our characters, of who we used to be together. I had to speak as he spoke, walk as he walked. I had to make him come alive on the page. The writing was an incantation, and the incantation helped me find peace.

But the magic worked two ways. My father had cancer when I began writing about him, and while I was working on the book, he got better. He went into remission, and his doctors believed he could fully recover. He was strong and healthy for some years. Then, not long after I turned the book in to my editor, his cancer returned. During the prepublication period of my book, he declined rapidly. The month the book about my father was published, he died. While I'd been writing about my father, he'd been strong. When I stopped, he withered.

Some years later Nikolai wrote me a letter that explained the workings of magic. He wrote that everyone, that all human beings, are actually magicians, but some more powerful than others. Our minds are our weapons, and we have more power than we realize. He explained the difference between black magic and white magic, namely that black magic will initially hurt the target but will turn around and damage the sender even more strongly. White magic, on the other hand, helps both the target and the sender. He said I could, by visualizing a person or situation, transform it through compassion (*"Om mani padme hum"*) or emptiness (*"Om gate paragate parasamgate bodhi svaha"*). My intention could change the karmic and metaphysical reality of my world. Mind and matter cannot be separated, he said, and we all have the power to transform our lives and relationships. It was a two-way street: The object of my thoughts would undergo a trans-formation, and I would undergo a transformation as well, because everyone is connected.

He wasn't commenting specifically on the act

of writing in this note, and I don't know if he believed that magic could explain what happened as I wrote and published the book about my dad. But we both understood that we, as writers, were magicians. We were powerful in ways we might not even realize.

In Providence we were writing all the time. Nikolai was in school and writing his memoir. I was writing a new book, a novel, and teaching as an adjunct writing instructor in Boston, taking the train north in the evenings. We were working seven days a week, and yet each month we struggled to scrape up enough to pay our bills. The stress of it wore on us, and we fought more and more about money. Neither of us wanted to think about the practicalities of life. We wanted to live in our books, where we worried about nothing but character development and the right turn of phrase. But we had two children under five years old, and there was no choice except to take responsibility for our finances. I'd been on my own for my whole adult life and had more experience than Nikolai when it came to paying bills, and so it fell to me.

I was terrible at managing our money. I didn't know how to do it at all. My solution to this lack of comprehension was denial and avoidance. I was in denial about the fact that we were broke and avoided finding a solution. My life raft became credit. I applied for a credit card and began to use it for groceries and other necessities. This eased the tension a little, although I still dreaded going to the mailbox each afternoon, knowing I would find a fistful of past-due bills. Soon this credit card was maxed out, and so I applied for another one. Miraculously, I was approved. Again I felt as if I'd been given a reprieve. When the second card was full, I repeated this process, until I had five credit cards that were charged to the limit. I paid the minimum balance each month but couldn't pay more, and so these debts grew as the interest accumulated. I would go over our expenses and try to understand what I was doing wrong, but we weren't living outlandishly. We simply weren't earning enough.

I felt both powerless and powerful about the role that money played in our relationship. Because I would (eventually, after lots of mistakes) be better at managing our money and because I had a career, I knew I would never have to be financially dependent on my husband. This gave me confidence that I could always stand on my own. I remembered my father and his criticism of dependent women, and I felt that I had avoided that fate, that I had not become "that kind of woman." And yet, at the same time, I longed to be taken care of by a man, to feel secure, and for my financial well-being—which was really the well-being of me as a person—to be respected. But I wasn't able to depend on Nikolai in this regard. He spent freely, and always expected someone—his parents or me—to rescue him financially. He couldn't understand the correlation between work, money, and respect. While being in charge of our finances put me in a position of power, I didn't always like being there. I couldn't ever be vulnerable, or in need, with my husband.

And yet while the practical problems were stressful, the romantic ones were corrosive. By the time we arrived in Providence, the romantic story I'd invented had all but crumbled. In Bulgaria I could tell myself that we were momentarily waylaid and that our "real life" hadn't started yet. But in Providence real life hit us hard. The dream life I'd imagined I would have with Nikolai was nothing at all like what I was actually living. The dream life could not accommodate exhaustion; the dream life could not accommodate money problems; the dream could not accommodate needy children. The very nature of the dream had been unreal. And so when reality arrived and the dream I had of my marriage began to die, I found myself wishing I could stop everything and start over.

As part of his financial-aid package at Brown, Nikolai taught an undergraduate workshop each semester. He told me about his students and sometimes brought home their workshop stories for me to read, and so I knew a little about his class. For example, I knew that on the first day of the semester, when everyone went around the table and made introductions, one of the students had identified himself as a "*Mayflower* descendant," a term that Nikolai didn't understand and, with my being midwestern and of Italian descent, one I rarely encountered. Another student was a world-class cellist and another a Russian whose parents were, Nikolai speculated, "rich ex-Communists." Danny DeVito's twins were at Brown that year, as was Donatella Versace's daughter. We joked about how cool it would be if a DeVito child and a Versace child got married. It would be an off-the-charts Italian dream couple.

Nikolai's class began at five-thirty on Thursdays. Usually he was home around eight, or if he went out for a beer after, he'd be back at ten. But on the last day of the spring semester, he was going out for sushi with his students after the workshop, a kind of farewell party. I knew he'd be out for dinner, so I put the kids to bed, had dinner alone, cleaned up, and went to bed, expecting to hear the front door open any moment. Hours later I woke up and found his side of the bed empty. I glanced at the alarm clock: It was two-thirty in the morning. He still wasn't home.

I got up, found my phone in my bag, and called him. He didn't pick up. I texted him and got no reply. I went to the window and looked outside, to see if our Toyota was parked in front. It wasn't. For a moment I considered calling the police, but then I didn't. Clearly he was still out with his students, and so I decided to wait another hour. I went back to bed, took a book from my bedside table, and began to read.

I woke the next morning with my lamp on and the book across my chest. I felt a nagging sensation that something wasn't right and realized, when I looked at Nikolai's side of the bed, that he hadn't come home. I jumped out of bed and went to the front window. The car was there, and, sure enough, so was my husband. I stood over the couch, where he had fallen in a pile, his coat still on and his black leather boots on his feet. The keys to the Toyota were on the floor. It looked as if he'd just made it to the couch and collapsed there. *That,* I thought, scooping up the keys, *is one mother of a hangover.*

I didn't have time to talk to Nikolai. I'd do that after I got back from the school drop-off. I made some toast and hot chocolate for the kids' breakfast, poured coffee into a mug to bring in the car, and helped Nico get ready for school. Alex didn't want my help. At seven years old, he loved to be independent. He dressed himself, packed his own school bag, tied his own shoes, and got his own cereal. Nico, at four, still loved to be dressed. She waited for me to pull up her cotton tights and slip on her shoes and put on her sweater. When she was ready, I took her in my arms and carried her outside.

Alex waited by the car. I unlocked the door, and he climbed into the backseat. I went to put Nico in but found that her car seat had been unbuckled and tossed into the cargo area. A green flannel blanket lay in its place. I leaned over the seat, pulled the car seat back into place, and was wrangling the straps around Nico, when Alex said, "What's this?"

I didn't look around right away, and so he repeated himself.

"Mama!" he said, more loudly this time. "What's this?"

I turned to see what he'd found. There was a bright blue condom package in his hand.

"SweeTarts," I said, taking the package from his fingers. It was torn and empty, the condom gone. Used.

"Can I have one?"

"Not now," I said. "Maybe after school."

Alex wiggled onto the seat and buckled himself in. He slid his backpack down by his feet, shoving aside a Louis Vuitton wallet lying on the floor. Another condom package, also bright blue, lay next to it, this one unopened. A credit card, a driver's license, a student ID, and a handful of change—a whole mess of quarters—were scattered over the floor.

"Can I have those quarters?" Alex asked.

"Sure," I said, distracted by the wallet. I picked up the quarters and dropped them into Alex's outstretched hand. Then I shoved the student ID, driver's license, and credit card inside the wallet and climbed into the front seat, where I took a closer look.

"Twenty-five, fifty, seventy-five," Alex counted from the backseat.

"Hey," Nico said, realizing she'd missed out. "I want some monies, too!"

The Brown student ID showed a picture of a pretty blond girl with huge blue eyes.

"These are mine," Alex said. "I found them."

I looked over the credit card—*what kind of student has a platinum card?*—and saw a long Slavic name, a name with so many consonants that I wouldn't have been able to pronounce it. Nikolai, who could speak Russian, would be able to pronounce it perfectly.

"One dollar. One twenty-five."

"I want one, too!"

"Give her a quarter, please," I said.

"They're mine," Alex groaned. "You gave them to me."

I examined the driver's license and read the date of birth. The Russian girl was nineteen years old. Her height was five-ten, and her weight was 122 pounds. These dimensions left my imagination to create a tall, thin, blond nightmare.

While Nikolai had mentioned that he had a Russian student in his class, he hadn't mentioned that the Russian student was a beautiful nineteen-year-old blonde with enormous blue eyes. I looked over my shoulder at Alex and Nico, sitting in the backseat, sorting out their booty. The flannel blanket that had been lying across the seat was scrunched up between them. An equation scrolled through my mind, and the equation was this: Blanket + an empty condom package + car seat thrown in the back + a nineteen-year-old blond Russian student + Nikolai out all night. The sum of this equation was not anything good.

I drove Alex to school and then Nico to day care, trying to keep my cool. *There are many possible explanations for this,* I thought as I drove home and parked the Toyota in front of our little white house. *I'm sure Nikolai will explain everything.* I unbuckled my belt, leaned back into my seat, and, suddenly I had what I will call a WTF moment. It was a moment when I would take a step away and look at the larger picture of my life and think, *WTF am I doing?* This kind of moment happened every so often in my life with Nikolai. I'd had a WTF moment at Maichin Dom, although I hadn't yet had the acronym in my lexicon then. Now, as I looked over the Russian girl's perfect teeth and her four-hundred-dollar Louis Vuitton wallet, a very strong, very angry WTF moment hit me. WTF was I doing on this beautiful Friday morning in Providence with a ripped condom wrapper in my hand and a blond nightmare in my mind?

Nikolai was still sleeping on the couch when I opened the front door. I went to the kitchen to make more coffee and then returned to the living room, where I sat on my favorite faux Eames chair, a yellow pleather affair I'd bought at the Salvation Army thrift store.

"Nikolai," I said. I leaned over and pushed his shoulder to wake him up. His eyes were blood-shot and puffy, and he smelled of cigarettes. *Of course,* I thought, *all Eastern Europeans smoke.*

"Hmm?" He opened an eye and looked at me.

"Coffee?" I asked, offering him a sip of mine.

He shook his head.

I dropped the wallet and the ripped condom wrapper on the floor. We hadn't bought a coffee table yet.

"We need to talk about that," I said.

He sat up. "What's that?"

"That's what I want to know."

We sat there for a good minute, me at the edge of my chair, him on the couch, the wallet and condom between us. Finally Nikolai cleared his throat and said, "I don't know what that is."

"Really?"

"Really."

We sat there for another full minute. The silence between us was like the rest in a piece of

133

orchestral music—a pause between big, raucous kettledrums.

"No idea at all?" I said.

He shook his head. I bent over and took out the driver's license and read, "Nzxhsarradvhda." He gave me a look, part derisive, part pained.

"You mean Nadezhda," he said.

"Is that how you say it?" I said. "Na-desh-da? Because I can hardly stand to read such an ugly word, let alone pronounce it."

"Hope," he said quietly.

"Excuse me?" I hadn't expected him to say that word then, at that moment, and tears sprang to my eyes.

"Nadezhda. It means *hope* in Russian. And in Bulgarian, actually."

"Wonderful," I said. "So what's her wallet and"—I nudged the blue wrapper with my shoe—"*that* doing in the car? The kids found them. Alex asked me what it was. I said it was fucking SweeTarts."

"Nothing happened," he said, going into defensive mode.

"I woke up at two-thirty," I said. "You weren't here."

"My students went out for sushi with me. And we had a little too much to drink, and then I drove them home."

"You and like all ten of your students were in the car?"

"No, just a few of them," he said.

"So you were driving drunk all around Providence with a carload of undergraduates until three in the morning?"

He covered his eyes with his hands. "I know it sounds bad," he said. "But I took Nadezhda home. She must have dropped her wallet."

"And that?" I said, looking at the blue wrapper again.

"She must have dropped that, too."

We had a long, tense discussion that turned into, over the next hour, a major fight. He became adamant that nothing had happened and that I was wrong to suspect him. Meanwhile I went through all my doubts about him, the ones I'd been collecting since the Red Suitcase Incident. I outlined the pattern of behavior that had begun even before Nico's birth, in Iowa City, with my journals, and continued with his J-1 visa requirements, and continued after Nico's birth. I was beginning to understand that this pattern of behavior was deeply rooted in his personality. It had always been there, but I'd chosen not to see it. It was like looking at a favorite painting and finding that the perspective was off, the shadows fell the wrong way, with no correspondence to the angle of the sun. The flaw had been there all along, only I had been too blinded by love to see it.

By the end of our fight, our positions had

solidified. He denied that anything had happened, and I was left with the equation I'd worked out in the car. I had a choice. I could leave or I could stay. Leaving would mean pulling apart everything I'd worked to build—breaking up my family and my home. Leaving would mean admitting—to myself and everyone else—that I'd been wrong about Nikolai, that I had bad judgment, that I was unable to maintain a healthy long-term relationship. It meant there was something inherently problematic with me for choosing a man who wasn't honest with me. It meant that I was damaged goods myself. I'd been married and divorced once already. I'd put my children through a lot of difficult changes in the past years. I was too ashamed of my past failures. I couldn't do it again.

But staying married created an equally damning situation. Staying married meant that I must suspend my instincts and my own perceptions about what was true and what was false. Staying married meant that I accepted all the past deceptions—the minor ones, like Nico's vaccination shot, and the major ones, like Nikolai's J-1 homestay requirement. It meant that I tacitly agreed to accept whatever future deceptions came up. Even if there were no future deceptions, it would mean being forever suspicious. But worst of all, staying married meant that I must push all these feelings of doubt and uncertainty about him down, below the surface of my life, and put on a happy face. It meant living with it. It meant making things work, come hell or high water. Reader, I chose to stay married.

But that didn't mean that I was happy to stay. I wasn't. And, as masking my feelings has never been my strong suit, we began to fight regularly. During many of our fights, I threatened to leave. I told him we should get divorced. The word was uttered in the way the word "bankrupt" is said at the board meeting, the way "terminal" is said at the doctor's office. It was a locked-and-loaded word. A final-solution word. It was more than a collection of consonants and vowels, but a demon I'd conjured into our lives.

This demon was powerful. It gave me a rush of control over my anger and unhappiness when I said it. But it also terrified me. It brought back memories of my parents' divorce and left me with a low-grade anxiety, one that kept me awake late into the night, adrenaline coursing through my body. When I left Sam, I hadn't considered divorce with the same terror, partly because Alex was only a baby and wouldn't remember it, but also because Sam and I were so young, and so immature, that it had almost seemed like we'd been playing at being grown-ups. But with Nikolai it was different. I had carefully considered my feelings. I had wanted to be his wife.

I'd wanted to give him a child. I'd wanted to be faithful to him. I'd wanted to keep my promises. I'd wanted to be with him forever. I might not have understood our Bulgarian wedding vows, but I understood what it meant to be committed. And I had been committed to Nikolai, one hundred percent.

To keep the demon away, I learned the art of avoidance. I avoided talking to Nikolai about sensitive topics (our lack of sex, lack of money, blue condom wrappers). I avoided friendships with happy couples, finding it difficult to be confronted with other people's marital success. I avoided the present moment and imagined the future. In the future we would laugh more. In the future we would make love twice a week. In the future we would see that at all these troubles were just a phase, something we'd made it through together. I lived for the day we would put everything behind us and be happy again.

After the Russian Girl, I insisted that we go to therapy. Things were becoming so tense that I saw regular discussion with an objective observer as a good solution. Nikolai didn't want to go, but finally he agreed, so long as he went alone to a therapist of his own choosing. And so we each found therapists at different practices on the East Side of Providence. I began seeing someone on Wednesday nights, while he was home with

Alex and Nico, and he was scheduled to go on Thursdays, while I stayed home with the kids. Nikolai saw his therapist twice. Then, for some mysterious reason, he stopped going.

"What happened?" I asked one Thursday night when he was supposed to be at therapy.

"Hmmm?" Nikolai was playing online chess, and it was hard to get his attention.

"I said why did you miss your session? Don't you have an appointment now?"

"What session?" he asked, glancing up from the monitor.

"Therapy? You know, we agreed to go talk to someone about . . . *this?*"

"Oh, *that,*" he said, as if I'd just reminded him of the Batak massacre of the Bulgarians by the Ottoman Turks. "Therapy. What about it?"

"I gather you're not going tonight?"

"No," he said, clicking his rook into a corner and protecting it with a pawn, a maneuver he told me was called castling. "I'm done with that."

"Who is *done* with therapy after two sessions?"

"I am," he said. "My therapist told me I don't need therapy."

My therapist told me I don't need therapy. I couldn't get this line out of my mind. I repeated it to myself, even as I stood there watching him play chess. *My therapist told me I don't need therapy.* Why would a therapist dismiss someone after two sessions?

"Don't you think you should find another therapist, then?" I asked at last.

"Why would I?" he said, clicking on his knight and moving it to a square he called H7. "You wanted me to try, and I tried. It didn't work."

"Isn't the point of therapy to help our marriage?" I asked, growing frustrated. He was just sitting there playing chess, without even looking at me, as if I weren't even there. "Don't you think you should at least stick with it for more than *two sessions?*"

"Is it really that important?" he asked, glancing up at me.

"Yes," I said, feeling like the very stereotype of a disgruntled wife, my arms akimbo, my voice pouty. But it was important to me that he show he cared enough about our marriage to try talking to someone.

"Okay. I'll find someone else."

"Really?" I asked, and I could hear the hope in my voice, the sound of hope not yet being pathetic to my ears.

"Sure," he said, turning his back as he made another move. "I'll take care of it."

It took Nikolai months to find a new therapist, and when he did, it happened a second time: He began therapy, and then he stopped going. When I asked him again what had happened, he said the same thing he'd said the first time, *My therapist told me I don't need therapy.* Now it was two therapists who had told him he didn't need therapy, two therapists who had assessed him and, finding that he was perfectly normal, with no problems and nothing to talk about, told him to stop coming.

Despite his resistance to therapy, I continued. I didn't exactly like therapy. I found it too disruptive to the alternative narrative of my marriage I was trying to create. After a therapy session, it was difficult to go back to my life—my increasingly hypocritical life—without feeling like I'd opened a Pandora's box of discontent.

And yet these sessions forced me to look at my feelings systematically. They forced me talk to someone for one hour once a week about my marriage, forced me to examine myself, forced me to look my own significant faults—my need for control, my perfectionism, my anxieties about money, my stubbornness, and my insecurities. I wasn't easy, I knew that. My childhood left a legacy of distrust. I wanted the security of a family, but I had no real working model for one, and so I patched together ways of getting through that were not healthy and even destructive. I had, for example, a big hot Italian temper that bubbled up and burst forth in an explosive shower of screaming and throwing whatever was nearby. I needed to show, not tell, my fury. Once, when Nikolai had pushed the wrong button, I threw an entire bowl of tomatoes at the wall, leaving pale pink splotches of color on the white paint, abstract expressionism Trussoni style. I could be bossy and a know-it-all, and I often used extreme measures to decimate Nikolai in an argument, saying the meanest thing that came to mind so that he would storm off in a rage. I was always testing him, pushing him, waiting for him to break. I eventually came to see this behavior, which must have been as excruciating for him to live with as it was for me, as the result of my choice to stay married. I chose to stay even though I knew I wasn't being honest with myself. I chose to stay even though the dynamic we'd created was killing us. My contempt—for him and for myself—was a result of my choice to stay. But I couldn't leave either. And this tension between what I should do and what I actually did do tore me apart.

Marriage is not easy for anyone, my therapist once said. I wasn't alone—my therapist had counseled hundreds of married patients, each unhappy in her own way. *Take things slow,* she told me. *Forgive him and yourself. Let your love grow again. Get some distance from your anger. Give yourself space.*

Like how much distance? I wondered. A continent?

Pitch

I woke in a pitch-black darkness, and from the edge of this darkness came a shrill, inhuman scream.

I flung off the covers and sat up in bed, filled with a primal fear. I listened, my heart in my throat, for the cry to return. My first thought was of Nico, not my eight-year-old Nico but my hungry newborn Nico, whose wail had summoned me at all times of the night, needing, needing, needing.

In the fraction of a second it took me to regain my sense of time and place—*it was 2010, and I was in a drafty, ancient stone structure in France*—I heard the screeching again, sharp and keening. No, I realized, it wasn't a baby, not a catfight on the street below, not a soprano crying out for her lover, murdered in a plot to overthrow the kingdom: It was just *le mistral*, the northern Provençal wind hurling itself against the windowpane at a hundred miles an hour, slicing through the cracks in the shutters and seething into the darkness.

Our bedroom held the northwest corner of the fortress, shouldering the weight of the mistral's winds. This position lent the room a kind of high drama of heaving and puffing and moaning, the sorts of noises usually found in the bedrooms of newlyweds but that in our bedroom were (literally) only wind. In the first months at the house, the wind scared me so much that I hung a rapier—an antique sword with a fine, narrow blade I'd found in a cupboard on the first floor of the house—on the wall over the bed, ready at hand should I need it. But I never did. The wind was incorporeal, evasive, without ill intent. It woke me and then slipped away into the night.

I reached across the bed, to feel if Nikolai was there, but found only the cool cotton sheet. He was still downstairs, in his office, probably deep in one of his online chess matches. I stepped into a pair of slippers and made my way down the hall, stopping at Alex's room, where he and Fly were sound asleep, Fly breathing in loud, snorting bursts, Alex in soft, short ones. I glanced into Nico's room. She had made a circle of dolls and animals around the edge of her bed, her own variety of protection against bad dreams. Alex had done the same thing when he was younger, setting up lines of Thomas the Tank Engine trains at his bedroom door—Thomas, Percy, Diesel, Toby, and Bertie—as if creating a magical barricade between his world and everyone else.

The wind howled and blew, rattling the windowpanes, sending a draft of cold air through the hallway. I shivered and walked through the Paris-Lyon doors, down the slippery stone steps, until I stood outside Nikolai's office. I thought he would be asleep, camped out on his couch, but a bright line of light cut across my slippers. Voices rose from behind the door, muffled. Nikolai said something in Bulgarian. I'd learned a little of the language, and I knew a few phrases. Then a second voice spoke. It was a female voice, also speaking Bulgarian. From the sound quality and the fact that I could hear both people, I guessed Nikolai was on Skype.

I never spied on him, partially because I knew how painful it could be—my journals were never far from memory—but also because Nikolai didn't give me the opportunity. His computer was password-protected with a long and unpronounce-able Tibetan word, and his phone lock was set to random numbers. He locked up everything of importance in his office. But now, standing at the door, hearing his voice and a woman's voice mingling in the air, I didn't turn and walk away. I stood there. I listened.

It took a few seconds before I understood: This was not a voice I had heard before. This was an unknown person speaking to him on Skype. The woman laughed; Nikolai laughed. They were laughing together in Bulgarian. I held my breath, as if I might be able to understand what they were saying. I tried to remember all the Bulgarian phrases I'd learned while I lived in Sofia, but nothing came to me. Bulgarian jokes were often dark and filled with puns, with difficult turns of grammar, the kinds of jokes I would never understand, not ever. I pressed my ear against the door, too hard. The door pushed back, making a low creak.

Suddenly it flew open. I stumbled into the room. The computer screen was closed—he must have flipped the top shut before coming to the door—and the room was silent. Nikolai stood in the doorway, watching me. He wore a new black hat, not his top hat, but a black porkpie I'd bought him for Christmas. With his hat tipped over his eye and the room dark, he seemed less my husband than a trick of chiaroscuro, an outlaw from a Caravaggio painting. Of all the reactions I could have had, of all the things I might have done at that moment, I reached up and took off his hat. His hair was matted, unwashed. He stepped away from the door, leaving me holding his hat.

"What are you doing down here?" he asked.

"I heard you," I said. "On Skype."

"Really?" he said.

"Who are you talking to so late?"

"It's six o'clock in New York," he said.

"You were Skyping with a Bulgarian woman in New York?"

"Bulgarian?" he said, abashed. "That was English. I was talking to my editor. About my book."

Nikolai had written his second book in English,

a novel about his childhood as a piano wunder-kind, so it was possible that he could be doing edits remotely.

"I heard you speaking Bulgarian," I said. "Very clearly. Bulgarian."

His gaze was deadpan yet somehow amused. "You're just tired."

"Come on," I replied. "I know the difference between English and Bulgarian, Nikolai."

He regarded me for a minute, then joined me on the couch. "I'm worried about you," he said, looking me in the eye. "You wake up at all hours of the night imagining things. You have night-mares about the house. I think you're stressed out by the move to France. It's been too much for you. You need to take it easy."

I knew what was happening. Nikolai was projecting his feelings and thoughts onto me. It was something he'd always done, but usually in more or less harmless ways. If he were hungry, for example, he would say, *You're starving. Let's eat.* If he wanted to drink red wine, he would buy a bottle and, upon bringing it home, say, *You've been in the mood for Châteauneuf-du-Pape.* If he were stressed, he would say that I should relax. For him, the line between us, of our thoughts and feelings, had become so blurred that he didn't know where his feelings ended and mine began.

"*I'm* stressed out by the move?" I continued.

"*You're* the one installing locks everywhere. It's crazy, all these locked doors."

"You have to admit," he said, "you're not yourself lately."

"Okay, sure, but I'm not *stressed out* by the move," I said. "I'm happy we're here. I don't want to be anywhere else in the whole world but here. This is our home."

Even as I said this, a shadow of doubt came over me. How could it be true that I loved my home when I didn't trust the man with whom I was making that home? Here he was, trying to get me to doubt what I'd heard just two minutes before, trying to get me to doubt myself. It was like the Russian Girl in Providence: I knew the truth, but he denied it so passionately that I began to doubt the facts.

Nikolai put his hand on my shoulder and drew me closer, hugging me. The hug was awkward at first—we didn't know how to hold each other any longer—then soft and familiar. It was the first instance of gentleness between us in months, and I felt myself melt into him, my heart go liquid. Maybe he was right. Maybe I was stressed about the move. Maybe the language I'd heard *had* been English. Maybe it was better to believe him so that we could have this rare moment of tenderness.

Nico was thriving in the village. She made friends fast and was confident enough to play the role of the "American girl," even as she spoke French like a native child. I would walk her to the *pétanque* field to see her friends, or they would come to play at our house. Alex, however, didn't like to venture outside La Commanderie. I signed him up for the village soccer team, and he gradually made friends, but when the village boys invited him to play, he didn't go. Instead he burrowed into a corner of the attic, where he read hundreds of books and played hours of video games.

Every day at *le goûter*, the afternoon snack that French children eat when they come home from school, Alex and Nico did their homework for an hour at a wooden table on the second floor. Homework hour was built into *le goûter* and included the memorization of French poems, the creation of verb charts, and the completion of math worksheets. I subscribed to a children's newspaper, *Le Petit Quotidien*, and we read it aloud, writing unknown French words on graph paper, learning the language together. Our efforts were paying off. The kids were fluent in French. But as with everything else, my kids approached learning differently. Whereas Nico jumped in and spoke imperfect but functional French from the beginning, Alex watched and listened in silence until one day he opened his mouth and spoke flawlessly. Nico threw herself into life, learning through experience, while Alex studied life, mastering his surroundings from a distance.

These character traits had always defined them, but the move to France had made them more pronounced, pushing the kids to extremes. The kind of controlled stress I'd created—taking them out of the United States and dropping them into a tiny village in France—was supposed to make them stronger, more adaptable, smarter, happier. But as Alex became more introverted, I saw that he felt alienated as the foreign kid in his elementary school.

One solution I fell upon was to give Alex and Nico pets. We adopted our three cats—Napoleon, Josephine, and ChouChou—from an animal shelter in La Grande-Motte. ChouChou was a gray-and-white year-old male who'd been living on the street. Napoleon and Josephine were black kittens born of the same litter. We bought Fly, a sand-colored pug, as a gift for Alex's eleventh birthday. I hoped that Fly would help bring Alex out of himself and maybe dispel some of his loneliness.

Fly changed everything. Alex loved his pug the second he saw him. After Fly arrived, Alex had a new role: He was the owner of Fly the pug. He walked Fly. He played catch with Fly. He bathed Fly. He fed Fly. Fly joined Alex in the attic, snoring at his feet when he read *Eragon*. My quiet, shy boy began to open up, to smile, to get excited about teaching Fly tricks. Alex would call me to the attic to show me how Fly's leg twitched and thumped when he slept. "He's running in his dream!" Alex said, proud as a parent. Fly was Alex's best friend. I worried a little less about him with Fly at his side.

What did worry me was my son's relationship with his stepfather. Nikolai's attention, affection, and time were lopsided with our kids. He kissed Nico and nodded to Alex; he read Nico stories at bedtime and walked by Alex's bedroom without stopping. When he played games with Nico, Alex was a third wheel. I didn't want to believe that Nikolai was capable of favoring Nico, but it was obvious that he had trouble opening up to Alex. Never mind that Nikolai had known Alex since he was a baby and had watched him grow into a sweet, lovable child. Never mind that Alex called Nikolai "Dad." When Alex went to hug Nikolai, Nikolai patted Alex on the back and punched him in the arm, but he couldn't respond with emotion.

I didn't believe that Nikolai didn't feel love for Alex or that he didn't have all the usual emotions a man feels for a child he has raised, but I saw that he couldn't express his feelings. He couldn't say "I love you" to him or make him feel special or needed. When it came to expressing his emotions, he was blocked. I understood this block, because my mother had been very similar. She loved us, I knew that, but she rarely touched us, and when she did, I could feel how unnatural it was for her to show her feelings. She came from cool, sturdy Norwegians whose feelings were kept in reserve, whereas my father—whose rowdy Italian family was all passionate arguments and operatic gestures of feeling—had been just the opposite. Growing up, I gravitated to the expressiveness of my dad, and I had become a woman who experienced emotional life on the surface. Happiness, bursts of passion, artistic inspirations, disappointments, anger, and meltdowns were all out there on display for the whole world to see. An emotional experience would come, inhabit me with frightening intensity, and be gone just as quickly. Nikolai, on the other hand, had a flat, deadpan way of expressing himself and an emotional chill that I found foreign. In the ten years we were together, for example, I never saw him cry. I eventually began comparing him to my mother and translating my own expressive emotional behavior as being a version of my father. When I explained this comparison to my therapist, she smiled and said, "It's not so uncommon. Lots of women marry their mother."

But Nikolai was not always emotionally blocked. He showed love and affection to Nico, and I welcomed it. Still, the way he treated Alex continued to eat at me, and so I consciously began to pay more attention to my son. When Nikolai took Nico on a walk to the *tabac*, I took

Alex to Sommières, the castled village just ten minutes from our home, for ice cream. When Nikolai played the piano with Nico, I played Ping-Pong in the courtyard with Alex. Alex and I would cook together, making crepes or fondue, while Nikolai watched TV with Nico.

"I just want to point out," I said to Nikolai one night after the kids were asleep, "that you spent half an hour reading Nico a book tonight and didn't even say good night to Alex. You just walked by his door. No kiss. Nothing."

Nikolai looked at me as if I were speaking in Swahili.

"But you were with Alex," he said, defensive.

"You were reading to Nico, and so I went into Alex's room so that he didn't feel neglected."

"I didn't notice that he was feeling neglected."

"I wish you'd try a little harder to notice," I said. "He sees how much time you spend with Nico. He needs a mom and a dad."

"And I'm here," Nikolai said.

"Then why don't you do something, just the two of you?"

"I play soccer with him all the time," he said.

It was true—they went to the soccer field at the edge of the village to kick the ball into the net some Sundays, but being physically next to someone does not mean you are present. There was another level of presence—engaged, honest presence—that I hoped for.

"Okay, sure, but do you ever actually talk to Alex when you play soccer?"

"We talk all the time. Stop imagining things," he said, and for a moment I would doubt myself, doubt what I witnessed every day. I would think that maybe I was projecting my own childhood onto my family—imagining that Nikolai was like my stepfather, Andy, a man I became close to only as an adult. Sometimes I would wonder if my own family was a massive reenactment of my own childhood feelings, my confusions and insecurities, projected onto Alex and Nico and Nikolai. Maybe I was replaying my broken childhood over and over and over. Maybe my past colored everything.

But then I would watch Nikolai and Alex together, and I knew it wasn't my imagination. Nikolai might be physically present with Alex, but he was emotionally absent. It made me angry, watching this daily negligence, and hurt because I knew it was my fault. I had chosen this man to be Alex's stepfather. As a young woman, leaving my working-class background behind had seemed so important. I'd thought that by giving Alex an educated and cultured parent, a man who was from a different class than the one I'd been raised in, my son would end up in a better place. But Nikolai's brilliant mind didn't mean a thing when it came down to

154

the simple act of loving a child. It was emotional intelligence that meant something, and in this, Nikolai was subliterate.

"Alex is your favorite," Nico said one afternoon as we walked through the outdoor market in Sommières.

The Sommières market on Saturdays was a bustling congregation of farmers and local artisans with tables of vegetables, handmade soap, vats of olives, pottery, woven baskets, wheels of cheese, hand-dyed yarn, and local wines. We were walking along, my wicker basket loaded with vegetables. I was going to make pistou, a soup popular in the south of France, and I had bought bunches of fragrant basil. I'd also bought a bag of chocolate-dipped orangettes from Chocolaterie Courtin, my favorite chocolate shop in the world. There were mathildettes, caramel sel camargues, chocolate truffles, over twenty varieties of *tablettes* of dark, white, and milk chocolate. We stopped by Chocolaterie Courtin sometimes after I picked the kids up from school, for a treat. Nico wanted an orangette.

"After lunch," I'd said, and tucked the pack of orangettes deep in the basket. "These are for dessert."

"You would let Alex have one if he asked," she said, turning on me, her voice growing belligerent. "Whenever Alex wants something, you let him have it."

"Nico," I said, gazing down at her. She looked like a boxer in the ring, her face scrunched with emotion. "That's not true."

"Alex is your *favorite,* I know it, but that's fine with me. Daddy told me that you and Alex can't understand us because we're special."

"Special?" I asked, steering Nico away from the market to a low wall, where I dropped the wicker basket.

"Daddy says I can do things that Alex can't do," she said, her belligerence turning suddenly to wonder, as if she were showing me a sleight-of-hand trick.

"What kinds of things?"

She looked suddenly sheepish. "It's a secret."

"We don't have secrets," I said, and in fact we didn't. Nico could not keep a secret if her life depended upon it. Every year, no matter how often I asked her not to tell, she revealed my birthday and Christmas gifts before I could open them.

She looked hesitant, as if she knew she shouldn't tell me, and then she let it all go. "Daddy says that he comes from a magic family. Like Harry Potter. And because I'm his daughter, I'm magic, too. Grandma Yana's grandpa was bitten by a vampire, and now we're . . . *special.* Daddy says he's going to teach me everything, but I have to be older, because I'm special now, and I'll be even *more* special when I'm bigger. But Alex is not daddy's *real* son, so Alex can't be magic. But I can."

I felt my face flush with anger—or was it embarrassment? While I hadn't heard the story of my husband's vampire ancestry, this was the kind of magical storytelling that first drew me to Nikolai. He'd once told me that in a previous life he had stolen the fifteen-year-old me away on a horse and we'd ridden off together, far from our parents, to elope. I was always a sucker for a romantic escape.

"Your dad is only telling you a story. Just like Harry Potter. It's not true."

Nico looked at me, her eyes narrowed as if she were gauging whether I could be trusted. Nico adored her father. She believed everything he told her. It seemed suddenly cruel to disillusion her.

"Sometimes a story is just a story," I said, shrugging. "Your dad is a writer. He makes up stories. It's his job."

Nico nodded. She understood.

"Don't tell Daddy I told you," she said, suddenly sounding frightened. "Don't tell him you know about our magic. He'll be really, really mad."

I didn't tell Nikolai what Nico had told me, but I watched her—and her interactions with her father—with a new sense of wariness. There was something growing between them, something that excluded Alex and me, and I wanted to understand it. Nikolai had always been possessive—he'd needed to take control of Nico, to feed her as he wished and name her as he wished and vaccinate her as he wished. But now Nico was old enough to be influenced by stories of special powers and vampire ancestry, and he appeared to be using these narratives to make her believe she was different from Alex and me. What I didn't understand was *why.* We were a family. Our power rested in our unity. There was no need to divide and conquer, because we were all on the same team.

"Daddy says that if I pray hard to Buddha, I'll be able to fly."

Nico said this one afternoon not long after revealing her vampire lineage. Nikolai had begun to teach her about Buddhism. He'd set up an altar in a nook overlooking the garden, where incense rose around a statue of Ganesha, swirling over a bronze statue of Buddha, a number of small statues of Indian gods, a rosary carved of bone and another of wood. There was a double *vajra*, a small golden scepter, and a copper bell. Tibetan books were shelved below the altar, long and thin, unbound, manuscripts.

"Fly?" I said. "How're you going to do that?"

"Lebi—"

"Levitate?"

"Daddy said he saw someone levitate in India."

"Really?" I asked.

"It happened," she said, defensive. I had become the doubter, the story killer, which was an unnatural position for me. Who the hell was I to be anyone's reality check?

"But how did the boy do it?"

"Buddha helps."

Nikolai had amazing stories about his time in India. Many of these stories were in his novels, but because they were in Bulgarian and I couldn't read them, he'd told me a few. One was the levitation story he had told Nico. Another story was about a boy who was publicly beheaded and who, after the saber had sliced through his neck, bent over, retrieved his head, and put it back on. Nikolai swore that these stories were true, that he'd seen them with his own eyes, and I only had to go to India to see such things myself.

Nikolai had lived in India for nearly four years. He had become disillusioned with monastic life and left Dharamsala, and his Buddhist teachers, behind. What remained was a strong belief in the mystical and a rebel's refusal to follow organized religious practices. My husband considered himself a mystic. He believed in spells and curses and sympathetic magic. He believed in charms to attract good fortune and charms to protect himself from harm. He spoke of spiritual warfare, a kind of chess of the mind used to wage battle on a higher plane. While he didn't keep any of the habits of his monasticism, he continued to practice what he'd learned in India, particularly the more esoteric and mystical elements that he had described to me as being a form of ancient magic.

I believed in magic, too. Not in Nikolai's ancient magic per se, but in a kind of universal narrative, a law, like gravity, that held us all together. I had gone to Japan in my twenties with a strong interest in Zen. I meditated until I began writing seriously, and then my hours of writing became my form of meditation. I believed that the human brain—or at least mine—was not equipped to fully understand the workings of the universe, but that we could sometimes glimpse them. Science was one part of this, of course, but so was spirituality. I was open to learning what Nikolai could teach me.

For my thirty-seventh birthday, he gave me three magic tools. Packed in a box, I found a *mala*, or a rosary with 108 amber beads; a *melong*, or divinatory mirror; and a scorpion protection amulet. There was a paper explaining the function of these gifts. The *mala* was a beaded necklace used for reciting mantras. Made of amber, the sacred substance of Scorpio, my sun sign, the *mala* would become infused with magic when I recited mantras, and it could be used as a sacred weapon. There was a description of a mantra I should repeat, noting that it would unlock wisdom and improve my memory. The *melong*, or mirror, was a shamanic magical instrument that could be used for divinations, sacred knowledge, and deflecting evil spirits and other forms of negativity. *Melongs*, he wrote, had been used for over five thousand years and were very powerful. The last item, a scorpion protection amulet, was an ancient image made by a tantric master and kept harmful spirits and ghosts at bay. He instructed me to hang it up outside a door, facing outward, for protection.

After I opened my gift, I made a joke. "Oh, a rosary! Just what every woman wants from her husband!" But in truth I understood the intention behind these gifts. He was sharing his most personal, most sacred secrets with me. He had unlocked a door and invited me in. He was offering me an apprenticeship in magic.

Nikolai made offerings of incense on the altar. He would place objects belonging to certain people on the altar if he wished to pray for them. I had been raised Catholic and grew up with the practice of prayer and confession, rituals that left in me a visceral need to communicate my thoughts with something larger, more powerful, than myself. Nikolai's altar filled that need. I would light a candle on the altar, or leave incense. The practice reassured me. After my father died in 2006, I put his photo on the altar, where incense and candles burned. Nikolai filled the altar with objects belonging to the people he loved. Once I found Nico's baby tooth before a statue of Buddha. Another time I found a clipping of my hair next to a cone of burned-down incense. The ends of the hair were charred, singed by a candle. I didn't know what he was doing, but I assumed it was a kind of prayer.

His prayers worked. After I had written my first novel, when Nikolai was in graduate school in Providence and we were living on the trickle of my part-time teaching salary, he had prayed for the book's success. He had said 108 White Tara mantras, asking that my book find a publisher. He taught me the words of the mantra, instructing me to say them aloud while I prayed for success. White Tara and Green Tara were the two aspects of the goddess Tara, also known as the Wish-Fulfilling Wheel, or Cintachakra. I chanted the mantra *"Om tare tuttare ture mama ayur punye jnana pushtim kuru ye svaha,"* imagining copies of my book stacked in the window of my favorite bookstore, imagining a reader opening the cover and beginning to read it, imagining good reviews. When the novel did sell, I couldn't help but believe that Nikolai had taught me to com-municate with the universe.

I was a receptive audience for my husband's mystical ideas, but even so I wasn't happy about the version of Buddhism that Nico was getting. Nikolai was a serious scholar of Tibetan and had read texts with the guidance of learned Buddhist teachers. And yet Nico was talking about Buddhism as if it were a Disney cartoon. I understood that the stories we believe have power over us. They work into our bodies and minds and change us from the inside out. What if one day these stories became something stronger, more real, than fairy tales? Nico was only eight years old and didn't understand her father's beliefs, but I saw his stories growing in her, and it frightened me. Even more frightening, though, was that I recognized, in my daughter, my own need to believe in the impossible.

Buttresses

Not long after the annual Fête Votive d'Aubais, on one of those scorching dry afternoons that sent villagers indoors for a siesta, I came home to find Nikolai sitting in our Citroën station wagon. The car was parked in the sun, its gray paint giving it the look of a metallic shark, only inside the shark sat Nikolai, looking troubled. I peered through the tinted window and into the car. The door was closed, and despite the heat all the windows were up. He gripped the wheel with both hands, his knuckles white, as if bracing for a long, steep drop. I paused, thinking through the possible reasons he might be sitting there. He'd told me an hour before that he was going to drive to Sommières, to go to Carrefour for groceries. He was supposed to bring the kids with him. But Nico and Alex were not there. Nikolai was alone.

I rapped the window with my knuckle.

The window descended, revealing Nikolai's face, his black hair wet with sweat, his eyes wide and blank, uninflected.

"What's up?" I asked him. I could hear the fear and confusion seeping into my voice. I could hear all the questions I was not asking, the *What are you doing sitting here in the car?* question, the *Why are you squeezing the steering wheel so hard?* question. His clothes were soaked in sweat, but who wouldn't be sweating? It was a steamy August day in the south of France, and the car was sealed up like an airless tomb. I was worried about him and wanted him to come out.

He bit his lip, as if he wanted to say something. "What is it?" I asked. "Did something happen?"

"I'm waiting for you."

"Why are you waiting?"

"To go to Sommières."

We hadn't discussed going shopping together. But he was waiting for me to accompany him.

"You want me to come with you and the kids to Sommières?"

He nodded. Yes, that's why he was waiting. He didn't want to be alone. He wanted me to come with him.

"Okay," I said. "Where are the kids?"

"In the house."

"I'll get them ready," I said. "You sure nothing's wrong?"

"I have stomach pains," he said softly. "I can't drive."

"Did you eat something?"

"I think I drank too much coffee."

"Too much coffee?" He was in such distress that I didn't think coffee could possibly be the cause. "How much coffee did you drink?"

"I don't know," he replied. "Enough."

I wanted to peel back the layers of his words—

the "I don't know" and the "enough"—and understand what was going on. He had always had trouble with anxiety, but our move to the village had triggered something in him, some latent terror, and I could feel him sinking into himself, descending further and further from reality. He would sit silent for hours at a time, staring out the window, doing nothing at all. He'd become listless and moody. He'd had a panic attack some weeks before and he'd stayed in the bathtub for hours, trying to calm himself down. He'd developed a fear of being alone—driving alone in particular—and had started asking me to accompany him when he left the house.

Like me, he'd begun having nightmares. In his dream we lived in a medieval village, a place exactly like our village, with all the same winding, narrow pathways, the same clay roof tiles and secret gardens. Everything seemed perfectly normal there—the sun was shining and the flowers were blooming—but something was wrong. The village was sinister and frightening. Evil. He walked and walked through the streets, trying to understand what was wrong, until suddenly he realized the problem: There was nobody there. The houses were empty. The streets were empty. The village was totally abandoned. He was the single person who remained. He looked more closely and found bodies piled up everywhere. A plague had struck, killing the entire population. I was dead, the kids were dead, everything had been lost. Nikolai was the only person left alive.

"Can I get you some water?" I asked. "Will that help?"

He nodded.

"Be right back," I said, but as I turned to go to the house, he grabbed my arm. "Do you remember," he said, looking me directly in the eyes, "when you made me go to therapy in Providence?"

"Well, I didn't *make* you go," I said. "We both agreed to go. It was something we did together."

"And I told you that my therapist told me to stop coming?"

"As I recall," I said, "two therapists told you this."

"Right," he said. "Well, I lied to you about that."

I blinked, taking this in. Of course I knew he'd lied about it. That two separate therapists would speak to such a complicated man for one hour and tell him never to come back again could not have been true. "You lied to me?"

"Yeah," he said. "I lied. My therapist didn't tell me not to come back. I *chose* not to go back."

This, I realized, was a breakthrough. If he could admit this, maybe we could go to therapy together. There was an English-speaking therapist in Calvisson, just ten minutes from Aubais.

"I chose not to go back," Nikolai continued, "because my therapist told me I should divorce you."

"What?" I felt myself draw back, as if I'd been slapped. "Divorce me?"

"She said that you weren't good for me and that I should leave you. The sooner the better. But I didn't want to leave you. You see, I know that we're meant to be together—we're *destined* to be together. I've known you for many lifetimes. I can't live without you in this one. I wasn't going to leave you. So I chose to leave the therapist instead."

I stared at him, not sure how to respond. "And what about the second therapist?"

"I never went to the second one," he said. "But she would probably have told me to leave you, too."

"Nikolai," I said, "therapists don't say things like that."

"Well, mine did," he said.

I was stunned by this revelation, partially because of *when* he chose to tell me—now, in the car, when he was most in need of help—but also because of the nature of the confession. Although he had admitted he'd lied, he was still not being fully honest about why his therapist would tell him to divorce me. What was behind such extreme advice? What had he told her? I wanted to believe he was trying to reach out to me, to be honest, but it seemed off somehow.

"Can you give me a few minutes?" he said at

last. "I just need to sit here for a while. Then we'll go to Sommières."

I walked away from the Citroën, to the other side of the courtyard, and sat in the sun. I needed a minute to myself before I went to get the kids ready. Alex and Nico would take one look at me and know that I wasn't all right, and appearing to be "all right" for them had become a priority for me.

Some crows sat at the top of the cypress trees on the other side of the courtyard. The first time I saw the cypress trees, they appeared to be just one big twisted tree, a massive cone of green lifting into the sky. But after closer inspection, I saw that three trees had been planted close together and over the course of decades had twisted up into one another, branches locking and trunks melding. Now the center tree had died. We hired a specialist to come, to remove it and take the wood away. *Impossible,* he'd said. *Take down one, and the others go with it.* And so we'd left it standing.

When an hour had passed and Nikolai still hadn't left the car, I called our new friend Jett to ask for help. I described the situation, summing up Nikolai's ailment as digestion problems related to stress, adding that he had a history of panic attacks. Jett said she had some experience with nerves herself and offered to stop by the house.

She arrived at our place with a bag of remedies, explaining that she alleviated her problems naturally, with over-the-counter treatments like Euphytose, Smecta, and valerian root. "Sometimes you just need to take the edge off, and everything feels better," she said. As I made Alex and Nico dinner, Jett spoke to Nikolai, giving him various remedies and talking to him in a soothing, maternal voice. They spoke for more than an hour, and by the end Nikolai seemed better.

Jett started coming over several times a week to talk to Nikolai. She would discuss his anxiety, give him pills and advice, and then stay to have a glass of wine with me. One day after she'd spent time with Nikolai, we sat out in the courtyard together. I opened a bottle of chardonnay and poured out two glasses and took a sip of the cool, mineral wine.

"He looks good, don't you think?" I asked.

She shook her head. "Looks exactly the same to me."

"He's not in the car at least."

"You're right," she said. "He's locked up in his office."

"But I'm sure it's just a phase. He'll get over this. I'm sure of it."

"It isn't something you just *get over,*" Jett said. "I know what it feels like. I've been there. It isn't easy to be a creative person. I think it might be best if I stop by to check in on him from time to time. I think it may help him to be around someone who understands his situation. And I won't tell him to divorce you, like his therapist."

"Did he tell you about that?" Our communication had become so strained that Jett probably knew more about his feelings than I did.

Jett smiled. "Unless, that is, you *want* me to suggest divorce?"

"I'm not sure anymore," I said, and it was true. I was beginning to wonder why I was holding on so tightly, why I didn't just open my fingers and let it all slide away. But of course I understood the reasoning behind my loyalty. I had made a Faustian bargain with my husband: He would sweep away my unhappy past and make me a part of his exceptional world. In exchange, I would give him my heart and my future. I had benefited from the deal—I had a family. I loved my children, my home, and the career I'd made with his encourage-ment. I loved being married to a handsome, brilliant artist. That he wouldn't make me happy was a part of the bargain I hadn't expected.

"Darling, look at you. You're a mess. You look exhausted. You're taking care of the kids, taking care of a husband who has gone into a tailspin, and meanwhile you have your own career to worry about. Something had better change fast, or you'll be the next one locked up in that Citroën."

"It will change," I said, taking a sip of wine. "That's why we're here. To change."

"Hmmm, maybe," Jett said, raising an eyebrow as if she were a doctor examining a broken limb. "What about sex?"

I looked away, embarrassed.

"You mean there isn't any of that happening either?" she said, shaking her head in disbelief, as if I'd told her that Nikolai and I ate raw pig brains for breakfast each morning. "That is the one thing I would not be able to live without. If that isn't working, nothing's working."

"You have a boyfriend?" I asked, realizing that she hadn't mentioned anyone before.

"Boy*friends,*" she said, emphasizing the plural nature of the noun. "Boyfriends, love. I have one who comes on Wednesday and another on Sunday afternoon, and then there are the ones who call when they're in the neighborhood, which gives things a more impromptu nature, which actually quite suits me, as I dislike planning. How many times a week do you make love?"

"Well, there aren't a lot of opportunities for intimacy with the kids around," I said. "And the move has been exhausting for both of us. And there's my book to edit, which is taking all of my time, and . . . you know. Life gets in the way."

"So how often? Once a week?"

"Usually," I said, too embarrassed to say that we hadn't slept together for months.

"Don't you find it difficult to manage? All that pent-up sexual energy and so forth? I would go out of my mind."

"Sure," I said, and it was true—I missed having a meaningful sexual connection with someone. I missed the easy, close affection Nikolai and I had shared in the first year we were together, before Nico was born. But it was gone, and I had no idea of how to find it again. Now we were like business partners, working to meet quotas. "We've been together a long time. Desire fades."

"If you say so," Jett said, as if she didn't have the slightest idea of what I was talking about.

I sat up in my chair, took a deep breath, and said, "I've been thinking about it, and I think that now is the moment to do something really special, something symbolic to help us get adjusted to our new life here."

"I should say that moving to a medieval village in the Languedoc is quite good symbolism."

"I was thinking of a renewal ceremony," I said. "We never had a real wedding. It might give us the chance to reconnect, if we renew our vows. We can just wipe out all of those problematic years. We can reboot."

"Reboot?" Jett said, her voice incredulous.

"Why not?"

"My dear," she said. With her huge black eyes and her deep voice, there was something divinatory about her. She was a temple priestess with too much eyeliner, a forty-five-year-old single, childless, sun-ravaged sorceress. She stood, wobbled on her plastic sandals as she walked to the trash bin and tossed the empty bottle of chardonnay inside. "Do you really think that any man gives a damn about a *renewal ceremony?* It won't change a thing. My advice: You want to reboot your marriage? Go to Barcelona for the weekend. I'll watch the kids. Eat fabulous food, stay at a fabulous hotel and fuck his brains out. That's all the renewal you need, darling."

Barcelona was three hours away from our village by car—far enough for a romantic weekend without the kids but close enough that we could get back to the village if Jett had trouble. I was excited about our romantic weekend, believing that Jett had made a very good point. How could we expect our marriage to work if we didn't sleep together more often? Sex wasn't just an accessory to a relationship. It was the center of who we were as a couple, something that held everything else together. While the attraction I had felt for Nikolai in the beginning had died, that didn't mean it couldn't be rekindled.

The day before our trip, I drove to Montpellier, found a small lingerie boutique on an ancient street near the university where Rabelais had done his studies, and spent a small fortune on seductive ammunition: black lace panties, a matching push-up bra, a garter belt, and black silk stockings. The expense of my lingerie was in exact proportion to the intensity of my desire to make the weekend "work"—in other words, to have great sex and create a meaningful connection with my husband.

Friday night in Barcelona, we checked in to a small hotel with views of the city. Instead of going out, I suggested we order room service and spend our first night in bed. I wanted to surprise him with my new gear.

"I'm going to take a shower," Nikolai said promptly, and locked himself in the bathroom. I opened some cava and sipped a glass while I stripped off my clothes and slipped into my fancy underwear. With the lingerie in place, I stood before the full-length mirror and examined myself. The mirror didn't lie. I could see very plainly that I had the healthy body of a young woman. And yet I was surprised. For the past years, I had begun to think of myself as old, like one of the village widows. I felt haggard, used up in a way that had nothing to do with sags or wrinkles. I was young in body but old in spirit. Without love my soul was shriveling.

But the young woman in me wasn't going under without a fight. I'd developed an active fantasy life over the past years. Sometimes I would meet a man somewhere, feel attraction to him, and then think about him later, even develop what I came to think of as a virtual crush: I would look him up online, exchange a message or two, remain distantly, electronically linked. These virtual crushes gave me the false sense that I had a circle of male friends, men who might actually want to cross over from virtual to real. There were a few times when this had happened and an actual friendship developed with one of my online acquaintances. There was Jonathan, a writer whom I met for dinner a few times in New York City. He came to one of my readings and accom-panied me to a book party. There was another man, Brent, also a writer, a fun, die-hard bachelor who told me about all the women he dated. After the incident with the Russian Girl, I was more open to the idea of meeting men and was curious about how I would feel when I was with them. I hadn't thought of it at the time, but I was opening myself up to the possibility of being with someone else.

I poured a second glass of cava while Nikolai shaved. I heard the rattling of metal on porcelain, a pair of tweezers being placed on the sink. He must have pulled a few wayward hairs from his otherwise totally bald chest. He disliked chest hair and would pluck out every last one, but I didn't mind it. There was something warm and comforting about a hairy man, like wrapping up in a cashmere sweater. I wished he would just finish up in the bathroom and come keep me company. Two glasses of cava in ten minutes, and I was ready for love.

But Nikolai wasn't finishing up. I heard the shaking of pills—the antianxiety remedy Jett had given him, most likely. Mineral water swished into a glass. There was a rush of water from the toilet flushing. What was going on in there? It was taking forever. I lay on the bed, feeling a bit woozy all of a sudden. I poured another glass of cava, a sure solution to dizziness, and waited.

I stretched a leg into the air. The seam of the silk stocking stretched from heel to thigh, latching onto the garter belt. Sexy. I twisted around onto my back and wiggled my legs up into the air, stretching. In the mirror I looked like a dominatrix doing yoga, my body pinched and sculpted by wires and clasps.

"Almost done?" I called at the bathroom door.

"In just a minute!" Nikolai replied.

There was a commotion in the hallway. A door slammed, and the people in the next room returned. We'd shared an elevator earlier, after we'd checked in. The couple had been speaking in rapid Spanish, and as the four of us crowded into the elevator, I'd secretly looked them over. The woman was dark-haired and sultry, dripping with gold jewelry, a big diamond on her finger, the man short and muscly with a nice watch, probably a businessman of some sort, someone who drank bourbon with the boys after work. I'd looked them over and made a mental profile of how happy they were compared to Nikolai and me. I played that game often, the couple index, comparing other people's happiness with my own. My assessment in the elevator had been this: *Recently married. Still in love. No kids. Staying in Barcelona for a long weekend after a business trip.* They got an eight on the couple index. Nikolai and I were currently at three.

Whatever their reason for being at the hotel, there was no doubt about how they intended to spend their evening. Within three minutes of their return, the panting and squealing began. Before I could refill my glass of cava, the businessman slammed Ms. Sultry against the wall and was pounding out a steady rhythm high-lighted by high-pitched directions in Spanish.

"*Sí, sí!*" she squealed. "*Sí, mi amor!*"

He pulled her away from the wall, and I strained to listen as he threw her onto the bed. At least I imagined he'd thrown her onto the bed—it could have been the couch or even the floor. But wherever he'd thrown her, the noise only increased. The woman's voice rose higher. There was a crack (the sound of his hand on her ass?) and a crash (a lamp hitting the floor?) and then more highly percussive screwing and shouting before it all came to a well-deserved, perfectly synchronized climax.

We didn't have sex like that, and in the past years our sex life had all but ceased. I wanted to change this, believing that if I could fix our lack of intimacy, everything else would fall into line. But it wasn't so easy to "fix" the problem. I had lost desire for him. When he reached across the bed, his fingers were as welcome as a spider crawling on my thigh. I didn't know what was wrong with me, why I couldn't be the way I'd been in the beginning. For a while I tried to disengage and sleep with him despite my feelings. These encounters left me empty, as if making love were a transaction, another chore to check off my list. Sometimes I would even mark a day in my calendar, reminding me that it was time to make love to my husband, a little star to prompt me. I had always believed that will-power and determination could get me through anything, but I came to see that desire is not\ about soldiering through. Desire is a complicated and deep and mysterious thing that two people create together. It cannot be forced into existence. At least *I* wasn't capable of creating it once it had vanished.

In Providence I had been determined to put our sex life on track. I speculated that our sleeping schedules—Nikolai went to bed late and I went to bed early—were keeping us apart. And so I decided to try something different. I asked Nikolai to go to bed at 11:00 p.m., which was late for me and early for him. I'd suggested this believing that if we spent half an hour, maybe an hour, reading or talking together before we went to sleep, we would sync into a kind of biological rhythm. Like female roommates who are on the same menstrual cycle, Nikolai and I would synchronize desire. Our sex drive would be aligned. We would find physical and emotional connection again. It was inevitable that we'd fall into each other's arms. We were only inches away, two warm bodies under a single blanket.

And so we went to bed together each night at 11:00 p.m. Once in bed, we touched feet and shared pillows, talked about the kids and work. For a while it seemed promising. Yet when Nikolai touched me, I pulled away. It was an instinctual, animal reaction, the kind of reaction the tongue has to bitter medicine: *Sorry, I'm too tired,* I would say. I turned off my bedside light and went to sleep. When he tried again, I reacted with the same violent refusal. I didn't want him near me. Whereas once I had wanted his touch, now it repulsed me.

Why had I lost desire? Why didn't I want to be intimate with him? This was a riddle I couldn't solve. He was good-looking, had a nice body, wasn't bad in bed, and sex made things much better between us. I wanted a deep and fulfilling sexual connection with him, but there was no spark, no flame, no fire. Nothing. I didn't want him to touch me. When we had sex, it felt like a violation and a punishment. I ended up being cool and distant, passive and unavailable, which led Nikolai to tell me—in the middle of our many arguments—that I was frigid.

He was right and he was wrong. I rejected him sexually, yes, but I was not frigid. Something in me had shut down in relation to him. It wasn't a matter of physical attraction. I looked at him and I saw that he was a gorgeous man. But when it came time to be intimate with him, it was not physical impulses that ruled me, rather emotional ones. It was here, in our troubled sexual life, that the evidence of our emotional distance was most clear. The lack of trust, the emotional betrayals, our inability to parent together, the disparities between our views on work and money—all of these pressures came together to create a wall between us. It was an instance of my body telling my heart that something was deeply, essentially wrong.

And yet I kept trying. As I lay on the bed in Barcelona, I tried to understand what in the hell I was doing in my sex-kitten outfit, drunk and alone, listening to another couple make love. I felt even more alone, even more isolated, than I had back at home. There I was, done up like Betty Page, wishing to God that I were somewhere else than in that bed.

Nikolai came out of the bathroom and slipped

under the covers, smiling, his eyes filled with expectation. But my mood had changed. Twenty minutes earlier I'd been game, but now the moment had passed. He was ready, but I was done. I felt my flesh prickle with resistance as he slid his hand over my thigh. My stomach turned as he kissed my neck. But I didn't resist him. I had made the preparations, had booked the room and bought the lingerie. It was too late to back out now. And while I went through all the motions of intimacy, my heart remained locked away, unreachable.

Once it was clear that our move to France hadn't worked miracles, the renewal ceremony became my new delusional quest. Like Scheherazade telling her 999th tale, I still believed that death could be avoided by the reinvention of our story. And the next chapter was this: a renewal ceremony to clear out all the years of unhappiness, wipe away the deceptions, the anger, the resentments, and the fantasies in one clean sweep. It would be a concrete, measurable, exterior proof that our relationship was improving. I needed such proof. I needed to go through the motions, to say the words and hear him say the words, to believe that we could change. I needed to make my efforts manifest, to see them play out physically, to make other people witness them. When the interior is weak, the exterior must appear strong. With the center hollow, the walls must be thick.

"How about poems?" I asked Nikolai one afternoon as we sat in the courtyard. After the Citroën Incident, he had gone off caffeine, exchanging espresso for pots of valerian-root tea, an infusion meant to soothe the nervous system.

"Poems?" Nikolai asked, fingering a black bag slung over his chest. Ever since Jett had given him antianxiety remedies, he'd taken to carrying the pill bottles around in a black messenger bag. A folder with his vital records (birth certificate, passport, medical records, and so forth) was stuffed in the side pocket. The bag accompanied him at all times, even to the bathroom, and Lord and Lulu joked that Nikolai was guarding top-secret documents in his bag, that he must be some kind of spy protecting classified state secrets. They called it his CIA bag.

"The vows. For the renewal ceremony. We could write them ourselves. Maybe poems?"

Nikolai was playing chess on his phone, his thumbs jabbing at the screen. He'd been playing online chess a lot lately, working on his opening, middle game, and endgame.

"Hey, hello?" I said. "Did you hear me?"

"Hmmm," Nikolai said, a sound that meant, *Just a second, let me finish this,* and after a barrage of thumb jabs he put the phone down and looked at me, a flush of victory in his cheeks. He must have won. "Sorry. My ranking rose over twenty-two hundred," he said.

"Is that a big deal?"

"Very," he said, wiping his forehead with the back of his hand and working his black top hat—his courtyard costume—over his head. "Grand masters are at that level."

At the time I didn't give a damn about grand masters or chess rankings, but it is clear to me now that this moment in the courtyard was one of missed connection. We were talking past each other, thinking only of ourselves, and had no idea of just how careless we'd become: The vows—and my project of renewing our marriage—were the most important thing in the world for me just then. His chess ranking gave him a solid measure of his skill and talent, something he needed to feel good about himself. But neither of us could see the other's needs.

"Were you saying something?" Nikolai asked.

"Vows," I repeated. "What do you think about writing vows?"

There was an utter blankness in his eyes, an almost comical lack of comprehension. The same look that I surely had when he spoke about chess.

"You know—*vows?* Renewal ceremony?" I said, biting my lip, trying hard not to get frustrated or hostile. I needed him to show some sign of life, something that proved he wanted to be part of this artistic collaboration called marriage. My biggest fear was that I was masterminding the whole thing while he didn't give a fig about it. "Weren't you listening?"

"Sure," Nikolai replied. "You asked me about your dress. Why not wear that purple one?"

I had, in fact, mentioned getting a new dress about thirty minutes before. He had registered one small part of our conversation. That was good enough for me. I picked up where I'd left off.

"I wore the purple one when we got married the first time. It's vintage. It was old even in 2002. But I wasn't talking about the dress. I was talking about writing our vows."

"Oh," he said. He looked desperate, as if he wanted to say the right thing, perhaps to please me, perhaps to end this increasingly uncomfortable conversation. "Why don't *you* decide about the vows?"

"Okay," I said. "I'll take care of the vows. Although you need to write what you want to say to me, of course." When Nikolai didn't answer, I said, "Are you sure you want to do this? It *is* supposed to be for both of us, you know. If you're not into it, that's fine. We can just call the whole thing off."

"Of course I want to do it," he said. "It's just that you're so much better at this kind of thing than I am."

It wasn't the first time I'd heard this line of thinking. It went: Because I was the more practical, organized, and capable one, I should take care of it. So it had been with our finances, and so, too, with managing the house. It would have been easy enough to stop being cast in this role—all I had to do was refuse. But I realize now that I found reassurance in being competent. Being competent meant I could make sense out of chaos. It meant that—with a little planning and organization—things worked. Maybe an unstable childhood, or the years of being stuck in Bulgaria, had created my need to believe that I was in control of my life, because I clung to my role as the competent one in our marriage, even when it left me exhausted and resentful.

And so I threw myself into organizing our renewal ceremony. I set about searching for the right location, but that wasn't going to be too hard to find. The French countryside was so beautiful that we could have the ceremony almost anywhere. There was the village château, or the beach at La Grand-Motte, or the mountains. Jett suggested Château des Hospitaliers, a winery in Saint-Christol, a village just ten minutes from Aubais. The winery made a distinctly southern French wine, with big, jammy fruit and spiciness. The vineyard was on land once owned by the Knights Hospitaller, contemporaries of the Knights Templar. After the Templars' downfall, their lands and wealth in the region were given to the Hospitallers.

The vineyard had a large, modern tasting room with a banquet hall. We would serve flutes of Boreale, a sparkling rosé *méthode traditionelle*, made on the property. When I stood in the space, looking out the huge windows, my eye followed the undulating hills of planted Syrah and Mourvèdre and Carignan. The vines went on forever, fading into blue sky.

I found an Anglican priest, a ruddy-cheeked Englishwoman who lived in a nearby village, to perform the ceremony. She was a glowing, benevolent lady, and I knew the moment I saw her that she was just the kind of person who would consent to marry two churchless foreigners. She was so kind, so good-natured, that it seemed she would be the perfect corrective to the gloom and morbidity of our first wedding ceremony in Sofia.

We met in Sommières to discuss the details, at a café overlooking the Vidourle River. We ordered *boules* of ice cream and cups of espresso. The priestess, as I'd begun to call her, settled back in her chair and examined us with her wise, piercing blue eyes.

"I think it is a wonderful idea to revisit your commitment to one another, and to ask God to bless your union," she said, working her spoon into her ice cream. "Marriage is a sacrament, a holy agreement. Is there a specific reason you chose to do this ceremony now?"

"We just moved here," I said. "We're starting over. It seems like the right time."

"And you?" she said, looking at Nikolai, perhaps noting that I had been answering her questions alone. "What is the purpose of this ceremony for you?"

Nikolai shrugged. "A fun party?"

I laughed, perhaps a little too loudly, although he probably wasn't kidding. His favorite part of this whole thing would be when it was over.

The priestess chuckled. "Well, I'm only officiating the ceremony. The reception will be up to you." She scooped up more ice cream. "Will you be exchanging rings?"

"Yes," I said. "We will."

"Good, good," she said, waving her spoon at Nikolai and then at me. "And vows? You must have some ideas about how you'd like the ceremony to proceed. Have you considered the blessing? What church do you belong to?"

Nikolai looked at me, waiting for me to save him. He was an ex-Buddhist monk raised in atheist, Communist Bulgaria who didn't believe in God any more than he believed in Santa Claus. I had been raised Catholic, felt an affinity with Zen Buddhism, and took an all-inclusive approach to spirituality and life: stay open to everything, allow the possibility of every kind of miracle, embrace every experience so as to not miss anything.

"We have a nondenominational approach to spirituality," I said. "We'd like to bring Eastern and Western religious ideas into the ceremony, if you don't mind."

The priestess looked confused. "Meaning?"

Nikolai leaned forward. "Well, we'd like to have a Buddhist text read. And we'd like to ask you to take some of the usual language out of the ceremony."

"Many couples remove 'obey,' " she said. "That is quite normal. Some people say 'love, honor, and cherish.' Is that what you mean?"

"Well," I said, "I think he was hoping you'd remove the references to God."

The priestess blinked. She put her spoon down. "You realize that I am an Anglican priest. That my beliefs are part of the ceremony."

"Yes, of course," I said. "He just wants to make everyone at the ceremony comfortable. His parents and my parents and . . . well, everyone."

"Your parents are . . . ?" she asked, looking pointedly at Nikolai.

"Atheist," I said.

"And you are atheist as well?"

"He's Buddhist," I said.

"Is that what *you* mean to say?" she asked Nikolai. I was speaking for him, and she didn't like it. It was an annoying habit, one I'd picked up after years of explaining Nikolai to others, trying to protect him from people who didn't understand his long silences, his defensive behavior, his nervous tics, and his refusal to answer questions directly. I'd become a kind of bodyguard, shielding him.

"Something like that, yes," he mumbled.

"Well," the priestess said, smiling gently, as if unsure of how the whole thing would work, "why don't you write the vows and send them to me. I'm sure we can figure something out."

The renewal ceremony became my point of focus, the spot on the horizon leading me forward. Each step closer to renewing our vows was a clear and objective proof of progress. I sent out invitations, arranged for my mother and stepfather to fly to France, invited friends from Aubais and New York. I bought a silver silk dress that was more sophisticated than anything a first-time bride could wear. I bought high-heeled shoes so I would be tall enough to meet Nikolai's lips when the priestess concluded the ceremony. The kiss would be the moment of grace, that one magical moment when the world would stand still and I would know without a doubt that I was really, truly loved.

Why I needed this moment of grace is a question I've asked myself time and time again since the renewal ceremony. If that magical moment hadn't occurred in all the years of my marriage, what made me think that a transformation would take place now? What tenacious part of me held on to the hope that a ceremony would bring about a miracle? Why wasn't I able to take a hard look at my marriage, see that it was dead, and move on? Was it a flaw in my thinking? An emotional defect? Was I too insecure or too needy or too weak to understand that love could not simply be conjured on demand? I couldn't answer these questions, but it didn't mean I stopped asking them.

Once I'd even consulted an astrologer to help me understand the purpose of my relationship with Nikolai. I asked the astrologer to look at my chart and tell me what he saw about our relationship. I was born on November 9, 1973, at 2:31 a.m. in La Crosse, Wisconsin, USA. Scorpio with a Virgo rising. The astrologer and I spoke on the phone one afternoon.

"Wow," he said at the beginning of the call. "Yours is not a chart for the fainthearted. It is an intense, hard-core, magical chart. Every soul chooses its incarnation, and your soul chose a most tumultuous and difficult one. Hats off to you, sister. This incarnation will not be easy, but here's the good news: You are here to learn human experience at a deep level and to live a true, real, solid, meaningful, loving, connected existence. Your soul's intention is to find a love that works. In order to get that love, your soul is on a journey to root out all that is *not* love: all that we humans—and I don't mean just now, but traditionally, in the form of arranged marriage or superficial connections for money or power—believe to be love. Human love, over history, has not been authentic. Your soul wants authentic love. No matter what your parents did or did not do to you as a child, it wouldn't matter in your case. Your soul was sent into human form to redeem itself by growing through hell. If it doesn't crush you and you can make it through this, you will understand things other people do not. You have chosen the hellish underbelly of relationships in order to learn the reality of love. Once you learn it, you will never need to do it again. Not in this life, not in another one. Your desire is to get to the bottom of things, and if you get this right, you can help yourself, and others around you, define what true love is. Only a small fraction of humanity actually experience true love. There might be divorce. There might be reconciliation. It all happens to give you clarity, to describe what love *is not,* to create hope. The goal for you in this life is to come to the point when you will no longer tolerate anything that is not love."

A few days before the ceremony, I walked through the house looking for Nikolai. The door to his office was locked, and so I went up the winding stone staircase and past the bedrooms to the altar.

Nikolai was reading a Tibetan book when I walked in. A stick of incense burned, sending tendrils of smoke into the air, giving the room an earthy, spicy scent. His face was tranquil, touched by candle-light. He was beautiful. I forgot that sometimes, in the rush of our daily lives and the cloud of discord between us, how handsome he was. He looked up, meeting my eye. I was disturbing him.

"Sorry," I said, standing at the door. "But I wanted to check if you've had a chance to write something for the ceremony?"

"The what?" Nikolai seemed fixed at some indefinite space in front of him.

"Ceremony," I said. "Renewal ceremony. You're gong to write something to say to me. And I'm going to write something to say to you? Vows? Remember?"

"Oh, yeah. *The vows.* I'm planning to write something." He looked up at me and gave me a brilliant, glowing smile. "Don't worry, baby."

"Great," I said, relieved. I walked over and kissed him. He would write something beautiful for the renewal ceremony, something that expressed his love for me and his optimism for our future, something to make me believe that we could overcome every difficulty together. He was a writer, after all. That was his gift.

My mother, my stepfather, my brother, and his wife were staying at the house the day of the renewal ceremony. We spent a lazy morning together, drinking coffee and talking in the courtyard until the hot midday sun chased us inside. Nikolai joined us but said little. He didn't understand the culture of my family—their midwestern lack of pretension, the value placed on understatement, their practical let's-cut-through-the-bullshit approach to life. He sat silently at the table as we talked, just as I had sat silently during his family discussions.

I wondered what my mother thought of all this drama around my marriage. Back home you didn't pick up and move to another country when things got rocky. You complained to your friends or baked a casserole or had a few too many beers after work. You kept a stiff upper lip, and then, if that didn't work, you had a reckless affair and a messy divorce. But the kind of elaborate acrobatics I was going through—moving to France and having a renewal ceremony—were totally foreign in my culture.

It wasn't easy for me to talk to my mom. She was a reserved and cool person, someone who didn't feel comfortable with physical displays of love or discussions about feelings. I was always more needy, and more verbal, than made her comfortable. When I was in my twenties, I would challenge her way of thinking, more out of a compulsion to get her to react to me than to cause a fight. I needed demonstrations of love from her, to hear what she felt, but she couldn't give me that.

When I met Nikolai, she didn't offer an opinion about him. When I asked what she thought, she said he seemed "very nice" and left it at that. Maybe she didn't want to interfere in my choice, or maybe she knew that I was so headstrong that I would do whatever I wanted no matter what she said, which was probably true. But it was more likely that Nikolai was just too alien. With his talk of philosophy and politics, he was exotic to my family. That's what had attracted me. And so my mom stayed out of it. Now, on this visit to France, she was there, ready to participate in my renewal ceremony. She wanted me to be happy.

Jett met us at Les Hospitaliers. She stood by the table of food in her loose black harem pants and a loose black blouse, camera in hand, ready to take pictures.

"I can't understand for the life of me why someone would want to get married once, let alone do the whole thing over again," she said. Then, glancing at Nikolai, "What the hell happened to him?"

I shot a look at my husband. He had been up all night and was exhausted, the bags under his eyes giving him the look of a French bulldog. His hair stood up on end, and he had his black CIA bag, pills inside, thrown over his shoulder.

"He's not doing much better, eh?" Jett noted, looking him up and down.

"Actually, he *is* better," I said, feeling my

defenses rise. I was protective of him, especially now, when we were about to start this new phase of our marriage. "He's just feeling a little nervous about the ceremony."

"Well, good thing his parents are here," she said, glancing at Yana and Ivan. "They can take the load off your shoulders for a while."

I glanced at Nikolai, standing with Yana and Ivan. It was true—their presence was a big help. Nikolai really relaxed only around them. They looked happy to be at the ceremony, happy that Nikolai and I were trying to make our marriage work. Yana and Ivan had cleaned up after Nikolai's first marriage failed. Nobody wanted to avoid another divorce more than Nikolai's parents. Except, of course, me.

The priestess, dressed in a long white robe, met us at the back of the room, her face flushed from the heat. She embraced me and then tried to hug Nikolai, who leaned to the side, giving her a quick air hug before stepping out of her reach. He hated to be touched, especially by people he didn't know. The priestess led us to the far end of the hall, where there was a small pulpit surrounded by rows of metal folding chairs.

"We have about fifteen minutes," she said, placing a Bible on a lectern. "Should we run through everything once before we begin?"

"We might need to read these over a few times," I said, giving her the vows. I had waited for

Nikolai to give me the vows he'd written for me, but when I didn't have them earlier that morning, I'd written them myself. So both sets of vows— his and mine—were . . . well, mine. I'd taken care to make sure his vows to me were loving and tender and hopeful. I'd made sure to promise myself the world.

The priestess stood behind the pulpit welcoming the small gathering of family and friends. The creamy stone, pale and smooth as butter, gave the space a warm glow. Alex and Nico were there, dressed in pretty clothes, their hair combed. My mom and stepfather were there; my brother and his wife were there. Lulu and Lord were there. Jett was there. Friends from New York were there. Nikolai's parents were there. The people closest to us had come to show their love and support. This was the big day.

The priestess began. "Friends and family have gathered here today from the United States and Bulgaria and England and, of course, France to celebrate the union of Danielle and Nikolai." She looked around, as if to confirm that everyone was in fact there, and then she went on. "This is a special day. This couple has made a decision to continue on their path together, to strengthen their commitment, before all of you and before God."

I could feel Nikolai stiffen at my side. He glanced at me: *Hadn't we said no "God" in the ceremony?*

197

The priestess introduced Nikolai's mother and my mother, who were going to read a Buddhist text together. They walked to the front of the room, near a window. Between them the rows of vines swelled and receded over an undulating hill. As they read, I glanced at Nikolai. He was clenching and unclenching his left hand, making a fist and releasing. I bit my lip, wary. He was covered with sweat, his shirt soaked with it. He was going to faint or, worse, have another panic attack, this one more public and more disastrous than the others.

"And now Danielle and Nikolai will repeat their vows."

Anticipation welled up in my chest. This was it. Our moment. The first day of the rest of our marriage. Suddenly a thick band of afternoon light fell over the room, giving me the feeling that the words we were about to say were blessed by all the universe—God in heaven, the sun in the sky, our families and friends, the grapes in the fields. The priestess led me through my vows, and I repeated them, word for word, looking at Nikolai. *I promise to love and honor and cherish.*

I tried to make eye contact with Nikolai, so that he knew I was saying those words to him, but he wasn't looking at me. His gaze was fixed at some point beyond the priestess, a hard, determined look, as if his survival depended upon keeping his eyes trained upon that wall. He was so uncom-fortable that I wanted to reach out and wrap my arms around him and comfort him. Maybe this whole remarriage thing was too much for him. Maybe I should have just left everything alone.

The priestess glanced at me, raised an eyebrow, as if to say, *I'm just going to keep going as if everything is normal, okay?*

On cue I plucked the gold band from the tray and slid it onto Nikolai's finger. The priestess smiled, turned to Nikolai, and began to lead him through the vows.

" 'I, Nikolai,' " she said.

Nikolai looked at the wall. He hadn't heard her.

" 'I, Nikolai,' " she said again.

Nikolai mumbled something—his name, maybe—his voice so low that I, standing right at his side, couldn't hear him.

The priestess furrowed her brow. " 'Do solemnly swear.' "

Nikolai swallowed, hard, and cleared his throat. He wasn't able to actually say the vow.

"A little louder, please," the priestess whispered, and Nikolai mumbled something, a few weak sounds, and then she went on to the next line. " 'To love and honor this woman.' "

Nikolai swallowed. He cleared his throat, then cleared it again. "Umm," he said, his voice no louder than before. He coughed and took a deep breath and cleared his throat. He mumbled a few words.

She chuckled. "Let's try again," she said. " 'I, Nikolai, do solemnly swear to love and honor this woman.' "

Nikolai stared at her as if she'd asked him to turn water into wine.

The priestess's pale skin flushed the slightest shade of pink, the same pale, effervescent rose as the sparkling wine waiting for us in the tasting room. She smiled stiffly at Nikolai and, leaning close to him, whispered, "You need to look at her." She placed her hands on Nikolai's shoulders and turned him forty-five degrees, toward me.

The priestess was doing the best she could to keep the ceremony going. But I, standing at my husband's side, felt as if these moments would stretch out forever. He was mumbling. He could hardly speak. He made an incomprehensible jumble of sounds, but those sounds were not vows. I glanced over my shoulder at my mother, who looked utterly confused, as if she were trying to decipher a foreign language. I felt an overwhelming urge to step in front of Nikolai and say his vows for him.

"I . . . umm, swear to . . . ummmm . . ."

Our eyes met. They were the same wide-set green eyes of the man with whom I'd fallen in love. They had the same color and the same shape, but they were utterly alien. I understood suddenly that I was looking into the eyes of a stranger. We had, over the course of our years together, become different people. I didn't know this man anymore. I didn't want to remarry him. In one glance everything—the delicate castle of cards I'd built, all the fairy tales I'd told myself—collapsed.

The priestess shot an embarrassed glance at me but, seeing my alarm, took pity and decided to draw the whole uncomfortable thing to a conclusion. With a deep sigh, she skipped to the blessing and ended the ceremony.

In the tasting room, everyone took hold of flutes of Boreale and clinked glasses. My mother smiled, and my friends raised their glasses. Jett came to my side and put an arm around my shoulders. "Well, my dear," she said, sipping her wine, "it seems that you've just married yourself."

Leaving our guests to celebrate, I headed out of the room, past the tables loaded with food and flowers, past the priestess unbuttoning her white robe, past Nikolai and his parents, to the bathroom, where I locked the door. I hadn't known until the lock clicked that I was on the verge of tears. But as soon as I was safely inside, I slid onto my heels and buried my head in my hands. The tears came all at once, hard and violent. All the tears that I hadn't cried for eight years, all the sadness I'd tried to wish away, all the disappoint-ment—all of this rushed upon me as I cried over my beautiful, broken dream.

Le Mistral

T he woman warrior returns!" Jett called as I stepped through the gate. "Come, have a celebratory drink."

I'd been in the States for three weeks, promoting my novel. I'd returned to Aubais that afternoon, and after spending a few hours with the kids, I drove to Jett's place. She lived in a *maison de village*, a two-story house with windows opening onto a flower-filled courtyard. It was April. Honeysuckle climbed a trellis and daffodils bloomed in clay pots. It was six o'clock, time for an aperitif. Jett sat in a chair by a fountain. She pushed another chair in my direction.

"Miss our local nectar?" Jett asked, pouring me a glass of wine.

"More than you might imagine," I said, taking a long sip of rosé. I was exhausted. I'd hit nine-teen cities in three weeks, had given readings in bookstores, interviews on television and radio. I'd been on so many flights and slept in so many different beds that I hardly knew where I was from one day to the next. We had a babysitter at the house to assist while I was away, but I'd asked Jett to drop by as well, to check in on things.

"I stopped by to make sure the place hadn't burned down."

"Well, it might as well have. It's a disaster," I said. "Laundry everywhere."

"Typical man," Jett said, sipping her wine. "They're like children. Thank goodness I do not have *that* headache. Actually, children I wouldn't mind. Children develop."

I laughed and drank, happy to be with Jett. She didn't seem to have any inhibitions. She did whatever she wanted, whenever she wanted to do it. There were times that I wished I could be more like her. Jett had been urging me for many months to take a lover, even offering the use of her house for the purpose. I had never taken her| up on the offer. But in New York I'd met a man I will call Jack at a book event, and we spent a night out on the town together. This guy was a big sexy mess, a writer and musician (yes, I have a type) with a mop of curly blond hair, huge blue eyes, and cherubic lips. Although I didn't actually have sex with Jack, I was unfaithful to my husband in every real sense of the word. I had willingly—joyfully, in fact—picked up a man in New York City.

"About bloody time!" she said when I'd finished telling her about Jack. "I'm only surprised this didn't happen sooner."

"Really?" I said, realizing I hadn't put up such a good front after all. "You thought it would happen?"

"Oh, my dear," she said, touching my knee.

"Nikolai has had this coming for ages. He has a beautiful wife and does nothing at all to take care of her sexually. He doesn't make an effort." Jett leaned back in her chair. "I think it's fantastic, simply wonderful, that you let your hair down on your book tour. Lord knows every *male* writer who's been on a book tour has had an affair."

"Well, I didn't actually have an affair," I said, just to clarify.

"Wait, wait. I'm confused: Did you sleep with him?"

"It didn't actually get that far," I said. "Although I'm sure it would have if we'd had the chance."

"Oh, my," Jett said, looking stricken. "What a disappointment. Well, will you see him again?"

"We're on different continents," I said, taking a final sip of my wine. "Not very practical."

"Being practical," Jett said, her black eyes meeting mine, "is your biggest flaw."

"Actually, I think I should just tell Nikolai about what happened," I said.

"What?" Jett shrieked, nearly spitting out wine. "Have you lost your mind?"

"Nothing else has worked for us," I said. "Moving here didn't change things, the renewal ceremony didn't change things, being financially secure hasn't changed things. A beautiful house hasn't changed things. Maybe this will shake things up. He might start to value me a little if he thought he could lose me."

"Darling, listen," Jett said, taking my hand. "This is not the kind of thing you should disclose to your husband." She looked me in the eye. "Believe me, I applaud you. It was high time you did something for yourself. I would even say you should have gone further and that you should try to stay in touch with this fellow. Every Frenchwoman worth her salt has a lover or two. But this idea that you have to be *transparent* is only going to make things worse. Besides, how do you know he's not doing the same?"

The village church bells chimed. It was seven o'clock. Time for Alex and Nico to have dinner. Usually the kids called when I was away, but my phone had been silent. I dug in my bag, looking for my phone, but it wasn't there. I checked my jacket. It wasn't there either. It was most likely in the car, on the passenger seat, where I sometimes threw it when I climbed in. I stood, grabbed my bag and kissed Jett good-bye before heading out to the car.

"What the fuck is this?" Nikolai said, pushing my phone in my face.

I'd just walked through the gate, returning from Jett's place.

"What. The. Fuck. Is. This?" he said again.

After the Red Suitcase Incident, I'd suspected that he snooped around on my phone when he had the chance, just as I suspected he went into my computer. Up until recently I had done nothing that could have raised his suspicions, and yet I felt that he was watching me, sifting through my messages and my browsing history and my phone log and my text messages. I had no hard proof of this, but only the strange feeling that something in the order and arrangement of my privacy had been rearranged whenever I left Nikolai alone at home.

Now that there *was* something incriminating to find, I had been careful. On my way back to France, I'd cleaned out my phone. I looked through the messages, meticulously deleting anything that could have been damning, especially the messages between me and Jack.

"Are you going to answer me?" he said, shaking the phone at me. "What the fuck is going on?"

"Don't talk to me like that!" I said, stepping close and lowering my voice to a whisper. "The kids might hear you!"

I beckoned for him to follow me, and we walked to the ancient well. I felt a sudden urge to jump into its wide, deep mouth and disappear.

"I want details," he said.

"Details?"

"Details. About what happened on your book tour."

I reached for my phone, but he pulled it away.

"Give me the phone," I said, stepping closer to him.

"I know everything," he said, giving me a triumphant look.

"Everything about what?" I replied, making another grab for my phone. He held it over his head. "There's nothing to know."

He crossed his arms over his chest. "You're a liar."

"I don't know what you're talking about," lied.

"I am talking about this," he said, and pulled up a message I'd written to Jack.

I met Nikolai's trembling, enraged gaze. I said, "What in the hell are you doing snooping through my phone?"

This was not the reaction he had expected. "That isn't the point."

"It is *exactly* the point," I said. "You were spying on me. What kind of relationship is this anyway? You say I'm a liar, but *you're* the one sneaking around. It explains why I've never trusted you. You're a *spy!*"

Nikolai blinked, blinked again, his skin flushing red. "Don't try to turn this around on me," he said.

"This would never have happened if you'd respected my privacy."

"Who is Jack?"

"Tell me how you got into my phone, and I'll tell you," I said.

Nikolai said, "I know your passcode."

"How?"

"We were both born in 1973," he said.

"Oh," I said dumbly. I had not chosen the most cryptic of passcodes. "But how did you . . . ? There were no messages in my phone."

"You didn't think to empty your trash folder," he sneered.

"You're right," I said, getting mad. "I wouldn't think to empty my trash folder, because I would never expect that my husband was a spy and that I would need to hide every last thing from him!"

"Who is Jack?"

"Why does it matter?"

"It matters, that's why it matters."

"I met him in New York," I said. "And we went out together."

"Out?"

"And he invited me to a bar, and I went," I continued. "And drank a little too much. And that's it."

"That's it?" he said, his voice rising in disbelief. *"That's it?"*

"That's it."

"What else happened?" he demanded. "Specifically."

"What do you mean?"

"What I mean is," he said, "did you fuck him?"

"No," I said. My response was immediate and confident. I wasn't lying. We hadn't been exactly chaste, but we hadn't rented a room either.

"I don't believe you," he said.

"I'm telling the truth."

"You're such a good liar that you believe your own lies."

"I did not have sex with Jack on my book tour," I said. "Not him or anyone else."

"What about in the bathroom?" he asked, holding up my phone with the message on the screen. "You refer to locking yourselves in the bathroom."

I knew then which message he had found. In it I told Jack that I was thinking about the day we'd spent together, how we'd walked through the East Village, gone to a bar, and locked ourselves in a bathroom. I wrote that I was thinking of leaving my husband, and that I loved him (Jack, not my husband), and that I wanted to see him again. It was the kind of romantic bullshit that was my signature at the time: naïve and girlish and filled with visions of escape. I was wrong to have written this letter, not only because I was married to Nikolai, but because it wasn't true. I wasn't in love with Jack. I didn't have the strength to leave Nikolai. I was sad and disappointed and worn out from trying to be happy, and so I reverted to my old standby belief that falling in love could make everything better. I had gone off with Jack in New York because I'd wanted to feel loved, even if it meant doing something childish, like locking myself in a dirty, graffiti-stained bathroom with a guy called Jack. Even if it meant writing an inauthentic love letter to a man I hardly knew.

"That bathroom thing isn't what you think it is," I said finally.

"What do two people do when they lock themselves in the bathroom together?"

"Do you really want to know what happened in the bathroom?" I said. I hated being interrogated, even when I deserved it. *"Because it is not what you think."*

"I want to know," he said.

"We snorted coke together."

He stood, silent and in shock, his mouth agape. "You did drugs with some random guy in a bathroom?"

"Yes," I said, as if testifying. "That's correct. We locked ourselves in the bathroom of a bar and did cocaine. Quite a lot of it, actually."

I'd been right: Nikolai had not expected that I, who could barely tolerate cigarette smoke, who didn't like pot and got tipsy after a glass of white wine, would do anything of this nature. I watched him trying to reconcile this information—this new version of me—with the image he held of me. He was trying to understand how the woman standing before him was related to the one he'd married. And he was right to be confused. I was not the woman he'd married. The woman he'd married was an idealistic twenty-eight-year-old so in awe of him that she'd followed him blindly into the abyss. The woman standing before him was a disillusioned and unloved woman whose last bit of hope had disappeared.

"It's so stupid," he said. "Not even you could make that up."

"I'm sorry," I said. "I'm so sorry. I felt alone. I was angry and sad. I just wanted to *feel something*. I don't know why I did that. I wish I could take it back. We're so *unhappy*. We're like strangers. We don't even talk to each other anymore."

"So that was your revenge?" he said. "Going off with some guy?"

I shook my head. "I didn't plan it," I said. "It just happened."

Which was true and not true. While meeting Jack had been a random encounter, I'd been the perpetrator, the active agent who'd made it all happen. I had wanted to feel something intense and sexual and romantic, something that would help me forget my unhappy marriage, and I had targeted Jack. At the time it felt as if I'd just floated into the situation, but I had not simply floated into Jack's arms. I was lonely and disappointed and looking for someone to make me happy. I was proving to myself—through concrete and unambiguous actions—that I was fearless enough, and beautiful enough, and young enough to have a fling if I chose to do so.

If you had asked me at the time if this was my intent, I would have sworn up and down that it wasn't. I would have said that I loved my husband and adored my marriage and that leaving it was the last thing I wanted. But it wouldn't have been true. The truth was that I dreaded my life. The truth was that I was running from the dream I'd made. The truth was that I wanted to destroy the dream. But I couldn't allow that truth to be true.

After the failed renewal ceremony and my book-tour tryst, the narrative that we were "starting over" died and a new practicality took its place. I no longer believed that I could re-create what we had lost. I accepted the reality that our relationship was broken and that it was unlikely I could fix it.

Instead of fixing us, I tried to see marriage in a different way: Our relationship was not about *love,* it was about *family.* It was not about creating a better marriage, but digging in and protecting what was left of the one I had. I began to see myself as the mechanism in a family machine, one designed to raise two children and provide an environment for work and health. The family machine needed to function, and discussions of love were inefficient and irrelevant. There could be contentment in this version of marriage, and for a while I found comfort in this weird way of seeing things. My work, my kids, and my home kept me going. And while this caused less frustration and heartache, in giving up on love I abandoned that precious thing that had motivated all my actions: hope.

On weekends I would pack up the kids, and the three of us would leave Aubais, going to Nîmes or Montpellier or Paris, leaving Nikolai at home. That I was replicating a pattern—taking off rather than being strong enough to confront the problem head-on—didn't occur to me. I just wanted out of there. I wanted to feel good again. I wanted to feel the sun on my face, eat a picnic lunch with the kids, and be happy for a few hours. I didn't care where we went, just so long as we were away from the toxic zone of our home.

During that period I began imagining various endings to my story with Nikolai. All of them relied upon a magical escape, some fantasy that would change my life. In one fantasy I found the hidden Templar gold under the fortress. It was not hidden in the *cuve* below the kitchen, not even close. The Templars had been too clever to put it there. It was at the bottom of the old well, tucked into a corner of the old olive press. The well had been abandoned long before we moved in, maybe even before the age of modern plumbing. The first time I looked into it, I dropped a stone, listening for water, but the stone hit chalk. It was dry, but that didn't mean it was barren: The treasure must be down there, waiting at the bottom. I had read in the *Midi Libre* a few months before that a couple in the village of Millau had discovered a stash of gold coins in their basement, a pouch secreted away during the French Revolution, when the rich were hiding their savings before losing their heads. The Templars had been the victims of a plot by the king, and many of them were murdered on a single night, Friday, October 13, 1307. Those Knights spared death were tortured until they confessed crimes they hadn't committed. But the Knights Templar had been made of strong stuff. Not one of them had disclosed the true location of their gold in La Commanderie. Their treasures had stayed hidden. Waiting for me. I would find their gold and buy myself a new life.

And so it went: I dreamed of unrealistic solutions to my unhappiness. I could live in that delusional state of mind for a while, but at the strangest moments, when I was taking the kids to school or buying baguettes at the *boulangerie*, the truth would hit me: *I am alone.* Married, with two children, but utterly and completely alone. My father was dead; my mother was far away; my husband and I were cogs in a family machine. In these moments I would stop, take a breath, and close my eyes, feeling the prick of loneliness pinch and disperse through my body. A depth would open in my heart, a funneling darkness so deep, so insatiable, that everything—the kids, the house, the car, my work, faith, everything—fell inside, leaving just me. I wanted to fill this darkness. I wanted to surround myself with curtain walls and bulwarks, with layer upon layer of armor. I wanted to build a wall so thick that nothing, and no one, could touch me.

In February 2012 my friend Diana invited me to join her for a ski trip to Austria. Nikolai didn't ski and didn't like airplanes, so he stayed home with our new nanny, Sveti, a Bulgarian woman in her fifties. Yana and Ivan had interviewed Sveti in Bulgaria and sent her to help us with the kids, believing that this could ease our growing marital problems. It was an open secret that Nikolai and I were desperately unhappy. Anyone who stepped into our home could feel it. And so Sveti arrived, like a savior from the east. She was kind to Alex and Nico and became a reliable driving companion for Nikolai. With her arrival the dynamics of our marriage shifted. I could ask Sveti to help me with laundry or cleaning, instead of expecting my husband to lend a hand. If I needed help with the shopping or the laundry, Sveti was there. If I couldn't make dinner, Sveti stepped in. Finally someone had my back.

We met Diana and her two boys near Innsbruck, at an alpine lodge tucked between two steep mountains. Great bristling pines splotched the white slopes green. The views from the ravine were stunning, majestic, with snowcapped peaks and wooden chalets. We took the gondola up the Stubai Glacier to the heights of the Alps, where the air was so cold and clear it seemed as if I'd never really breathed before. While the kids learned technique with instructors, Diana and I took long runs, stopping to warm ourselves at ski stations, picking the kids up late in the afternoon and going back to the hotel for dinner.

Diana and I spent a lot of time talking on the chairlifts. She lived in London and was in the middle of a bitter divorce. She had been separated from her husband, Joseph, for over a year, and she'd just learned that he'd become involved with one of their nannies. Diana's husband was fifty; the nanny was twenty-five. Diana had been keeping me up to date about the proceedings with weekly calls, and the situation was not improving—they were spending tens of thousands of pounds in legal expenses and were locked in a stalemate over custody, alimony, the liquidation of their Kensington apartment, the boys' school fees, retirement accounts, life insurance, division of stocks, and maintenance.

Thank God Nikolai and I are not going through that, I thought whenever I heard the gruesome details of Diana's divorce. The "thank God I'm not them" sentiment was something I felt every time I heard about a nasty breakup. They were everywhere, these couples who fought like savages over property or summer visitation. A friend had just told me the story of a woman who had pounded up her own face with a brick and gone to the police to report that her husband had beaten her. I heard another story of a man who not only took his wife's engagement ring back but stole all her jewelry, every piece, and dumped it into the river. Such people made my parents' divorce, which I had always considered the nastiest separation in the history of all separations, look pleasant.

These stories put my marriage in perspective. Nikolai and I might have been struggling, we might have been unhappy, he might have had a fling with one of his students, and I might have gone overboard on my book tour, but we were educated, civilized adults. Even if we ended up separating, we would never resort to such mean and vengeful fighting. We would talk things through. We would be compassionate and understanding, logical and calm. He'd been a Buddhist monk, after all, and I was determined not to repeat the mistakes my parents had made. We would be different. Of that I was sure.

Late one night the kids and I came back to our hotel room to find a red light blinking on the phone. There were three or four messages waiting from Nikolai. It wasn't that unusual. There were always messages waiting from Nikolai, as well as dozens of text messages and missed calls on my cell phone. Since my book tour, he'd begun interrogating me whenever I left the house, asking me who I'd met and what we did. He wanted a confession from me, a remorseful admission of guilt. But I had nothing to confess. Other than the fact that I no longer loved him.

When I called back, Nikolai answered on the first ring. His voice was anxious.

"Where were you?" he said. His breathing was loud and irregular, as if he'd been running.

"At dinner," I said. "There's a buffet between seven and nine. Just like last night."

"I called ten times, and you didn't answer."

"We were skiing all day," I said.

"What about the kids?"

"They were skiing, too," I said. "We came here to ski. They're in ski school every day, learning."

"I don't understand why you guys left," he said.

"Yes you do," I said, exasperated. "We're skiing in Austria with Diana."

"What's so special about Austria? Why can't you ski here?"

"Because there's no snow in the south of France," I said.

"Then why didn't you let me come with you?" He sounded like a child who hadn't been invited on a playdate. "Why did I have to stay behind? I wanted to come."

I was trying to keep my temper. "You were welcome to come with us. You said you didn't want to come. You don't ski. You hate flying."

"You tricked me into staying here," he said. "You're always finding a way to take the kids and leave me behind. Who's with you? A man?"

"You know I'm here with Diana," I said. It was getting exhausting, having to defend myself at every turn, but some part of me must have felt I deserved it, because I didn't hang up. I listened. I tried to reason with him. This was the price I must pay to keep my life from falling apart. I felt I owed it to Alex and Nico to hold on as long as humanly possible, to endure, as if marriage were a marathon. One thing I'd learned from my childhood was that sometimes, when things are bad and it didn't seem like I could endure another day, holding on would get me through. My life had become an endurance test: How much could I bear before I broke?

"Who else did you meet there?" he asked, his voice lowering to a whisper. "Austrian business-men? Friends of Diana's?"

"You're not serious," I said.

"London stockbrokers? Hedge-fund guys? I know the kind of men Diana likes. Tell me. Is she setting you up with someone? Who's there with you?"

"You are being totally ridiculous," I said. "You know I'm here with the kids. Diana is here with her boys. It's a family vacation. That's all."

"I don't trust you," he said. "Not after New York."

"New York has nothing to do with it. You've been paranoid and jealous since the minute we met. What happened in New York just gives you an excuse to act like a psycho," I said, glancing over my shoulder to see if the kids were in earshot. They were. "I don't want to talk about this now."

"Put Nico on the phone," he said.

I gave the phone to Nico. She sat on the bed and answered a series of yes-or-no questions. I could only imagine what he was asking: *Is your mom alone? Does she leave you in the room alone? Is there a man there? Does Diana have a boyfriend?*

I began bracing myself for the fight that we would inevitably have when I got home. It would go something like this: It might have been out of line to call me so many times, and his calls might have been accusatory and paranoid, but it was my fault. I had left him to go to Austria, and so I was to blame for making him feel abandoned. I should apologize for putting him through hell.

As Nico answered her father's questions, Alex shot me a sad, knowing look, one that said, *Of course Daddy wants to talk to Nico and not me,* and my heart sank. Neither of us fully understood then that Alex was lucky to be spared that kind of attention. In some ways Alex's invisibility was a shield.

• • •

Nikolai met us at the airport in Montpellier. I stacked the suitcases onto a cart and shepherded the kids through the terminal and out to the Citroën station wagon. Nikolai peered at us from the driver's seat, his eyes shaded by his black porkpie hat. He said something in Bulgarian, and Sveti jumped out of the car to load the bags into the back. *Of course,* I thought, shaking my head in exasperation. *Let the nanny carry the luggage.* I had come to resent him for his unapologetic dependence on women, his reliance on me and his mother and Sveti. In my resentful state of mind, I translated this as a lack of masculinity. I would focus on every little thing that bugged me, mentally picking apart his flaws. Sometimes in the heat of a fight, I ridiculed him openly, calling him a pussy or a loser. I was mean and petty, trying to humiliate him, to make him feel how much I resented him. Such hazing rituals had become more regular *chez nous*, and although he did his share of name-calling, I was the Queen of Ridicule. I ripped into him and then ridiculed him for being wounded. There was no warmth or tenderness possible in this kind of contest. When I hurt him, I never actually felt that I'd won. In fact, I felt, at those moments, like the biggest loser on the planet: I might have scored the point, but I was losing the match. Real love could never live in such fierce conditions.

The kids and I helped Sveti with the bags, and when we'd shoved everything in, Sveti returned to the front seat of the car. I slid in with the kids, the three of us pressed together in the back. As we pulled away from the airport and drove onto an access road near the highway, Sveti glanced back at me with concern. She said something in Bulgarian, and Nikolai pulled the car over.

"Sveti says you should sit in the front seat. That's your place."

"No, that's fine," I said, realizing that it was in fact rather strange for the babysitter to sit up front with my husband while I sat in back with the kids, but then again everything about our family's situation had become unnatural in the past years. "I'll stay back here," I said. And in truth I would rather have stayed in the back with Alex and Nico anyway. I loved spending time with them. It was the least stressful and happiest part of my life.

But Nikolai, perhaps feeling Sveti's disapproval, insisted that I get in the front seat. I untangled myself from my children and took my place by Nikolai. Now that we were all in our proper seats, Nikolai began his first round of questioning.

"How was Austria?" he asked, glancing in the rearview mirror at Alex and Nico.

"Amazing!" they said in unison.

"So did you ski?" Nikolai asked.

"Of course!" Alex said. "We skied every day."

"That's *ah-MAAA-zing!*" he said in an over-the-top Mister Rogers voice.

"I went down a black run," Alex said, his pride evident.

"A black run?" Nikolai exclaimed, his enthusiasm tangible. *"Ah-MAAA-zing!"*

"And I lost Stinky in the airport," Nico said.

"What?" Nikolai said, his eyes wide with fake incredulity. "You lost Stinky?"

Stinky was Nico's favorite stuffed animal, a hippo she slept with every night. Nico sat up on her knees, straining against her seat belt, the emotions of the experience coloring her voice, and said, "It was *terrible!* I left him at the play area in the airport, and we didn't know he was gone until we were on the plane! And Mama had to run out past security to get him! I thought I would never see him again!"

"It's a miracle we didn't miss our flight," I said, and it was true: I'd barely had time to get back through security before they closed the door to the plane. Nico loved Stinky so much that we all lived in fear of the day we actually lost him.

"It's like in New York," Nikolai said. "When she left Stinky in Central Park."

"Did I lose Stinky in Central Park?" Nico asked, amazed.

"You were about four years old," Nikolai said. "And we went to the Central Park Zoo. When we were driving away, you let out a shriek, and we realized that you'd forgotten Stinky on a park bench. I turned the car around, drove as fast as I could back to the park, ran to the bench, and rescued Stinky. You were so happy!"

I stared at Nikolai, taking in his version of the story. The details of the situation were correct—Nico had left her stuffed hippo on a bench in Central Park, and she'd screamed at the top of her lungs when she discovered it was missing. Nikolai had indeed turned the car around and driven back to the park, but he'd been driving the car, and so it had been up to me to run into the park and retrieve the hippo. I'd played a significant role in saving Stinky, and here he was, taking all the credit.

"Nikolai," I said, "that's not how it happened."

He gave me an odd look, part confusion, part annoyance. "Of course it is."

"You didn't go into the park," I continued.

Nikolai looked at me as if I were crazy. "Yes I did," he said. "I ran to the zoo and hunted until I found Stinky."

"Where did you find him?"

"What do you mean?"

"I mean where was he?"

"I don't know," he said, thinking this over. "Where Nico left him."

"You don't remember," I said. "Because you were driving. You stopped, and I jumped out of the car and went into the park to get Stinky."

224

"That's not what happened," he said.

"Yes it is," I said, absolutely certain that I had the facts right. But even if I didn't have the facts right, I was fighting for credit, fighting to be seen, fighting to be recognized for my role as Stinky's savior. "Stinky was sitting on the third bench from the zoo entrance."

As we continued our drive toward home, I stared at the highway, going over the incident in my mind, replaying the sequence of events. It was just one small and insignificant episode out of thousands of small and insignificant episodes in our lives, an unmemorable and random incident, but suddenly it took on a greater importance. It became, all at once, the single frame in the movie that had captured the whole narrative. We were living together, experiencing our day-to-day lives in tandem, but we had totally disconnected experiences. We both thought we were the heroes of the story. We both remembered saving Stinky. My husband lived in one story, and I lived in a different one.

I glanced into the backseat and saw Alex looking at me with interest. He'd been there, in the car, sitting next to his sister, watching quietly as his parents reacted to her missing-hippo emergency in Central Park. He remembered what had happened, I was sure of it. I loved his perfect repose, the tranquillity of his watchfulness. I wasn't going to ask him to report his version of what had happened with Stinky. Asking him to correct Nikolai or to correct me would be asking him to take sides, to contradict one of us. Any judgment he made would unsettle his equilibrium. It was that very suspension that kept him aloft between his parents, that weightlessness that protected him from us. And this fragile balance was the one thing too sacred to break.

We rode the rest of the way home in silence. It was such a stupid thing to argue about—who'd saved Nico's hippo?—but this small, silly thing tipped a scale inside me. At home I grabbed my coat and walked through the courtyard. Aubais was warm compared to Austria, but I threw on my jacket anyway and headed to my car. The prospect of going back into La Commanderie and returning to my life with Nikolai there was too much for me. I fought back tears. This is what my life had come to: Even before I got home, I needed to leave again.

Driving would clear my mind. I got into my car, opened the windows, and turned on the French news. I pulled out into the village and drove down past the bulls. It was blue, blue skies for as far as I could see. I drove past an olive grove filled with barren trees. My eyes were brimming with tears, and I could hardly see, but I was driving faster and faster, taking the corners without slowing, daring fate to put me in harm's way. Maybe it was for the best. If I were to die in an accident, no one could blame me for giving up on my marriage. I wouldn't be a terrible wife. I wouldn't have to explain my failure to my children. I could escape without making the hardest decision of my life: to leave.

In Sommières I parked by the Vidourle River and called Diana. She'd just made it back to London, and I could hear her boys running through the apartment, screaming and laughing in the background, and for the first time in all the years I'd known Diana, I envied my friend, truly envied her. Not for her expensive things or her apartment in Kensington or her fat maintenance check. I envied her freedom.

By the time I asked her to help me find a lawyer, I knew that I'd made up my mind. I was going to take a separate path. I was getting ready, packing my hopes and expectations away, and preparing for my journey out of there. The question was only how and when that path would materialize. In the meantime I would wait until the right moment arrived. I would camouflage my impulses. I would live my days as if I were the same woman I'd always been. But I wasn't the same woman. I was a woman planning, scheming, waiting for the right moment to flee.

The Knight

Petro and Silvia were a couple we knew only slightly, but we happened to be in Paris the same weekend, and so we met them for dinner near the Palais Garnier, the enormous Second Empire opera house in the 9th arrondissement. As we joined their table, I looked them over, curious. We had met them just a few times before, and always with other friends. Petro was a banker, and Silvia was an artist. Bulgarian by birth, they had four children, lived in Switzerland, and owned a summerhouse in the Corniche in Cannes. They were thirty-eight, the same age as Nikolai and me, and had been married for eighteen years. On the couple-happiness index, they would get, at first glance, a seven.

They had reserved a table for six. Two men sat with them, a film critic for *Cahiers du Cinéma* and a young Parisian filmmaker named Pierre. As Silvia introduced us, Nikolai shot me an uncomfortable look, a *What the hell are we doing here?* kind of look. Nikolai didn't want to spend time with Petro and Silvia to begin with, let alone meet these new people. He'd told me on the way to the restaurant that he was only going to the dinner to please me, that he wasn't in the mood for stuffy restaurants or stuffy people. I was always dragging him out to these stupid dinners, he said. I should be grateful he was there at all.

I sat on the red leather banquette, and Nikolai slid next to me. There was more than enough space, and yet he pressed himself right up against me, sitting so close that our legs and hips touched. I inched away, to get some space, but Nikolai moved with me, as if our bodies were stitched together. I could feel his every movement, grating, rubbing, scratching me. He tapped his foot under the table and wiggled his knees. His cologne—the same expensive cologne I'd found so alluring when we met—was now too strong, cloying. His leg bumped my leg; his arm brushed my arm. He was tap-tap-tapping his foot under the table. He was too close to me. He wouldn't stop touching me. If I could just inch a little to the left, I would be much, much more comfortable. I tried to slide over, and he moved even closer. He was trying to trap me in the banquette. He was letting me know how irritated he was that I'd forced him to have dinner at this restaurant with these unknown people. I glanced at him and gave him a look, exasperated: *Can you give me some room, please?* He ignored me, and I felt an urgent desire—a wild, primitive need—to leap up, jump over the table, and run as far away as I could.

Petro ordered wine—a few bottles of burgundy, white and red. The food came. We drank and ate. The lights were low and the conversation filled with talk of art and films and books. I began to tell them about Nikolai's work, talking up his books, hailing his new novel as a masterpiece, the kind f brilliant social novel that wasn't written anymore. "It's like *A Clockwork Orange* meets Orwell's *1984*," I said, smiling and proud, the supportive wife. That's how we'd come to deal with the disparities in our careers. *It was just luck,* I would say, downplaying my success. Instead I praised his books, pushing him into the spotlight, while I didn't mention my work at all. Sometimes at the end of a dinner party, no one had the slightest idea of what I did professionally. I could talk about the kids and I could talk about our house, but if I began to talk about hitting the bestseller list or the book tours in Italy and Spain, Nikolai would fall into a funk. The slightest aroma of my success would sour his mood.

Of course, when we met, he was the successful one. This hadn't caused strife or jealousy between us: It didn't matter who scored, because we were on the same team. His first book in English—the memoir of his time in India that he wrote in Providence—had done well and gotten strong reviews. Then Nikolai's second book in English—a novel about his life as a pianist—had been published. It hadn't sold well, and although it was well received, there was not a review in the bible of book reviews, the *New York Times*.

He'd spent years writing the book, and he felt slighted. It is a writer's biggest fear, the one thing that is sure to produce megadoses of anxiety: the possibility that our work might be ignored. He came to my office some months after the book was released and leaned against the doorway. "I didn't expect this to happen," he said. By "this" he meant "nothing." He hadn't expected *nothing* to happen in the *New York Times Book Review.* My heart sank. I wanted to tell him that I could fix it, that I could call up someone in New York and make the review happen. But I couldn't. Fortune did not owe us equal bounty or equal review space.

At the restaurant in Paris, I sat back against the soft leather watching operagoers making their way to the Palais Garnier. Black-tied, satin-gowned, they were a horde of beautiful people walking through the glow of a warm Paris evening. It was like a parade of Renaissance courtesans and jesters and knaves, and I—inside the restaurant, glass of wine in hand—longed to be part of the carnival. How perfect everyone seemed out there, I thought. How free.

After dessert we walked out into the street. The opera had begun; the avenue was empty. "We're going to a party," Silvia said. "It's at a friend's place in the second arrondissement. Why don't you come along?"

I looked at my watch. It was only ten o'clock,

too early to go to sleep. "Sure," I said, and instantly I felt Nikolai's fingers grip my wrist. He didn't want to go. He hated parties. A party would be crowded. There would be strangers and uncomfortable silences, and all sorts of potentially disturbing encounters. "Just for a little while," I added, to appease him.

"Great," Petro said and, before I knew it, he had hailed a taxi and we were on our way to the 2nd arrondissement.

The exact maneuvers of the taxi from the restaurant to the party have faded, but I remember the moment I saw the Frenchman—that scorching-hot monsieur from the beginning of this story—with a precise, telescopic clarity, as if the lens of my mind had been focused and waiting for him to appear all my life. He opened the door to his small, mansard-roofed apartment on the top floor of an old Parisian building, and there he was, the most magnetic man I'd ever seen.

"Hello," he said in French-accented English. He kissed Silvia's cheeks before going on to kiss mine. He smelled of cedar and musk and leather, and I was suddenly overwhelmed by a desire to stop, to let the others pass by, and stand at his side as he greeted his guests.

"Who is that?" I whispered to Silvia as we stepped into the apartment.

"This is his party," she whispered back. "He's a

friend of Pierre's, a young filmmaker. Handsome, *n'est-ce pas?*"

Handsome to say the least. He'd leaned against the wall, and the dim candlelight washed over him, illuminating his high cheekbones and dark eyes. He had wild caramel-brown hair, a Roman nose, and full lips. Everything about him seemed a study in artistic messiness, as if much thought had gone into the disarrangement of his hair, his wrinkled jean jacket, his unshaven chin. He was thirty at most, probably younger, but with a seriousness in his expression that gave one the sense that he suffered from some long-standing existential aggravation. He had been born handsome, and as if to spite the gods who'd given him this gift, he did everything in his power to downplay his beauty.

I watched him while he performed his duties as host—putting on music and pouring drinks and opening the window to cool off the room—all the while feeling that there was something strange about him, something foreign yet familiar, a feeling of déjà vu. Then it came at me, quick as a slap to the face, a realization so strange and yet so obvious that it left me momentarily confused: That strange yet familiar feeling was *desire.* I wanted to push this French guy, this total and complete stranger, against the wall and rip his clothes off.

There were bottles of champagne and glasses

of whiskey with ice, and loud electronic music, and by the time midnight rolled around, I was dizzy from it all—the champagne, the dancing, the magnetic attraction I felt whenever our host walked by.

"What do you know about him?" I asked Silvia later that night, when champagne had made me bold.

"Well, I know he is getting over a bad breakup," she said. The champagne had thrown her off balance, too, and she leaned heavily on a chair. "Pierre says he's been a bit depressed. Drinking too much. Doing some drugs. Sleeping around. You know—post-breakup Band-Aids."

"Dangerous," I said.

"Yes, very," Silvia said. "Oh, and he's twenty-six years old."

I did a quick calculation: thirty-eight minus twenty-six. That was a twelve-year difference.

"Come on," Silvia said, taking me by the arm and walking me over to the Frenchman. Soon the three of us were talking and drinking another glass of champagne together. When Silvia walked off to dance, I told him stories of the bull runs in Aubais, about the hedonism of the fête, the way the village transformed from a quiet village into a bacchanal every August.

"Everyone is drinking and dancing and making love in the streets. Actually, there's a saying that the population of Aubais always grows nine months after the fête—new babies born."

"Sounds like fun," he said, smiling at me.

"You should come south next summer," I said.

"Maybe I will," he said, looking into my eyes as if trying to read something hidden behind them.

I glanced up and saw Nikolai, standing across the room staring at us as we spoke. I would definitely have to pay for talking to this guy when we left. I took a step away, turning my back so that Nikolai couldn't see my face.

"Something the matter?"

"My husband isn't happy that I'm talking to you," I said.

"How do you know?"

"I know," I said.

He glanced over toward Nikolai. "We're just talking."

"He can see that I'm enjoying myself."

"You aren't allowed to have fun?" he asked, perplexed, as if this were the strangest thing he'd heard all evening.

"I can have *fun*," I said, "but not too *much* fun. Especially not with you."

"Why not with me?"

"Well, because . . . well, *look* at you."

"Ah, he is jealous."

"He's probably thinking, *What's he saying that's so funny? What is she laughing at now?*"

"You don't laugh like this all the time?"

"No," I said, giving him a smile. "Not often."

"You should laugh more often, " he said, moving closer to me.

"If you say so," I said, trying to get away from the subject of my husband.

"Come," he said, looking like a mischievous child. He leaned close to my ear and whispered, "Laugh."

"Laugh at what?" I said, whispering back.

"It doesn't matter," he said. "Just laugh like I told you a very funny, very dirty joke."

I considered this a moment and then laughed, a boisterous and bold laugh. A laugh filled with hope and inspiration and joy and light. The kind of laugh that can change the composition of the universe. Following my lead, he laughed, too, and soon the very act of laughing was funny in itself, funny enough to spur us on until we were genuinely laughing, laughing so hard that tears came to my eyes. Laughter had created a conspiracy of happiness between us.

"What's your name?" I asked, realizing that I hadn't asked earlier.

"Hadrien," he said, smiling sweetly, his face flushed.

"Hadrien," I said, turning the word over as if it were a golden coin. "Like Hadrian's Wall?"

"Exactly," he said. "Hadrien. Like the emperor."

An hour later the party had moved down to the rue Montmartre, to Silencio, a club owned by the experimental filmmaker and Transcendental Meditation proponent David Lynch. The club was an exclusive venue for film, performance art, music, and dancing, with daily screenings and events. Silencio was created as a space for artists, and while it was difficult to get into if you were, say, a hedge-fund manager, I'd applied as a novelist and had been given a black membership card with the word SILENCIO in silver. We walked past a long line outside the club, stopping near the bouncers. I flashed my membership card, a black velvet cord was swept aside, and we were waved into the darkness.

We stepped inside among a pulsing mass of people. Silvia was drunk, falling over her Louboutin heels, Hadrien on one arm and Petro on the other, a beautiful woman accompanied by gladiators. I glanced at Nikolai, but he wouldn't meet my eye. He was furious. He didn't want to be at Silencio, and he wanted me to know it.

Suddenly Silvia grabbed my hand. "Ladies' room!" she said, and although I could hardly hear her above the noise, I followed her through a narrow hallway, to a powder room with huge round mirrors. Silvia took lipstick from her bag and, after putting some on, gave it to me.

"Don't worry about Nikolai," she said. "Petro doesn't dance either."

"Is it that obvious that he doesn't want to be here?"

"He'll loosen up," she said, giving me a reassuring smile.

"That is pretty much impossible."

"He can talk to Petro about stocks or something."

"Nikolai isn't interested in stocks," I said.

"Really?" she said, looking at me with surprise, as if to say, *What man in his right mind is not interested in stocks?*

"I'm going to have to hear about this all day tomorrow," I said, knowing that the night would be fuel for many future arguments. "He's never going to let me forget about it."

"But you like dancing, don't you?"

Of course I liked to dance. I loved it. I used to go out dancing all the time before I met Nikolai. "Actually," I said, "I do."

"Then don't let Nikolai stop you," Silvia said, flipping her blond hair over her shoulder. "That's how Petro and I have stayed together. I don't prevent him from doing what makes him happy, and he doesn't stop me from doing what makes me happy."

"Sounds ideal," I said, feeling as if she'd just spoken scripture from some esoteric relationship bible, one that I could not quite interpret.

"Well, nothing is ideal, especially when you have kids. But it works for us."

We walked back out into the club and found Nikolai, Petro, Hadrien, and Pierre at a table.

Silvia sank into a chair and began talking to her husband, forgetting that she'd wanted to dance. I looked to Nikolai. "Come dance with me!" I said over the music, giving him a hopeful smile.

Nikolai regarded me with a flat expression, as if I'd asked him to jump off the Eiffel Tower. He shook his head. *No way.*

"Why not?" I asked, remembering the fête in Aubais. He hadn't danced with me that night either.

He shook his head a second time, a definite negative.

"Please," I said, giving him a look that could only be considered a final plea, a look that said, *Let's have fun together. Let's be foolish together. Let's forget that we have all these problems and dance until the world fades away.*

Nikolai shook his head a third time, an answer so clear that I couldn't possibly mistake his meaning. He wasn't dancing, and there was nothing I could do to change his mind.

I looked around to see if Silvia was free, but she was talking to Petro. Hadrien sat alone, seeming bored. I considered him a moment, and then I stepped close to this young, beautiful Frenchman and asked him if he wanted to dance. In the same way Nikolai had chosen me in Iowa City, I chose Hadrien.

Tu aimerais danser? Would you like to dance?

● ● ●

"That was all so *pathetic,*" Nikolai said the next day as we settled into our seats on the TGV at the Gare de Lyon. He took out his book, Céline's *Journey to the End of the Night*, and put it on his lap. "Mindless," he pronounced. "And worse. It was all so cliché. Champagne and clubbing? Do Petro and Silvia think they're original, throwing money around in crass places like that? It was terrible. And thanks to you we were stuck with them all night."

The train left the station, gaining speed. I loved to watch the city recede and the countryside approach, the fields of rural France spreading out from the window, the hills topped with cottages and the valleys clotted with sheep. From Paris to Lyon and from Lyon to Nîmes. The land rushed by, so idyllic it seemed cut from a children's picture book.

I pretended to read a magazine, but all I could think about was the Frenchman. His features were burned into my mind. I remembered the broad forehead, the thick eyebrows, the straight Roman nose. I didn't want the image I had of him to slip away, to flutter off in some gust of forgetfulness. Had he smelled of cedar and leather? Or was it musk? Had he actually kissed my ear when he'd whispered to me, or had I imagined it? Had he touched my hand when we danced? Such questions had been on my mind as Nikolai pulled me out of the club and to the street, where he'd hailed a cab and gestured for me to get inside the car. Such thoughts had been on my mind as we lay in bed, Nikolai asleep at my side. Everything about Hadrien seemed dreamlike, unreal. The facts I had were these: I knew his first name, and I knew where he lived. I knew he was a friend of Pierre's. Other than this, I had no concrete information to go on.

Nikolai and I sat in excruciating silence. Finally, near Lyon, he set aside his book and looked at me. He cleared his throat and said, "How drunk were you last night?"

"Very," I replied, without looking up.

"What do you remember about the club?"

"Not much," I said, although of course I remembered everything, every last detail.

"Well, I can tell you that you acted totally ridiculous."

"I did?"

Nikolai was, I realized, offering me a way out. If I claimed that I remembered nothing, he might let it go. This was my escape route. Nothing happened if I couldn't recall it.

"I don't remember."

"It's good you don't. You were stupid, but you were led into it by Silvia. She is such a cliché," he said. He was doing what he usually did when outsiders threatened us: He cut them down and buried them before they could be a problem. "The rich housewife playing the artist."

"That she can manage to paint with all of those kids is pretty extraordinary, if you ask me."

"She's not a real painter," he said.

"Sounds like you're jealous," I said, and Nikolai shot me a look of reprimand. I'd broken our unspoken tradition, one that had bound us together for years, of criticizing other couples. Some nights after we'd been to a dinner party, we would come home and gossip about who-ever happened to be around the table. We would dissect their careers, their marriages, their kids, their finances, their lifestyles. We weren't always cruel, but sometimes we were, and I now understood why: Ripping apart these people was the only way Nikolai and I could feel good about our own marriage. Diminishing someone else's happiness made our misery bearable. We had to tear down the castles of others to make our own castle strong. But I didn't want that anymore. Now the castle I wanted to tear down was my own.

"I don't want you to see Petro and Silvia again," he said, looking up. "Those people are toxic."

"We just met them," I objected. "They're fun."

"I don't like how you behave around them," he said. "You're not yourself with them. You're too good for them. They change you."

"Change me?"

"They make you less special," he said. "I don't like your behavior when you're with them. It's childish. And desperate."

"Maybe I *am* childish and desperate," I said, realizing that this was true. For years I had childishly avoided confronting the truth head-on, which had made me desperate.

"Well, you were last night, dancing around like a teenager," he said. "It's embarrassing."

"We were just having fun," I said. I'd rolled my *Paris Match* into a truncheon and was gripping it like a weapon. "And the club was full of people, most of them having fun and none of them teenagers. By the way, that's David Lynch's club. You like *Eraserhead*."

"You were out of control," he said.

"Whose control was I out of?" I replied. "Yours?"

"Since when do you like going to clubs?" he said. "You used to like spending the day at the Louvre."

"We always do the same thing. I don't want to keep going in the same circles my whole life."

"With those people," Nikolai said, a look of snobbery on his face, "you're just going backward."

Nikolai returned to his book. I unrolled the *Paris Match* and tried to read. But I couldn't concentrate. My mind kept going back to Hadrien and then, even further back, to a fact that I had all but deleted from the story of my marriage to Nikolai. I didn't think of this eliminated episode of my life, just as I didn't speak of it to anyone during my second marriage. It was the unspoken past, something that lurked below the surface of my marriage to Nikolai. As a novelist, someone who created characters and killed them off, I had the luxury of editing out whole lives in my books, but no matter how I wished to expunge a scene from my own story, I couldn't: I had been married to my first husband, Sam, when I fell in love with Nikolai.

Sam and I had been unhappy and on the verge of breaking up, but it was Nikolai's presence that gave me the courage to leave. I hadn't had an affair—I wasn't cut out for that kind of long-term deception—but once I understood my feelings for Nikolai, the day we met in the library and kissed in the European-history section, in fact, was the day I left Sam.

Sam had been beautiful and dangerous when I met him—six feet four with dyed-blond hair and shocking blue eyes, a body full of tattoos and piercings—and nonconformist in the extreme. He wore a beat-up leather jacket, wrote free-verse poems, and played pool like a genius. I fell for him in a single burning instant. In Sam I'd found someone kindred, someone I recognized. He was a free spirit who had read more books than anyone I knew, could write a beautiful love letter, and—most important to the lonely twenty-three-year-old I was—he loved me.

We had been together only a few months when I got a job teaching English in Japan. If Sam wanted to come with me, he needed a spousal visa, and so we decided to get married. We were in love in the way that twenty-three-year-olds love: selfishly, narcissistically, with a shortsighted passion that implied that we weren't going to live past thirty, so why the hell try? We applied for a marriage license one day, and a few weeks later we were applying for a spousal visa, and a few months later we were living in Japan, and a few months after that I was pregnant. We were happy together. We were playing by our own rules. I kept my name. We didn't wear rings. Our parents didn't know we were married at all until a year after we'd eloped, when we were living on the island of Kyushu. We never imagined ourselves being married in the traditional sense, and so we didn't consider it strange to hide the truth. And besides, we didn't care what people thought. Our love was ours, and we decided what it meant.

After I became pregnant, everything changed. Our freewheeling, bohemian marriage turned into a relationship of the more traditional sort: We were man and wife with a baby boy on the way. Suddenly I needed more than a cool and romantic guy. I began to ask for more from Sam. I wanted him to go back to school and get a degree. I wanted him to get a real job. I had changed, and I wanted him to change, too. By the time Alex was born, I was no longer a wild child flouting convention, but a woman with a deep commitment to her son and his future. I wanted my child to have everything I hadn't. And Sam, it seemed to me, was happy just the way we were.

Of course, there was much more behind the split with Sam than this—I see that now—and I often wish I could go back in time and explain those reasons better. If I could, I would return to the day I left, when Sam and I sat together in the basement of our Iowa City house. Sam was crying into his hands and saying, "Why are you doing this?" and all the while I just sat there, stupidly silent, watching him cry. He told me he hated me and that I was ruining his life, and still I said nothing. I didn't have the words to describe the swirling, contradictory emotions I felt. I just knew I needed to go. I believed that my future was waiting for me. I couldn't afford to let it pass me by. "I'm sorry," I finally said, and I *was* sorry, so sorry for what I was doing to him, but despite the regret I felt, I couldn't stay another moment. I'd fallen in love with a magician who would make all my dreams come true.

Out of control. This phrase stayed with me for days after we left Paris. Out of control, the laughter. Out of control, the dancing. I had been *out of control,* free, on the other side of the boundaries of my marriage. My husband had said these words as an insult, but in my ears they were liberating. I had been so tightly under control, so bound up in what I must do to keep things going, that I'd controlled myself into a straitjacket. The memory of being with Hadrien, the lightness of it, the simplicity of it, rushed over me, and I would momentarily be transported. With Hadrien I had laughed. It was nothing more complicated than that. I would remember our laughter when I drove Alex and Nico to school; I would remember it when I went to work and before I fell asleep. It was simple. With Hadrien I'd been happy.

I didn't know how to get in touch with Hadrien, and so I searched for him on online. Hadrien was Pierre's friend, and Pierre was a friend of Silvia and Petro. Surely they were friends on Facebook. This web of connections would be my glass slipper, the tool by which I would find him. I looked through Silvia and Petro's lists of friends on Facebook, but I didn't find Hadrien. I had no idea of his family name, which meant it wouldn't be possible to find him by doing a general search. And so I sent a friend request to Pierre, and then sent a message: COULD YOU PLEASE PUT ME IN TOUCH WITH HADRIEN? THANKS. Some hours later Pierre sent me

Hadrien's e-mail address. It sat in my in-box, waiting.

Did you like dancing with me at Silencio? I wrote to Hadrien a few days later. A message came back within an hour: *No. Our time together was too short. Je voudrais t'entendre rire.* To which I wrote, *I'd like to hear you laugh, too.* To which he responded, *That is what I hoped you would say.*

We began to exchange short messages. He didn't ask anything of me, not to speak to me on the phone, not to see me again. His messages were always as light as the sound of his laughter. This softness was so different from the way Nikolai and I communicated. Even in the beginning, every gesture had been as cerebral as a game of chess, overintellectualized, urgent, economical. His Christmas letters were the most honest and emotional expressions between us, and they were urgent, filled with need. With us it had always been about efficiency and success. We fell in love right away; we married within six months; we had a baby soon after. No time to waste. In the past decade, we had become two hardened warriors, not two lovers. I wanted to take off the armor. I wanted to be vulnerable. I wanted to open my arms without feeling a dagger between the ribs.

For weeks Hadrien and I wrote messages to each other. And then, one month after we met, he wrote, *When are you coming back to Paris?* I wrote back: *As soon as I can.*

To go to Paris. To dance. To laugh. To see Hadrien again. These became my most pressing wishes. I remembered the party at Hadrien's apartmen and replayed the evening in my mind over and over.

Laugh.

Laugh at what?

It doesn't matter what. Just laugh like I told you a very funny, very dirty joke.

I wanted to go back to Paris, if only to see whether this man was for real. I wanted to know if he could make me feel the same way a second time.

And then an opportunity arose. My stepfather, Andy, would be flying to France from Wisconsin the first week of April to visit the kids and help me do some work on the house. Andy was an expert handyman and builder, and he'd offered to come to La Commanderie to repair some leaking pipes in the bathroom. The visit had been planned months before. Andy would be arriving in Paris on Sunday, April 1, so while it wasn't exactly a lie when I told Nikolai that I was going to Paris to meet my stepfather at Charles de Gaulle, it wasn't exactly the truth either. It was a half-truth, and only the first I would use to justify what I was doing.

As soon as the word "Paris" left my mouth, Nikolai knew what was going on. He began to reel off the reasons I should stay at home: *The kids need you, you should be working on your new book, there's a party in Aigues-Vives.* But I had found a viable excuse, and so I insisted that Andy needed me at the airport. Andy was doing us a *huge favor* by coming to do repairs at the house, and I owed it to him to be there. And since I was going to Paris, I added, I would meet Silvia for dinner Saturday night. This, of course, made Nikolai furious, not only because he'd told me not to see Silvia again but because he suspected the truth: I was not really going to Paris to meet my stepfather at the airport, or to see Silvia, but to meet the man who had captured my heart.

One afternoon Nikolai cornered me in the kitchen. "Tell me again why you're going to Paris," he said.

"I told you, I'm meeting Silvia on Saturday night," I said. "And picking up Andy on Sunday."

"Where are you going with Silvia?"

"We're going to dinner at Hôtel du Nord and then going dancing at Silencio."

"Dancing," he said, rolling his eyes. "Is that guy from the party going to be there?"

"What guy?"

"The guy you were dancing with the last time we went to Paris."

"I don't know if he'll be there," I said, which was technically true: I had no definite plans to meet Hadrien. Not yet.

"*Come on,*" Nikolai said, his voice rising. "You're obviously going to Paris to see this guy."

I gave him a look that said, *Drop it.*

"I don't have plans to see him."

"But if you're in Paris, you *might* see him," he replied, as if trying to get me to admit, in some roundabout fashion, my intentions.

"Well, we'll both be in the same city," I said. "So there's always the chance I'll run into him."

"I don't want you in Paris if there's *any* chance you're going see this man."

"Why would it matter if I saw this guy in Paris?" I said finally. "I am an adult. I can see whoever I want."

"Because that guy clearly wants to fuck you."

I raised an eyebrow. "And how do you know that?"

"Pheromones," he said.

"Excuse me?" This was a new topic, one Nikolai hadn't brought up before. "Phero-what?"

"Pheromones," he repeated.

"Are you serious?"

He looked at me as if deciding whether he could trust me with this sacred information. "You know what pheromones are, don't you?"

"I think so," I said, although I'd never given

much thought to the subject before. "They're hormones, right?"

"Pheromones are chemicals that living things emit and can be detected by other living things. There are fear pheromones and hunger pheromones and sex pheromones. That guy you danced with was giving off intense sexual pheromones around you."

"You can detect them?" I said, amazed.

"Some people can," he said, suddenly conspiratorial. "In India I knew people who could read someone's pheromones like a text."

"Wow," I said, so impressed by this information that I momentarily forgot that he was trying to keep me from going to Paris. "I had no idea."

"Some people give out too much pheromone," he said. "Like Jett, for example. Overwhelming."

I stared at him, not quite sure what to say. All this sounded utterly crazy, but for some reason I believed him. "And me?"

"You have very particular pheromones," he said. "Not too strong, but the type that attracts a certain kind of man."

I started to laugh but restrained myself. "You're joking, right?"

"That French guy is the kind of man who is attracted to your type of pheromones," he said. "And that's why you're not going to Paris."

Soon the very idea of Paris became a point of contention. "Paris" was a code word for trouble.

He sulked about Paris. He gave me dark, silent looks that said, *Don't go to Paris.* He refused to join the kids and me for meals because I was going to Paris. I would find him sitting in the courtyard, his black hat pulled low over his eyes, anger seething from his skin. He gave me an ultimatum: *Go to Paris, and it's over.* But I wasn't backing down. I had made a decision. I wanted to meet Hadrien again, to look him in the eyes and see if I felt all the overwhelming feelings I'd felt when we'd met. I had believed for so long that I couldn't feel genuine love again, that some part of me had been crushed under the weight of my marriage, that I had to know the truth.

Although the original impulse had been to verify my feelings for Hadrien, in the course of fighting Nikolai my reasons for going to Paris had changed. Now Paris was my right to choose my fate. Paris was a jailbreak. Paris was power. However wrong I might have been to deceive him—it *was* wrong, and I knew it was wrong—Paris was freedom. The following weekend I packed some clothes and headed out to my car.

Even as I walked away from La Commanderie, I understood that my decision could have grave consequences. I hoisted my bag over my shoulder, knowing that everything could change once I stepped onto the train platform in Paris. I could lose everything. The stable life I'd created for Alex and Nico, my decade-long marriage, my life in France—everything could be turned upside down. Yet I had to go to Paris, no matter what the cost. It might be my downfall, this reckless quest to understand my heart, but I couldn't hide from it anymore.

From the train, the sun-scorched buildings of Nîmes transformed into the flat planes of the southern countryside. I leaned back in my seat and sent a text message to Hadrien: ARE YOU FREE TONIGHT FOR A DRINK? He wrote back that he was free after seven. I suggested we meet in the 6th arrondissement, near the studio I'd rented for the weekend. We could go to a café and have a glass of wine and talk. If the drink went well, I would invite him to dinner with Silvia and me. And if that went well, I'd ask him to go dancing at Silencio. I hadn't thought through what could happen beyond that point.

As the train drew closer to Paris, I created all kinds of justifications for what I was doing. I told myself I had the right to sit in a restaurant with anyone I wanted. There was nothing wrong with a married woman having a glass of wine with a man, I told myself. This wasn't the thirteenth century, after all. And even if this meeting did turn into something more significant than a glass of wine, then so be it. If I wanted to have an affair, then I would have an affair. Every Frenchwoman worth her salt had a lover or two, Jett had said. Why not me?

Suddenly my phone buzzed. It was a text message from Nikolai.

—YOU FORGOT YOUR SCARF AT HOME.

I texted back right away: DARN! IT WILL BE CHILLY IN PARIS. . . .

—BUY A NEW ONE. I DON'T WANT YOU TO GET A COLD. YOU ALWAYS GET SICK WHEN YOU DON'T HAVE A SCARF.

—HOW ARE THE KIDS?

—THEY MISS YOU. THEY KEEP ASKING WHEN YOU'RE COMING HOME. WHEN ARE YOU COMING HOME?

—I JUST LEFT!! I'LL BE BACK WITH ANDY TOMORROW NIGHT. MAKE SURE THEY BRUSH THEIR TEETH.

—OKAY. LOVE YOU.

—ME TOO.

Suddenly the tower of self-justification I'd cultivated began to crumble. Who but Nikolai knew that I always took a scarf with me when I traveled? Who else knew that small, intimate detail about me? Not my mother, not my children, not my friends. No one. My relationship with Nikolai was the most intimate one I'd ever had. And there I was, ready to throw it away over some sexy young Frenchman who liked to dance. What was wrong with me? Had I gone mad? Maybe everything—the trip to Paris and the desire I felt for this man—was a big mistake.

I glanced over the text messages again. I

couldn't have known that this exchange about a scarf would be the last warm communication between Nikolai and me, our final kind gesture as man and wife, a sort of parting gift. It was strange that he'd texted LOVE YOU and even stranger that I'd replied ME TOO, when we both knew that I was doing everything I could to escape him.

I stood behind the door watching Hadrien for a long time. It was an elaborate Parisian door from another century, with an arabesque of old ironwork scrolling over the glass. I pressed my hands against the pane and looked harder, trying to understand, to intuit, what I should do. Hadrien stood across the street on the rue Saint-André-des-Arts, reading *Le Monde*, his hair swept aside, his bearing elegant. He turned the page of the newspaper; he ran his fingers through his hair; he folded the newspaper under his arm. Maybe he was wondering what was taking so long—I was supposed to have met him outside the apartment building ten minutes earlier—because he pulled out his phone, checked to see if I'd sent a message, and then slid it into his pocket again.

I'd intended to make a good impression. I'd intended to sweep out into the street with pretty clothes and high heels and *le brushing* I'd had at the corner coiffeur. Instead I'd frozen. I couldn't leave the entrance. All I could do was stare through the dusty glass and wonder what I should do. All of my future and all of my past seemed to collect in that glass. I had two choices. I could walk up the stairs to the studio, grab my bag, and take the evening train home to my family. Or I could walk out the door to Hadrien. I couldn't have both. I couldn't divide myself in two, one half living in a loveless marriage and the other half falling in love with Hadrien, any more than I could cut my body in two, my head going one way and my heart the other. I would have to make a decision, and that decision would change my life.

There he stood, across the street, reading *Le Monde* under a streetlight.

Then, suddenly, something came over me, and I knew I couldn't go back. I knew what I felt, and I knew what I wanted, and I wasn't going to be afraid to act. I would open my arms to this, wherever it might lead. I would give myself permission to fall in love.

I pushed open the door, the squeak of the hinges catching Hadrien's attention. He glanced up and smiled, and I felt a rush of recognition. It was as if no time had passed, and we were standing together laughing in his apartment, laughing for no reason but the silly pleasure of it. In that instant I knew I was making the right decision. And without a second thought, I walked up to him, put my arms around his neck, and kissed him full on the lips.

It was a warm spring evening, and I didn't need a scarf after all. We found a café around the corner, on the boulevard Saint-Germain, taking a table on the sidewalk. I ordered a glass of white burgundy, and he ordered a beer. While the openness of our first meeting had not completely disappeared—we'd been writing messages back and forth for the past weeks—this was only the second time we'd met in person. We were strangers sitting at a marble-topped café table, unsure of how to begin.

"You speak English well," I said, to break the silence.

"I went to stay in Ireland as a child," he said. "I learned English there. I loved it, but I complained to my parents the entire time. I called and asked to come home. I didn't really want to leave Ireland. I was only hoping my parents would miss me."

"Did it work?" I asked. "Did they let you come home?"

"No, with my parents that kind of thing never worked," Hadrien said, leaning back in his chair. He took a sip of beer. "You came to Paris alone this time?"

Just then my phone buzzed. Nikolai had been sending text messages in a steady stream all afternoon, messages like WHERE IS THE CAN OPENER? Or NICO CAN'T FIND HER HAIR-BRUSH, questions that Sveti could have answered, but now the tone of the messages changed. They became more direct, aggressive, and they began to arrive every few minutes. WHAT ARE YOU DOING? WHERE ARE YOU? WHAT TIME ARE YOU MEETING SILVIA? When I didn't answer these questions, he sent texts about the kids, knowing I couldn't ignore them. CALL ME. NICO WANTS TO TALK TO YOU.

I pushed my phone to the bottom of my bag. "You should join me for dinner. I'm meeting Silvia and Pierre at a place called the Hôtel du Nord," I told Hadrien.

"That's near the Canal Saint-Martin," he said. He was a native Parisian and knew every street and alley. "What time?"

"Eight-thirty," I said, taking a long sip of white wine.

"Will you be dragged away by your husband this time?"

"I hope not," I said.

Hadrien brushed a strand of hair from his eyes. "He looked like he was going to kill someone. Is he always like that?"

"I found out last year that he's been going through my e-mail messages. I suspect that he's been doing so for a long time, maybe even from the beginning."

"Did he find something?"

"Yes, he found something in my phone."

"And now he's trying to hold on to you?"

"It's complicated. We've been together a long time."

"And you have children."

"A girl and a boy." I suddenly felt self-conscious about my age. Thirty-eight years old with two children.

"They must be adorable."

"Let's have another drink," I said, trying to avoid the subject. I could hardly bear to think about how my actions would affect Alex and Nico. And so I didn't.

We ordered another round, and I asked him questions about his work and his life in Paris and his past and his family. He didn't ask me about Nikolai, and I didn't tell him, but I couldn't stop thinking about the dead cypress tree back at home. The trunk might stand, the branches might reach for the sky, but in the first strong gale the whole thing would topple to the ground. The center of my marriage was long dead. The wind had begun to blow.

We met Silvia and Pierre at the Hôtel du Nord, a dimly lit bar with marble floors and black-and-white photos of hotel guests taken in the twenties and thirties, when artists and writers spent time drinking near the Canal Saint-Martin.

Silvia and Pierre were having a drink at the bar, waiting for us. Silvia was perfectly put together, her blond hair bobbed and flipped, her dress short and pretty, and her legs long.

"Hello, darling," Silvia said, kissing me. "How are you? Good? Perfect! We've started without you." Leaning close to my ear, she whispered, "Nikolai has been calling me for an hour. I'm not answering."

"Thanks," I whispered back, biting my lip and looking at my phone. There were five missed calls from Nikolai.

We'd just settled at the bar and were ordering drinks when my phone began to buzz again. I knew that there was no emergency at the house, and I wanted to ignore him, but I couldn't. No matter how much I wanted to be myself without him for one night, the connection was too strong. I felt beholden to him, responsible. I excused myself and went to the bathroom, where I checked my phone. There were a series of text messages from Nikolai that went something like this:

Nikolai: TRIED CALLING. CALL ME BACK.

Nikolai: WHAT TIME ARE YOU MEETING SILVIA?

Nikolai: THE KIDS WANT TO CALL YOU.

Nikolai: IS PETRO GOING TO BE THERE?

Nikolai: CALL ME. I'M STARTING TO WORRY.

Nikolai: TRIED CALLING AGAIN. WHY AREN'T YOU PICKING UP? ARE YOU OK?!

Nikolai: SILVIA ISN'T PICKING UP HER PHONE. ARE YOU SURE SHE'S MEETING YOU TONIGHT?

Nikolai: WHAT'S THE NAME OF THE RESTAURANT?

Nikolai: CALL ME. IT'S URGENT.

What struck me as strange, other than the sheer abundance of text messages and missed calls, was that he already knew where and when I was meeting Silvia. I had told him exactly where we were going and when I would arrive. But he wasn't really calling because the kids wanted me or because he was curious about the restaurant. He was calling because I was slipping from his grasp.

I typed: AM HAVING DINNER AT HOTEL DU NORD. NO TIME TO CALL YOU! EVERYTHING IS FINE. HUG THE KIDS FOR ME. WILL CALL LATER.

Nikolai: CALL NOW. I WANT TO TALK TO YOU.

Me: I CAN'T TALK NOW. I'M ABOUT TO HAVE DINNER!

Then a message came from a French number: ÇA VA? WE ARE ORDERING ANOTHER DRINK.

It was Hadrien, texting me from the restaurant bar. I quickly wrote back: ÇA VA. BE RIGHT BACK!

Hadrien: DO YOU WANT A DRINK?

Nikolai: I WANT TO SPEAK TO YOU NOW. I'M CALLING. YOU BETTER PICK UP.

Me: CHAMPAGNE.

Nikolai: CHAMPAGNE?

I had accidentally sent Nikolai the text with my drink order. I quickly sent the message to Hadrien and wrote back to Nikolai: SORRY. AUTOCORRECT. REALLY CANNOT TALK NOW. CALL YOU LATER? XOXO

The addition of "xoxo" was meant to reassure him, to bring him down from what had become a full-blown freakout. I couldn't blame him. He was imagining the worst, and he wasn't wrong to be angry. I *had* lied to him. I *had* met Hadrien. And he knew it. Going to Paris was selfish, and it was hurting him, but at that point I was so unhappy, and so ready for change, that I didn't care anymore. I'd reached a reckless point where I no longer cared about what was going to happen. And yet for some reason I couldn't turn off my phone either. I had taken all the steps to come to Paris, I was out with another man, and yet I was still deeply tied to my husband.

When my phone rang, I answered.

But it wasn't Nikolai on the line. It was Nico. "Hi, Mama," she said.

"Hi, baby," I replied. Nikolai was using his best weapon: our daughter. "Everything okay?"

"Not good," she said, her voice a pout.

"Why not?" I asked, imagining her father sitting there at her side, listening.

"Because Alex is upstairs playing video games still, and he won't let me play for even five minutes!"

"Where's your dad?"

"Right here," she said.

"Well, why isn't he helping you?"

"He told me to call you."

"Go tell Alex to let you play," I said. "Tell him I told you it's okay. Tell your dad I said he needs to help you. Tell Alex to listen to your dad."

"Okay, Mama," she said, her voice brightening slightly, as if she had just a little more hope of dislodging her brother than she'd had before she called.

Nikolai took the phone. "Hi," he said, his voice calm, as if none of the recent text exchanges had happened. "Where are you?"

"You know where I am," I said.

"You're at the Hôtel du Nord?"

"Yes," I said. "Just like I told you."

"Seems kind of quiet."

"I'm in the bathroom," I said. I opened the door and stuck the phone out into the cacophony of the restaurant. "Better?"

"Who is there with you?" he asked, as if we hadn't covered all this many times. I felt my anger spike: *Who? Where? What? When? Why?* He was asking the same questions over and over again.

"Nikolai, you know who is here with me!"

"But I want to hear you say it," he said.

"I am at the Hôtel du Nord with Silvia," I said.

"And Pierre," he added. "Pierre is there, too, isn't he?"

"Yes, he is, and we're having drinks. In fact, they're waiting for me now."

"How do I know Silvia is really there?"

"Because I just told you she's here."

"What if I don't believe you?"

"Do you want me to prove that Silvia is here?" I asked. "Do you want to say hello to her?" I was getting so worked up, so annoyed by the questioning, that I stepped out of the bathroom and walked to the bar, where Silvia, Pierre, and Hadrien were finishing their drinks. I was so ready to prove that Silvia was there that I went right up to the bar and gave her my phone. "Nikolai would like to say hello."

Hadrien pushed a flute of champagne to me as Silvia took my phone, a confused look on her face.

"Nikolai, hello!" Silvia said, giving me a look that said, *I don't have to deal with my own husband—why should I deal with yours?* "Yes, yes, we're at the Hôtel du Nord. Yes, it's very nice. We're having dinner and then going dancing."

She shot me a look. *What should I say?*

I shrugged. *Whatever makes him happy.*

"Yes, of course, Pierre is here, too." She listened, and I could imagine Nikolai drilling her with questions. *Who? Where? What? When? Why?* "Yes, actually, he's here, too. You remember him, of course, from his party last month."

Suddenly I realized how stupid, how utterly stupid, I'd been to give Silvia my phone. I hadn't prepared her for Nikolai's Gestapo-style interrogation.

"Oh? She didn't tell you?" There was a long silence, and then Silvia said, "Well, really, I don't think it is such a problem, you know. We're just having a drink. Nothing more than that." She glanced at me again, her eyes wide with surprise, and I knew that Nikolai was losing it. "Give it to me," I whispered, gesturing for her to pass me the phone, and Silvia said, "Well, got to run now, darling. Here's Danielle!" And she dropped the phone into my hand as if it burned her fingers.

As I put the phone to my ear and heard Nikolai say my name, I understood all the consequences of my actions. I understood the pain I would cause my children, the disappointment of our families, the division of our house and our friends. I felt the loss of all the traditions we'd made—the Sunday lunches in the courtyard, the birthday parties and morning coffees. Everything, the family I cherished, would dissolve. I understood all of these things and then, as if fairy dust had been sprinkled over me, I forgot them.

"Listen," I said to Nikolai, "I can't talk now. Call you later." With that I turned my phone off.

The next day I met Andy at the arrivals area of Charles de Gaulle. My stepfather stood smiling, his suitcase in hand. I felt a rush of relief and then simple happiness to see him. He'd come all the way to France to help, and I was grateful that he was there.

Andy came into my life twenty-five years before, when he and my mother fell in love. Both Andy and my mom were married at the time, and both left their spouses for each other. I had disliked Andy in the beginning, believing his appearance on the scene responsible for the destruction of my family. While I blamed Andy during the divorce, I came to see over the decades I'd known him that he was good for my mother and that there were far deeper reasons for my parents' split. As a little girl, I couldn't see the whole picture. I couldn't understand that blame wasn't so easily assigned. Over the years Andy and I had become close. Now I couldn't imagine life my without him.

We set off for the train station on the lower level of the airport. We boarded the TGV for Nîmes and found our seats. I sat near the window, watching the countryside speed by. In this high-speed transit between Paris and the south, I could feel myself readjust from the woman I'd been with

Hadrien to the one I would have to be back home. I could not have imagined, when we'd planned Andy's visit months before, that it would coincide with the breakup of my marriage. It seemed to me in that moment that Andy and I had come full circle. I had watched his life change when he met my mother. Now he would stand witness to the upheaval that lay ahead in my own life.

As the train sped south, I remembered my night with Hadrien. After dinner at the Hôtel du Nord, we went dancing, staying at Silencio until the early-morning hours. We walked hand in hand along the rue Montmartre, making our way to Hadrien's apartment, the small garret where we had met weeks before.

"I am not going up there," I said when we arrived at his building. It was a ridiculous thing to say, as we were almost at his front door.

"A bon?" he said. "Is that so?"

"Not tonight."

"You're sure?" he asked, taking me by the waist and pulling me close.

"Definitely not," I said. "No way."

"Really?" he said, leaning closer.

"Absolutely."

And then he kissed me, a long, lingering kiss that made my entire body tingle. There it was: All I'd been missing. Pleasure. Desire. Passion.

"Okay, I'm going up there," I said, following him up the winding steps to the seventh floor.

As we climbed the steps to his apartment, I knew there was no going back to my old life. I was going to be happy. I was *choosing* to be happy. The consequences of my choice would be severe, I knew this, and yet I wasn't afraid. I was more afraid of losing the clarity I had won, the vision of who I was and of who I could be, and the strength I'd found to make this new woman come into being.

I sat up a little taller in my train seat when I thought of the night Hadrien and I had shared. We lit candles in his bedroom and kissed each other in the shadowy, flickering light. We opened the window so that the cool air swept the room. We spoke to each other in a mixture of French and English, and I felt that we were creating a new language, one that only he and I understood. I slept soundly, peacefully, untouched by nightmares, and in the morning I knew: I could live a new life. I just had to begin.

I didn't know where the night would lead. I had no idea if Hadrien would be more than the handsome man who gave me one perfect night in Paris. But I was changed by this single night, renewed, made strong again. In fifty years, when I'm an old woman, I will look back at this night and know that such beautiful nights are what make life worth living. I came to France to find love again, and I had found love. Only it wasn't with my husband.

Oubliette

After my weekend in Paris, the breakdown of my marriage was irreversible. Just as quickly as we had fallen in love in Iowa City—two unstable elements forming a new compound—so too did we fall apart, the bonds snapping. The undoing of our union might have been part of our makeup, built into the very chemical bonds that had fused us, but I never expected the dissolution to be so fast and so complete. Within six months Nikolai and I would be divorced, our kids would be separated, our possessions scattered, our family blown apart. La Commanderie would be for sale and many of our cherished belongings—the baby grand piano, for example—sold to pay legal fees. All that held us together would dissolve to nothing, like a dead star disintegrating in a void.

It was dark by the time Andy and I made it back to Aubais. The house was lit up, and from the courtyard I could see Alex and Nico come to a window, their faces bright with joy, and disappear down the stairs, running quickly through the house to the courtyard, hugging their grandfather and hugging me, looking for presents from Andy (Jelly Belly jelly beans and chocolate-covered cherries) and presents from me (Tom-Tom et Nana comic books). Fly bounded out after them, jumping onto my legs, clawing at my skin, yelping and whining with happiness, his tail curled up like a spring. Andy smiled at me with approval. I could see that he admired what Nikolai and I had created together—the house, the kids, this foreign life in France. It was different from the life he lived—and the one I grew up living—back in Wisconsin, but it was distinctly mine.

Andy deposited his suitcase in the guest room and walked upstairs with the kids, Fly's nails clicking after them. I looked around. The house was utterly still, shadowy, filled with an oppressive gloom. I wandered through the salon, where the piano gleamed, past Nikolai's office, and to the kitchen, but he was nowhere to be found. The rooms were immaculate, everything in its place. On the marble countertop, arrayed as if for a buffet-style dinner, were two homemade pizzas, one white and one red, a bottle of wine, a stack of plates, linen napkins, and silverware. I went to the counter to have a look. The pizza was hot, as if it had been taken from the oven just minutes before, and the wine—a white Languedoc Picpoul—chilled. It was eerie and quiet, a dinner party for ghosts.

I ran my finger over the edge of the plates, trying to understand why he would prepare dinner and then disappear. I took a glass from the cupboard and poured myself some of the white wine. It was the perfect temperature, as if it had been whisked out of the fridge at just the right moment. I leaned against the counter, and my gaze fell on the *meurtrière*, the narrowing arrow slit that cut through the oldest wall of the La Commanderie. I imagined how it used to be, eight hundred years before, when it was the point of defense of the village. *The knight positions himself near the wall, fixes his eye on the target, draws the arrow back, feeling the tension in the muscle as he steadies the arrow and releases.*

"You're back," Nikolai said, stepping from behind the door, startling me. I jumped and splashed wine on the counter.

"Why are you sneaking up on me like that?" I said, taking one of the cloth napkins and wiping up the wine. "You scared me."

"I made dinner." His voice was flat, without expression, his face equally cool, smooth and affectless as a mask.

"I see that," I said, taking a long sip of wine. "I'll tell the kids to come and eat before it gets cold."

"I want to talk to you," he said, his voice wavering just enough to reveal the anger behind his neutral tone, the rage behind the mask.

"Okay," I said, taking a piece of pizza and sliding it onto a plate. "Want a slice?"

"I want to talk to you," he said again. "Now."

I took my glass of wine and followed Nikolai

through the living room and upstairs to our bedroom. I stopped by Nico's room, where Andy was sitting on the bed with Alex as Nico demonstrated her Playmobil village. "There's pizza in the kitchen," I said, and then—when they had gone downstairs, out of earshot—I went to the bedroom, where Nikolai waited.

He closed the door and turned to walk the length of the room, pacing from the large wooden door to the window before he turned and walked back to the door again. This is what I had dreaded, this moment of confrontation, the moment of finality when we actually said the words "It's over." The end of the story had arrived, and it was a tragedy. There was not even the possibility of fooling myself this time.

I sat on the edge of the bed, holding my wineglass too hard, as if it were the hand of a friend. I was scared. The time of reckoning had arrived.

He paced the room. "I want to know everything."

His voice was terse, without pliancy. I didn't respond but watched him walk to the window, turn, and pace back again.

"I'm waiting," he said. "Start talking."

"You'll be waiting awhile," I said, defiant. There was no way in hell I was going to tell him what had happened in Paris. It was too precious, too special, too perfect to be described under these circumstances. It was mine. I wanted to protect it.

He paused and looked at me. "What does that mean?"

"It means I am not going to tell you what happened," I said. "It's private."

His cheeks flushed pink. He seemed to vibrate with anger. "You leave for the weekend against my wishes, you see the person I forbade you to see, and now you sit there and tell me that it's *private*." His voice was growing louder. "You are married. You. Do. Not. Have. A. Private. Life." He began to pace again, and his voice returned to the same cool, interrogatory tone. "I'm your husband. You have an obligation to tell me everything. Not just a part of what happened but everything, every last detail. Or this marriage is over."

"What do you want to know, exactly?"

"If you were unfaithful."

Unfaithful. I thought a lot about this word over the course of my marriage, trying to parse the real meaning of it. *Unfaithful.* Faith was belief, and unfaithful was a loss of belief. I had believed in us, had fought for us, had bet everything I had and everything I was on us. But this relationship, this *us,* had become toxic. It was nothing like the pure *us* of our beginning, the one built of admiration, trust, and truth. My time in Paris with Hadrien had allowed me to see how very far away from love we had fallen. It had allowed me to feel, under the detritus of my cold, dead marriage, a possibility of something true and strong. This warm light was a fire kindling, growing, waiting to burn. This realization was a revolution in my heart. For the first time in many years, I had been deeply, truly faithful to myself.

It wasn't the right moment to explain that to Nikolai. He continued to pace the room, walking over the stone floor, past the fireplace to the shuttered windows, where he turned on his heel and walked back. I sat very still, as if stillness would make him stop. Finally he leaned down and met my eye. He was over six feet tall, broad-shouldered and strong; I was five foot four inches, fine-boned, petite. There was no comparison in our physical strength. And yet for some reason I had never thought of him as a threat. I'd always thought of myself as the stronger one. I glanced across the room, at the old rapier hanging on the wall. I could grab it with one jump if I needed to. I drank the last of my wine and set the glass on the floor.

"Are you telling me you want me to look away while you have a lover?"

"I am resigned to stay with you for Alex and Nico, but I'm not resigned to be miserable anymore."

"You blame all your misery on me, but this is

a hundred percent your fault. Your mental problems are to blame for everything."

"*My* mental problems? *Mine?*"

"Yes, your mental problems." His voice had become soft, his whole manner changing. "You are bipolar. Manic-depressive. An addict who snorts cocaine in bathrooms with strangers. You're so unstable that you're a threat to yourself and your children."

"I'm the only stable person in this marriage," I shot back.

"It is clear that you are going through some kind of bipolar episode."

I stared at him, taking in this new twist on my personality. I knew what Nikolai was doing. He was rewriting my character. He was changing the adjectives to alter the noun. *Bipolar, manic-depressive, addict, unstable.* These words would circulate among our friends and families and lawyers, becoming his reason for what went wrong between us. I understood why he chose such strong, stinging words to describe me. If I were unstable, he was stable. If I were crazy, he was sane. If this mess of a marriage were my fault, he was innocent. But whatever words he might use, whatever new descriptions of me he might invent, there were no innocents in our marriage. I was at fault for the failure of our love, but so was he.

"That is ridiculous," I said, rising to defend

myself. "You know very well I'm not bipolar. I'm not even depressed."

"You're always unhappy. Unhappy with me. Unhappy with our marriage. We were fine in Providence, but you wanted to move all the way here and start over in France. Does that sound sane?"

"We were *not* fine in Providence."

"I went along with your *madness*—the move, that ridiculous renewal ceremony, everything—so that you wouldn't kill yourself."

I sat on the bed, watching him, too stunned to speak. I had never tried to kill myself; I had \ never even expressed the smallest desire to kill myself. I loved being alive. If an immortality pill existed, I would swallow it. If this was his version of me, no wonder we'd had so many problems.

"I saved you from yourself," he continued, moving close to me until he was right up in my face, his large green-hazel eyes close to mine. "You need me. I am the only one keeping you from committing suicide."

"That is absurd," I said, scooting backward on the bed, to escape. "I've never tried to commit suicide."

"That's because I'm here," he replied, inching forward. "To stop you."

"Before I knew you, I never tried to kill myself."

"I'll forgive you," he said, his gaze locked with mine. "I'll forget about Paris. We'll pretend it never happened. If you tell me everything."

I felt myself being drawn into the maddening rhythm of his thinking. Not so long before, I would have been able to shove my feelings underground, bury them and move on. I'd become so adept at it, that kind of emotional masochism, that it was almost natural. But now, here, at this moment, it was impossible.

"We can't forget about Paris," I said. "I can't forget."

His expression became soft, tentative. Time folded over, and suddenly he was the same man I'd kissed in the library in Iowa City. There was the liquid sincerity in his eyes, the hope. "Do you love me?" he asked. "Answer that at least."

I looked at my husband, really looked at him. I saw the man whose life had been intricately stitched to mine. I saw Nico's father and Alex's stepfather. I saw the man I'd followed to Bulgaria, whose work I'd championed, whose family I'd admired, whose lips I'd kissed. I loved what we'd created together, the big, towering edifice of our shared dreams, but the edifice was crushing me. I didn't love him, not anymore.

"No," I said. "I don't."

He lowered his head into his hands. "You're only saying that because you saw that guy in Paris. You saw him, didn't you?"

"You know I saw him," I replied.

"And you slept with him, too, didn't you?"

"I'm not going to talk about that. Not now. You're too angry."

"Well, we're going to talk about it," he said, slipping his hands over my wrists, lightly, his touch like the cool caress of handcuffs.

"No," I said, pulling away. "We're not."

He grabbed my wrists harder and pulled me off the bed. A burst of anger swept over me, and I pushed back, hard, a solid two-handed shove, giving it all my weight. I knocked him off balance, and he fell backward, hitting the wall. I went at him, pushing him again, hard. As he recovered his balance, I saw a flash of rage, a moment when reason and instinct squared off. He wanted to shove me back. He wanted to make me feel his anger. But he didn't touch me.

"Let me tell you what is going to happen," he said. "I am divorcing you. Do you understand? I am selling this house, taking the kids, and leaving this godforsaken village. This farce is over."

After he'd left, I sat on the bed staring at the rapier. I heard the kids come back upstairs, Andy coaxing them into their beds. I walked out of my room, composed, chilly with unexpressed emotion, and kissed Alex and Nico good night. I said good night to Andy, and then—turning all the lights off except the bathroom night-light—I walked past the Paris-Lyon door to the top of the stairwell. Sitting, I rested my head against the wrought-iron balustrade, my eye following the steep descent of the stone stairway. The night-light cast a shadow that faded as it fell downward, dissolving with each gradation. I kicked off a shoe and watched it tumble down, slipping into the murk, then kicked off the other. After a while Fly climbed onto my lap. I hugged him and buried my head in the folds of his skin. His pigtail curled as he licked my hand. The scenario that Nikolai had just described—of selling La Commanderie and taking the kids away—wasn't possible and yet, I was terrified. He was mad, and his anger made him irrational. When he'd had some time to think, we would sit down and talk everything through.

I put my head in my hands, massaging my temples. It was as if a dark fog had collected over my vision. My future, like the stairwell, had faded into darkness. I couldn't see even two steps ahead. There was only the present, that very moment with Fly in my lap, fear flapping in my chest, and nothing beyond. Somehow I felt that I could follow this uncertainty. The not-knowing would guide me. It was the not-knowing that warned me to be careful, to be strong as I went forward. I was walking out onto a rope stretched tight between my two lives. On the one side, there was my past life with Nikolai, and on the other was my future without him. The walk between these places was treacherous, and I knew, even as I made the first step in my migration, that once I crossed a certain point on the rope, a certain point where balance and gravity met, I would lose my connection to all those things that had once been so natural to me. I would lose this life, this structure, that had held me—however unsteadily—aloft. What waited ahead was uncertain.

We decided to meet in the upstairs kitchen the next evening. It was a neutral spot, yet private enough to keep the kids from overhearing. I wanted as little acrimony as possible, although after the fight in the bedroom the night before, it didn't seem likely. Nevertheless, I sincerely hoped we could find a way to talk to each other. I hoped we could have a civilized conversation, a logical conversation, a conversation concerning what I had begun to think of as the dismantling of our relationship. *Dismantling.* It was a cold, practical word, but it was what kept coming into my head as we sat there. *Dismantling.* As if we were taking apart some rickety old structure, salvaging the stained-glass windows and the elegant moldings, lifting out the valuables to be auctioned off. We were splitting up, yes, but it didn't have to be a destructive act. It didn't have to be a total demolition. It could be a renovation. What had happened to me during my parents' divorce wasn't going to happen to my children.

We would be smarter, Nikolai and I. We would protect our kids. We could plan away any possible damage. We could build a bridge over the moat, and they would walk across it all. With a little planning, we could focus upon preservation and reconstruction. If we were conscientious, we could go forward without destroying everything we'd made together. I was so disconnected from the reality of the situation—from how hurt and angry and aggrieved we were—that I honestly believed we could split up without a fight.

A few minutes before Nikolai and I were scheduled to meet, I walked down to our wine cellar, a roomy, cold cupboard cut into the rock under the stairs. The door was old and swollen with moisture and had an ancient, rust-coated latch. Peering into the cobwebby space, I saw my bottles of wine stacked and organized, piled up in wooden crates. There were bottles from local vineyards, bottles from the nearby Rhône Valley, the occasional old Bordeaux and vintage champagne. I collected wine not because it was valuable—there were many more cheap bottles than expensive ones in my cellar—but because I had chosen each and every bottle myself, making a collection so personal and private that only I knew exactly where and when I'd bought the Hermitage or the Mas de Daumas Gassac. The wine was my way of organizing and preserving my time in France, keeping it safely tucked away for the future. I felt like this about one bottle in particular. Way in the back, in the box of wine meant to remain untouched, I dug out a bottle of 2002 Bollinger champagne.

I placed the bottle of champagne on the kitchen table, and Nikolai narrowed his eyes, unable to ignore the symbolism of the gesture. Our wedding year was 2002, and this bottle of 2002 Bollinger was meant to be opened on our tenth wedding anniversary, which was two months away, June 5, 2012. When I'd bought the bottle, I'd imagined that drinking champagne from the year we were married would be like letting a genie out of captivity. I'd imagined that we would find something of our own beginning in the wine, maybe remember who we were back in 2002, when everything was so new and magical. I could never have imagined that we would be drinking it as we discussed the terms of our divorce.

Ten years before, we had just arrived in Sofia. I'd just learned I was pregnant and that we couldn't leave Bulgaria for two years. I had made a pledge to my not-yet husband to stay with him. *I'm not going to leave when things get hard.* What, I wondered as we sat down, would have happened if I'd turned around and flown back to Iowa? What if I'd taken a realistic assessment of the situation, decided it wasn't what

I wanted and left? How would my life—Alex's and Nico's lives, Nikolai's life—be different now? Of course it was impossible to know, and such speculations were useless. But what I did know was that my promise to stay had kept me fixed in place, making it harder and harder to leave. It would have been much easier to go then, in 2002, than in 2012.

I took two champagne flutes and set them on the table. I cut the foil and gave Nikolai the bottle, as was our custom, and he twisted off the cork, *pop,* and poured out two glasses of bubbling, golden-colored liquid. He sat on one side of the table, I sat on the other. The flutes sat between us, tall and elegant as soldiers on a battlefield.

"You really are a masochist," he said, nodding at the champagne.

"This might be our last chance to drink it together," I said, picking up a glass and taking a long sip, feeling a yeasty crispness in my throat. The alcohol would bolster me. The alcohol would get me through this. "We need to talk about what's going to happen."

"We're getting divorced," he said. "That's what's going to happen."

"Yes, but *how?* What you said last night—about selling everything and taking Nico and Alex. That's not possible."

"It is possible," he said, pulling some printed pages out of his bag. "Read this."

I took the papers and glanced at them. There was information in French about something called *divorce amiable*.

"Divorce by mutual consent," he said. "French law divides everything in half. Fifty-fifty. But if we choose, if we agree, we can create the terms of our separation and custody and then ask a judge to approve it. It's the fastest way."

"What exactly do you have in mind?" I asked. "Because it seems only logical that the kids stay at the house with me and you move somewhere nearby, so that they can see you regularly."

"That's not going to work for me," he said.

"What part of that doesn't work for you?"

"Moving to France was your fantasy, not mine," he said, shivering, as if the idea of France were too much for him to stomach. "You can't force me to stay here."

"Force you?" I said. "Nobody is forcing you."

"If Nico is with you, I'll have to stay," he said. "I'm leaving this fucking place as soon as I can."

"Are you serious?" I said. "Where will you go?"

"Back to Bulgaria," he said.

I almost jumped out of my seat. "Bulgaria?"

"Why not?" he said.

"Nico can't live in Bulgaria."

"She's half Bulgarian," he said. "There's no reason she can't grow up there."

"*Grow up there?* You've never even taught Nico

285

to speak Bulgarian, and now you want to raise her on the other side of the world? You're always saying how much you hate Bulgaria. What in the hell is Nico going to do in godforsaken Bulgaria?"

"I'm not going to listen to your racist diatribes," he said, but he didn't get up and leave. He stared at me, waiting, watching. This was not the calm, logical discussion I'd imagined.

"She can't go to Bulgaria," I repeated. "I'm here. Alex is here. You can't separate Nico from her brother. Or me."

"Alex can come to Bulgaria too."

"This is too extreme," I said, feeling my cheeks flush with heat, my blood shot through with champagne and fury. "They can't go live in Eastern Europe with you. Their lives don't need to change so drastically."

"Divorce is drastic," he said with a shrug, dismissing all the complexity of the situation with a single smug phrase. *"Divorce amiable* is the least drastic agreement you're going to get."

"Nico and Alex stay together," I said. "Those are my terms."

"Listen," he said, changing his tone, becoming suddenly conciliatory, diplomatic. "Under French law I can take half of everything. Half of the house, half of your book royalties. Half of everything."

I stared at him, taking this information in. We

both knew that I had earned over 90 percent of our income through the duration of the marriage—our tax returns proved as much. That I'd also done a large share of the housework and child-rearing was less easy to prove, but true nonetheless. Now he was telling me that he could walk away with half of everything.

"Not only that," he said, his voice filled with triumph. "But because you are the breadwinner, I can ask for maintenance and future percentages of your earnings."

"That isn't fair," I said.

"That's the law," he replied. He looked at his glass of champagne for the first time, picked it up and took a drink. "But as I said before, we don't have to take that route. *Divorce amiable* allows us to change that equation. If we make an agreement, I can opt to take less. Financially."

"Take less than half?"

"Significantly less."

Suddenly I realized what he was getting at. Nikolai would give me a break financially if I let him take Nico to Bulgaria. He was trying to buy me off. But it wasn't going to work. I'd rather lose everything than lose her.

"And what if I refuse to sign this agreement?"

"In France everything is split in half. But I promise you: If you don't sign, and this goes to trial, I will make sure there is nothing left to divide. I will spend everything we have before we make it to a judge. I will empty our savings. I will max out the credit cards. I will grind you down until you can't fight anymore. Until there's nothing left to fight for. Tell me: What is half of nothing, Danielle? Half of nothing is nothing. *Nothing.* If you fight me, you'll get nothing."

I sat back in my chair and fixed my gaze on my glass of champagne. The golden color of the Bollinger had faded. I picked up the glass and turned it in my fingers, feeling a strong urge to hurl it at Nikolai.

He stared at me, his eyes expressionless. "I'm offering you the best deal you're going to get. We sign a *divorce amiable,* Nico comes with me to Bulgaria, and nobody suffers. You get her all summer and on holidays. It's not the first time a father has had custody."

"And if I don't sign this agreement?"

"Then this is going to be a very difficult time for everyone."

"You're really willing to go that far," I said. It wasn't a question. I knew him. He hated to lose. He would torch everything, burn the house down, squander our treasure, to win. I had been trying for so long to avoid this kind of malicious game, had so twisted myself up inside to avoid coming to this point, that now that the armies were being called up and the tactics were being drawn, I found myself unprepared.

"Think about it," he said, standing and pushing

back his chair, leaving his glass of champagne half empty. "And let me know what you want to do."

Within forty-eight hours Nikolai's parents arrived in the village. He'd called them on Sunday night, after our big fight, and they had driven from Bulgaria to the south of France. It was a long trip, nearly two days of solid driving through Serbia, Croatia, Slovenia, Italy, and the coast of southern France. But when Nikolai called, they came.

The day before Yana and Ivan were set to arrive, Nikolai stopped by my office to tell me they were staying at the house. "They'll sleep in the attic, in the playroom," he said. But I knew this wasn't a simple family visit. His parents would come to the house and take Nikolai's side in the situation and try to convince me I was making a mistake. They would cajole me into coming around to their way of seeing things, or they would cut me out completely. I'd seen it before, in Sofia, when we had argued over how to care for Nico. Either I was with them or I didn't exist.

"Andy is here," I said. "There isn't enough room."

"Come on," he said. "There's more than enough room."

"They can stay at a hotel," I insisted.

"I'm not telling my parents to stay in a hotel," he said.

"Why do they need to come to Aubais in the first place?" I said, exasperated. "It's totally unnecessary. We don't need their help. We're both adults."

"They're coming," he said, crossing his arms over his chest, "because they don't want to leave me alone with you."

"Well, they've left you alone with me for the past nine years."

"They didn't know about your violent tendencies," he said.

I almost laughed. "Violent tendencies?"

"The other night," he said. "When you attacked me."

"When I *what?*"

"When you attacked me in the bedroom," he said, his hand slipping over his left side. "You probably broke my ribs."

I stared at him, abashed. Yes, I had pushed Nikolai, that was true, but I had not *attacked* him, and I had not used enough force to break his ribs.

"I can't even sleep I'm in so much pain."

"Are you serious?" I said, astonished that he would say such a ridiculous thing. "I'm half your size."

He gave me a look. "I knew you would deny it."

"You were just fine earlier," I said, looking at him more closely, as if I could X-ray his chest on my own. He'd been in perfect condition that morning, when he took the kids to school with

Sveti, informing me that I was no longer welcome to ride along for the morning drop-off. He'd carried Nico on his back out to the car.

"We are going to see a doctor," he said. "My parents want to be with me for the X-ray, as witnesses. They want to stay with me, to support me. They're worried that you'll resort to violence again." I must have looked as confused as I felt, because he added, "My parents didn't know how mentally ill you are. I've hidden that unfortunate fact from them, just like I've hidden the physical and psychological abuse I've endured during our marriage, but now that I've told them the truth and they know who you really are, they're coming to help me."

I listened, drawing the picture for myself: *mentally ill, violent tendencies, physical and psychological abuse.* His story was coming together, and although I was a character in the story, the heroine of it, the narrative was utterly strange to me. What had begun as a series of insults flung in anger in our bedroom had morphed into a living, breathing character. And that twisted character was me.

"Are you done?" I said, glaring at him.

"I'm going to set up the futon in the attic," he replied.

"Wait, this is not happening," I said. "The only reason you're bringing your parents here is so you can gang up on me." I was getting mad. It was already horrible, passing each other in the kitchen or in the courtyard, horrible to feel the twisting of our partnership as it ground down into one of animosity and antagonism. It would only get worse if his parents stayed with us. Then I would be cornered.

He stared at me a moment and said, "This is my house, too, and I'm inviting my parents to stay with us."

"If your parents sleep here," I said, "I'm leaving."

"Leave, then," he said, clearly glad to be rid of me.

"Okay then, I'll leave," I said, realizing even as I said it that I didn't have anywhere to go. I imagined packing a bag and showing up on the steps of Lord and Lulu's *maison de maître*. Or I could give Jett a call. We could share a bottle of wine and bitch about men, and I would feel better. Then I had an idea. The main reason Andy had come to France was to help me with some repairs around the house. But Andy had also come to Aubais to babysit the kids for Nikolai's birthday weekend. I'd planned a surprise gift for my husband: A long weekend at a music festival in Salzburg for the two of us. Everything had been arranged—hotel, flight, passes to the festival. The trip was an extravagant surprise, another love offering, one more attempt to make things better. With all that had happened in Paris, I'd planned to skip the festival, but now that his parents were on their way to France, I could use my ticket and leave. Andy would take care of the kids, and I could have a few days to think things through. I needed a moment to breathe and decide what to do next. I needed some space to think clearly. It gave me a way to avoid the situation just a little longer before coming back to reality. It was my specialty, running away, and I wasn't going to abandon it now, when I needed it most. And so I decided to go to Salzburg.

As soon as my plane landed in Vienna and I turned on my phone, I saw the missed calls from Andy. I hurried into the airport and called him back.

"Something weird is going on here," he said, and I knew then, before he said another word, that going to Salzburg had been a big mistake.

"What is it?" I asked. "What happened?"

"You know that Nikolai's parents are here," he said. "Well, after you left, they had this big to-do in the kitchen. They were really wound up about something."

"Where were the kids when this was going on?"

"Upstairs," he said. "They didn't hear anything, I don't think. But then, just a little while ago, Nikolai loaded a bunch of stuff into the car."

"What kind of stuff?"

"Suitcases and some toys. Nico's things, actually. And a bunch of boxes of wine from the cellar. Then they left."

A terrible sensation came over me, as if the oxygen had been sucked from the atmosphere. The whole world seemed to fold in and fold in again, crunching down on me.

"Left?" I said. Andy's words were perfectly clear, and yet I couldn't understand them any more than I could understand the German announcements echoing through the terminal. "What do you mean, *left?*"

"I mean they left," he said. "Gone. Left."

"I'm sure they're just in Sommières or something. I'm sure they'll be back soon."

"Well, when I saw him loading the car, I went out to the courtyard and asked him what he was doing. He said he was going to Bulgaria with his parents. And when I asked him if you knew about this trip, the guy just ignored me. Like I wasn't even there. Just looked right through me as if I was nothing, even less than nothing. Insulting. That guy's got some serious, serious problems. Rude, I tell you."

"Oh, my God," I said, realizing the extent of my error. Instead of standing my ground and making it clear that I would be a formidable opponent, I had been a coward. He'd brought in his soldiers, and I had retreated. I'd believed I was ready to fight, but I wasn't. I was simultaneously fearless and fearful. These two emotional states would form the poles of my behavior for the next months. It was Strong Warrior versus Retreating

Coward. I would morph from one to the other on a daily basis.

"How long ago was that?" I asked, my mind racing so fast I could hardly think.

"I'd say three hours or so ago," he said. "I called you right away, but I guess you were up in the air."

"Is Alex there with you?"

"Right here. We're playing Risk and eating popcorn. He's fine. Don't worry about him." He paused, as if unsure of how to ask. "Does this have something to do with that fight you two had the other night?"

I hadn't been able to tell Andy all the details of what was happening. I didn't know how to say the words "We're getting divorced." I had fought against the possibility of that outcome with such ferocity that I didn't know how to acknowledge it now that it was in fact real. And so Andy didn't know the full extent of the trouble I was facing. "Yes," I said, feeling shame burn through me. "It does."

"Well, was he planning to go somewhere?" he asked, his voice kind. "Because this seems pretty sudden."

Maybe it was his tone of voice, the gentleness of it, but a wall inside me broke. I told Andy everything that had happened, about the weekend in Paris, the fight, and why I had left Aubais. I told him how just before I'd left for Salzburg I'd found Nikolai in my office. He was going through

295

my desk, taking family documents—our marriage certificate, Nico's birth certificate, Nico's passport. When I asked him what he was doing, he said he was keeping these things "just in case." I tried to get them back, but he wouldn't give them to me. I made a grab for the passport, but he held it high in the air, so I couldn't reach it, and then walked away. I made him promise that he wouldn't use the passport, or any of the other documents, but he'd done exactly that. He waited until I'd left for Salzburg and took off with Nico. He had our daughter's passport and her birth certificate, so he could travel with her. I had been outmaneuvered. I felt like the dumbest person in the world.

"He lied to me," I said. "He told me he wouldn't go anywhere."

"Danielle," Andy said. "When people are mad, they'll do just about anything."

My hand shook as I held the phone to my ear. I pressed it closer to stop the trembling. Of course I knew that divorce could bring out the worst in us. It would push us to emotional extremes, set us up to fight a primal battle for children and shelter and sustenance. As I listened to Andy, the slow, sickening realization hit me: We were at war.

After speaking with Andy, I sat at a Starbucks in the airport and called Nikolai's cell number. I called four, six, ten times, but got nothing except his voice mail. My skin was hot, my shirt wet with sweat. *How could I be so stupid? How could I be so naïve? How could I be so dumb?* These self-accusations became a kind of mantra. I blamed myself. Nikolai had left with Nico, yes, but I had allowed it to happen. Fear and worry and out-rage—these emotions swirled through my mind, causing static in my thinking. I left ten, maybe more, voice messages, each one as impassioned and outraged as if it were the very first. I called and called, believing that eventually he would answer. Finally, after half an hour, he picked up.

"What," he said, his voice flat.

"Where are you?" I screamed.

"What do you want?" he said. There was not a hint of emotion in his voice. It was as if he were running out to the supermarket for milk.

"You need to turn around and go back to Aubais," I said, trying to calm down. "Andy is there waiting for you."

"I'm not going back to Aubais," he said.

"This is *kidnapping*—you know that, don't you? Kidnapping."

"I don't call taking my daughter to visit her grandparents kidnapping," he said.

"Driving an eight-year-old girl thousands of miles across Europe without her mother's permission after taking her passport *by force* is kidnapping!"

"Don't be hysterical," he said, and I imagined him rolling his eyes at his father, who was surely in the passenger seat.

"If you do not turn the car around and bring Nico back to Aubais right now, you will understand hysterical. Andy is waiting for her. He's going to call me as soon as she's home. If I don't hear from him in one hour, I'm calling the police."

"Go ahead," he said. "I've already been to the gendarmerie."

This floored me. I gasped. "You have?"

"My lawyer suggested—"

"Your *lawyer?* You have a lawyer?"

"My lawyer said that it is perfectly legal for me to take Nico out of France for a visit during the *vacances de Pâques.* My lawyer suggested that I file a report with the police, so that it is clear that I am taking Nico out of the country for a visit."

In the perfect opening to his endgame, Nikolai had anticipated my next move before I could make it. Now, even if I called the police, even if I went there to file a report, they would tell me that Nikolai was just taking Nico for a visit. I was cornered.

"When are you coming back?" I asked, hearing the defeat in my voice.

"In a week. Ten days at the most."

"How am I supposed to believe you?"

"Honestly, I don't give a damn if you believe me," he said. "I prefer not to speak to you right now. Your aggression is beginning to upset me."

"Let me talk to Nico." I was on the verge of tears, but I couldn't actually cry. Something was holding my tears back, some horrible constraint that, I realized as he handed the phone to Nico, was terror.

The phone scratched, and suddenly it was filled with the radiant sound of my daughter's voice. "Hi, Mama!"

"Hi, baby," I said. "Where are you?"

"We just stopped at McDonald's. I got a Happy Meal."

"That's great," I said, trying to sound as if everything were normal. Nico had no clue what was going on behind her Easter trip out of France. She sounded cheerful and excited, and why shouldn't she? She was going on an adventure with her dad.

"I hear you're going to Grandma and Grandpa's house for a visit?"

"And we're going to Venz, too."

"Where?"

"To Venz," she said, and I realized she was trying to pronounce "Venice." Why on earth were they going to Venice when Nikolai had told me that they were going to Bulgaria? What in the hell was going on? What other secret plans had Nikolai made?

"Nico, give me the phone," Nikolai said in the background, and abruptly, before my daughter could say good-bye, the phone went dead.

• • •

I later learned they left France on the *autoroute*, driving past Nîmes, Marseille, Nice, and Monaco, traveling along the Côte d'Azur into Italy. I knew the route well—the pebbled beaches and the rocketing palms and the sky so blue and hard that it seemed like blown glass. I knew a place to buy sachets of lavender that left the car with a sweet herbal scent, and I knew another place where the highway cut so close to the water that the car could tip into the immense green sea. I knew a bistro in Marseille that made good bouillabaisse and a bar in Nice with a postcard view of the sunset. I knew the spots of the Fauvist painters, those rocky terraces where sun and sea created pigmentation so bright it seemed pixelated, artificial. I knew the number of tolls on that road—four between Nîmes and Nice—and I knew the amount of change I needed to toss to pass through them. But I didn't have a clue as to how to stop Nikolai from stealing Nico away on this road.

The facts I gathered were these: Nikolai went to the bank to withdraw thousands of euros in cash from our joint account; he went to see a lawyer; he stopped by the police station to file his report. Then he packed the car and left France.

I put this timeline together over the course of many weeks, examining the paper trail he'd left behind. The bank statements showed that he'd bought something from our telecom company (a new iPhone 4), and something from the pharmacy (most likely his pills), and something from the *tabac*. They showed that he'd filled the car with gas in Sommières and that he'd loaded up on groceries at the Carrefour. He had rushed to get out of the country, and I support this impression by the fact that a speed-control camera clocked him driving fifty kilometers over the limit near Nice. A ticket arrived some weeks later with the license-plate number of our 2009 silver Citroën C5, recording the place and date and excess speed.

When I looked over the speeding ticket, I imagined Nico in the backseat, the window cracked, the wind unsettling her long brown hair. I imagined Stinky, her stuffed hippo, tucked under her arm. It was a warm spring in the South of France, and the smell of the sea might have made her think of the days we'd spent on the beach together, long afternoons of sand castles and beignets. Maybe she was excited to be on the road; maybe she thought the whole thing was fun. I knew how much she liked to look at the stamps that inked her passport—Bulgarian and American and French stamps—counting each one as she recalled a detail of the places we'd been together.

I called Nikolai back, and my call went to voice mail. I tried again, and then again, but he didn't pick up. Many more times that weekend, I called, and I always I found myself listening to a recorded message telling me, "*Je suis désolée la personne que vous recherchez n'est pas disponible pour le moment.*" I left messages, a dozen messages, so many pleading and angry and fearful messages, all of them asking for details of what he was doing, and when I could speak with Nico, and why he was doing this. All my messages went unanswered.

The blanket of silence and secrecy around Nikolai's movements led me to imagine the worst. I became so wrapped up in the dark imaginings playing through my mind that I couldn't eat or sleep. I was dizzy when I stood up and dizzy when I lay down. I wanted to do something, anything, and so I went to the music festival, and I went to a dinner party thrown by a friend of a friend, moving through the weekend as if in a trance. My impulse was to get on a plane and fly to Bulgaria, but I wasn't sure they were even there, as Nico had said they were going to Venice. And after Nikolai's report at the gendarmerie, there was no point in going back to France to get the police involved. I was stuck.

At the hotel in Salzburg, I set up my laptop and began to write backtracking messages to Nikolai, begging him to call me so that we could "work things out." I wrote text messages telling him we needed to look at the "bigger picture" and that I still loved him and wanted him back. Those texts are lost, but reading my e-mail messages now, I see that my tone was conciliatory, desperate, pleading. At one point I wrote, *"It is becoming very clear to me that you do not want to speak to me and that you have decided that you don't want to work things out. If our marriage is over, I need to know your plans so that I can start figuring out what to do next."* It is incredible for me to read this now, because we *had* decided what we were doing— getting divorced. It was plain that our marriage *was* over. I had a lover. Nikolai had a lawyer. We were not going to work things out. All that had been decided before I went to Salzburg and he left France with Nico. I closed my e-mail message to him with, *"I would greatly appreciate it if you would call me so that I understand what you are doing. I also need to understand what you want from me and how we will end this quickly without fighting and anger."* Without fighting and anger? How could there be no anger after what I'd done in Paris? How could there be no fighting after he'd driven off with Nico? I was furious and ready to go after him.|And yet I was using a gentle, reasonable approach. I was remaining calm. And I see now that this pose was a new incarnation of the Angry Warrior, one used to lure her enemy close. By being nice and offering a white flag, I could woo him into bringing Nico back to France. He was playing dirty, and so I was playing dirtier. This ruse marked me as a true Machiavellian or, to put it a better way, I was being a manipulative bitch.

But when Nikolai wrote back, it was clear that he wasn't buying it. He said that it was baffling to him that I would think that we could work anything out. There was nothing to work out between us. We were getting divorced, and that was that.

After days of trying to call Nico and having no contact with her or her father, I called Yana, who—to my surprise—answered her phone. Yana confirmed that Nikolai and Nico were in Venice with Ivan. Yana had flown home sooner so she could go back to work. That's all the information she would give me. She wouldn't tell me, for example, if Nikolai planned to stay in Bulgaria for one week or for one year. She wouldn't tell me, for example, if Nikolai was filing for divorce in Bulgaria or in France. Just as she had welcomed me into her life ten years before, now she closed me out, as if I were a stranger.

"Do you know that Nikolai did not—*does not*—have my permission to take Nico to Bulgaria?"

"But why does he need your permission?" Yana said in her heavily accented English.

"Because I am her mother," I said.

"It's your own fault," she said. "You pushed him to leave."

"Please tell him to turn around and bring Nico back home," I said. "Will you tell him I said that?"

Yana said nothing.

"Because if he doesn't bring her back to France in the next day or two, I am going to come to Sofia and go to the American embassy. Nico is an American citizen. They will not let an American child be taken like this. I'm serious."

"You think you are very frightening, eh?" Yana shouted. "You are very scaring us, yes? Come if you like, and bring the Americans. You're the big woman now, eh? Come and you will see if we are scared." She hung up and stopped answering my calls altogether.

"I need to go to Bulgaria," I said to Hadrien when I called him after my conversation with Yana. "I can't just sit here doing nothing. I have to go there and bring Nico back home."

"They won't let you," Hadrien said. "Even if you show up at their door, they won't let you in."

"I know," I said. "But what else can I do?"

"Come to Paris," Hadrien said. "Come here and we'll figure out what to do together."

In Paris I took a taxi to the 2nd arrondissement, where I climbed the narrow steps to the seventh floor to Hadrien's mansard apartment and collapsed into a chair, exhausted. I had barely eaten in days and had trouble sleeping through the night. I was so worried and angry that I could hardly think. Hadrien got me a glass of water, put his arm around my shoulders, and said, "Breathe, everything is going to be okay," comforting me until I was calm again. I leaned against him and closed my eyes, taking in the particular scent of him, wishing that I could stop feeling so helpless.

We sat together for a while, talking, his body warming me. At some point during the conversation, my mood shifted: the fearfulness and anxiety that had skittered through me for days became, all at once, the slow, sweet, predatory feeling of desire. I slid my hand under his T-shirt and felt his body. He was warm and soft, his skin smooth beneath my fingers. His dark eyes watched as I crawled over to the bed. I gestured that he join me. I undressed him, unbuttoning his buttons and unzipping his zipper and peeling off his socks; he undressed me, rolling my stockings down my legs, kissing my knee, my shin, my feet. I lay back in the bed and closed my eyes, feeling everything with a careful, hungry awareness. This warmth, this closeness, had the power to transform me. It had the power to open a pathway into the future, one through which I might have seen the years ahead, if I chose to look. If I had, I would have seen the beautiful afternoons together in the Jardin de Luxumbourg, the dinners at bistros where he would order his favorite food, giving me a taste for "Parisian cuisine, not that stuff from the south." I would have seen the nights walking through the narrow streets of Paris, wending our way along the rue Vivienne to his apartment, and our eventual move to New York City. I would have seen that we would be happy, he and I, for many, many years. But I didn't look into the future. In his arms I was wholly, com-pletely, in the present. After we made love, I was ready to go back to the terrible fight ahead of me.

"What am I going to do?" I asked, taking a sip of water. "I can't even get through to Nico. Yana said they were going to be in Bulgaria, but really I have no way of knowing where they are. They could be flying to India for all I know."

"We'll get through to her," he said, resting his hand on my shoulder.

"How? He won't answer his phone."

"I spoke to my godfather, who is a lawyer, to see if he could help you," Hadrien said. "He says you need to hire a lawyer who lives in the south, and you must go immediately to the gendarmerie and file a police report, to counter what your husband said. You have to give your version of events. I'm working on getting you the number of a lawyer in Montpellier."

"Okay," I replied. "I'll go to the gendarmerie as soon as I'm back home."

"You need to begin to present your case," Hadrien said, running a finger over my arm.

"Present my case," I repeated.

"You need to start recording everything. Keep a diary of what is happening. And don't write anything in an e-mail that he can use against you. From now on, every interaction between you and your husband is a legal record and is going to be part of your divorce case."

I took this in, knowing that it was a turning point. Now, suddenly, the relationship that had been the most intimate and personal part of my life was a legal encounter. Our actions were considered "evidence," and I was in charge of collecting it. But even as I determined to hold my position and engage in this fight, I felt an enormous sense of doubt about the meaning of the words "innocent" and "guilty." It was unclear to me that these words could mean anything at all in such a context as our breakup. If our marriage were a murder mystery, there would be no way to determine the murderer and no way to identify the victim. We were both the killer and the killed, the criminal and the corpse. That was the very nature of divorce: the annihilation of the innocent by the innocent. Or the guilty by the guilty.

The gendarmerie was just down the street from Alex and Nico's school in Sommières, not far from the market square, and although I'd passed by often on my way to the Saturday farmers' market, I'd somehow never noticed it before. It was one of those places, I realized, that you ignore until you need it. I stood at a gate and pressed the intercom button.

"*Oui, bonjour?*" a voice crackled.

"I want to make a complaint," I said in French. Everything would be in French once I walked through the gate, and I would have the verbal capabilities, as Nico liked to joke, of a French two-year-old.

"*Entrez!*" The automatic gate clanked and began to slide open.

I walked into the offices and was directed to the back, where a uniformed man sat behind an extremely orderly desk. He had dark hair and dark eyes and a large framed photo of a woman and a child on his filing cabinet. There was a nameplate on the desk. It read Henri Cabirot.

Henri gestured for me to sit, and then, after asking me why I'd come and pulling up a form on his computer, he began to ask me questions. When I told him the basics—that my husband and I were getting a divorce, that he'd taken my daughter's passport and driven off to Bulgaria—he said, "But why a divorce?"

"Well," I said, trying to figure out how to explain such a complicated story. I could have said that we'd moved to France to make a storyook life and that when this failed miserably, I fell I in love with a handsome Parisian twelve years my junior. Instead I said,

"I met a man in Paris, and my husband is angry."

"I see," Henri said. "He is jealous."

"Yes," I said.

"And you have children?"

"A boy and a girl."

Henri typed this into the computer. "Continue, madame."

"My husband told me not to go to Paris, but I went anyway."

"To see this man?"

"To see this man."

"It was *une question de liberté* for you, madame? To go to Paris if you choose?"

"Exactement," I said, feeling that someone finally understood me. *"Une question de liberté.* I went to Paris, and when I returned, my husband was very angry and . . ." I wanted to say "aggressive" in French, but I hadn't a clue how to say it, so I settled for "mean." ". . . *méchant.*"

"He beat you?"

"No, but he was meanly angry."

"No insults or threats?"

"Insults," I said. "And threats."

"What threats?"

"He said he would divorce me and take *everything*—the house and our children—and move to Bulgaria. My husband is Bulgarian."

"I'm sorry, but this is *la France*, madame, and in *la France* no man can do that to his wife. We are a civilized country. We have laws."

"So then he called his parents, and they came to Aubais from Bulgaria. They drove here."

"*Oh là là*," he said. "Such a long drive."

"Then he told me he was going to go to Bulgaria and he wanted to take my daughter. He took her passport from my office *by force.*"

"He beat you, madame?"

"No, but he took it and held it like this." I stood up and held my hand over my head, demonstrating how he had waved it high in the air, bully-in-the-playground style.

"*D'accord*," he said, looking more and more perturbed. "He took the child's passport by force. And?"

"We argued. I told him I did not want our daughter going to Bulgaria. But he left for Bulgaria anyway."

"With your daughter," he said.

"Yes, with our daughter," I confirmed.

"What was this date?"

"He left on the sixth of April," I said.

"When is the last time you spoke to your daughter?"

"I spoke to her April sixth for a few minutes. Now he won't answer his phone. I spoke to his mother, but now she won't answer either."

"You are afraid he will keep your daughter in Bulgaria?"

"Yes," I said. "That's my fear."

"I will tell you something, madame," Henri said,

straightening in his chair, preparing to give me some important information. "What he did—taking his child out of France to visit his family—that is not a crime."

I had known that this was coming. It was exactly as Nikolai had said it would be. But for me it *was* a crime, a crime of the worst kind: the wounding of a parent through the child. I was furious, and wanted my daughter back. I felt absolutely zero empathy for him. I couldn't understand that maybe, in his mind, he had no other option but to run away with Nico. Just as there had been no option for me but to go to Paris.

"It is only a crime," Henri continued, "if he does not bring your child back. What your husband has done is not illegal. It is simply very bad taste."

Bad taste—the worst condemnation one can receive in France.

"But you have to understand," I said, beginning to feel desperate. "I haven't been able to speak to my daughter for a week. He could be anywhere by now. There's no guarantee he's coming back. That is a big problem."

"I agree with you, madame," he said. "But in my opinion, when a man does this kind of act to his wife, it is not because he wants to keep the child. Children are too much trouble for most men. No. It is because the man wants *revenge*."

He looked at me, to see if I understood. I nodded. I under-stood perfectly.

Henri returned to the keyboard. "When does he say he will bring her back?"

"First he said one week. But it's been a week already."

"When is she due back at school?"

"The end of the Easter vacation," I said. "April twenty-second."

"Okay," he said, typing in this date. "If when the *vacances de Pâques* finishes and your child is not home in France and she is officially absent from her school, then the gendarmerie can do something for you."

"But that's almost two weeks from now," I objected. "I can't just wait here without news for that long."

"I'm sorry, madame. There is nothing else I can do for you."

I must have looked particularly forlorn at that moment, because Henri took a piece of paper and wrote something on it. "This is my personal number. You call me if there is any trouble." He pushed the paper toward me and smiled. "And I will wait to hear from you on the twenty-second of April, *d'accord*?"

In the days that I waited for Nikolai to bring Nico back from Bulgaria, I wandered from room to room of the fortress as if looking for something

I'd misplaced. I'd find myself in some part of the house, the dining room or the laundry closet, and suddenly wonder why I'd gone there to begin with. Had I needed dinner plates? Was there laundry to fold? Soon I didn't know one day from the next. I wasn't hungry, and so I didn't eat much. I wasn't tired, and so I didn't sleep more than a few hours a night. I couldn't think clearly, and so I stopped working on my new book. I didn't want to see anyone from the village, and so I avoided going outside La Commanderie, remaining home instead with Alex and Andy. The days were irregular, distended, indistinct. I didn't pay attention to where I was going and walked into doors, dropped coffee cups on the floor, cut my finger while slicing an apple for Alex. I fell down the stairs because I wasn't watching the steps, and I had bruises covering my legs and arms, dark flowers of broken vessels splotching my skin. They didn't hurt, all these cuts and bruises. Nothing hurt. Nothing had edges sharp enough to pain me. My heart had been ripped out and transported thousands of miles away, leaving me numb, bloodless. Nothing could get through to me any longer.

I blamed my suffering on Nikolai. He had gone crazy, I told myself. He had completely over-reacted about my weekend in Paris. He was doing all this to get (as Henri had suggested) revenge. But if I'd been able to look at the situation with some distance—something I could not manage until quite a few years later—I would have understood that he wasn't just out for revenge. He was in pain. He was losing me, and Alex, and he was afraid of losing Nico, too.

During that time of waiting, I went into my e-mail and looked up the Christmas 2003 messages Nikolai had sent me. I reread each letter, as if to convince myself that the man who had once written such beautiful love letters could not possibly hurt me now.

One afternoon I followed Alex up to the attic playroom. He was glorying in his Easter vacation, so many weeks of unstructured freedom. He had played in a soccer tournament, and now he was in serious pursuit of leisure. He'd set up camp in the attic, creating a magnificent wreckage of books and games and water glasses and bags of micro-wave popcorn and DVDs and Fly's toys. Fly slept among the rubble, snoring away as Alex played games on the computer. Some afternoons I would go upstairs with a book or a magazine and stay there with Alex and Fly. Being near my son was one of the few things that helped make me feel better while I waited, and so I tried to be close to him as much as possible, lying down on the couch when he was watching television or sitting in the courtyard when he played Ping-Pong with Andy. In my mind Alex and Nico were linked together, my *AlexNico,* and if one were here with me, the other would soon be.

On this particular day, I climbed the attic stairs and collapsed on the futon, winded. There weren't many stairs to climb, perhaps ten, but I was barely able to pull myself up. I was weak, and although it was my own fault—I'd virtually stopped eating and sleeping—I couldn't find the will to take care of myself.

The futon in the attic was hard, the cotton sheets cool. I pressed my cheek against the sheet and watched Alex. He was perched at the edge of his chair playing FIFA 12. I watched him for a long time, noting the way the blue light from the screen danced across his skin. In my malnourished, insomniac, magical state of mind, I could trance out for minutes, watching that light flicker over my son.

In the far corner to the playroom, there was a basket filled with Nico's stuffed animals. I got up, pulled the basket next to the futon, and began setting the animals up around the bed, piling stuffed bears and dolphins and frogs and cats at the outermost edge, a plush zoo. I drew a big stuffed frog close and inhaled. It didn't particularly smell like her—it didn't have the mixture of shampoo and condensed milk and salt of Nico—but it was *her* stuffed frog, one she'd slept with since the first year of her life. I pressed my face into its

316

belly, trying to find some trace of my daughter.

Finally Alex glanced up from his game, as if noticing me for the first time. A look of concern crossed his face, and I remembered the two-year-old Alex visiting me at Maichin Dom, that serious expression in his eyes when he said: *You'll get better now, okay, Mama? You're better, okay?* We had always had an understanding, unspoken, perhaps forged in the womb, that I would be there to care for him. When I couldn't, he stepped in to care for me. What he might not have realized was how much I depended upon him to keep me steady. He was twelve, and his blond curls had darkened to brown, but he was still my compass, that strong magnetic force that guided me.

"What's up?" Alex said.

I pulled myself up and propped my chin on my elbow. "Nothing's up," which of course was not true: Everything was up. Up in the air. Up in arms. Upside down.

He wrinkled his forehead, studying me. He knew the details of what had happened with Nico. Every night he sat at the dinner table as Andy and I discussed the trip to Bulgaria. He understood that Nico's absence hurt me and that I was anxious for her return. Still, I was not the type of person to lie around for an hour staring off into space.

"Are you sick?"

"I'm worried."

"About Nico?"

"About Nico," I said. "And about you. I'm worried that all this is making you sad."

"I'm okay," he said, and the way he said it—the confident smile, the indifferent shrug, his practiced ability to hide his feelings—almost made me believe him.

"Doesn't any of this upset you?" I said, pushing him to reveal something to me, some flicker of thought, a reaction.

He shrugged again. "Well, there's one kind of weird thing that happened before Daddy left," he said.

"Really?" I sat upright, facing him. "What was that?"

"Daddy and Grandma told me I should come and live in Bulgaria," he said. "They told me I could go with them when they left."

"What?" I said, feeling my stomach lurch. It was still hard for me to believe that they had taken Nico, let alone that they'd wanted to take Alex, too. "What did they say to you?"

"Daddy and Grandma came to my room and told me I could go with them if I wanted. They said that Nico was going to choose them and that I should, too. But I didn't want to go. I think they got mad about that."

"I don't know why they said that," I said. "It wasn't right. You can't choose something like that."

I was trying not to get emotional in front of Alex, but I was furious that they would put him in the middle. Even if Alex had wanted to go to Bulgaria, even if he had packed his bags and jumped into the Citroën of his own volition, they would have had no right to take him without my consent. Just as they'd had no right to take Nico without my permission.

"I told them I choose you," he said, meeting my eye. "I choose you."

"Come here," I said, gesturing for him to sit next to me on the futon. He came and leaned against me. I wrapped my arms around him and hugged him. He was still thin as a twig then, a short boy with a lot of growing ahead of him, but I could see the person he would be one day. It was folded into him, his height, his future, waiting to unfurl. In just a few months, after school let out for the year, I would send him to stay with Sam for the summer break, hoping to spare Alex the worst of the divorce. In August, Alex would call to tell me he wanted to stay with his dad for the 2012–13 school year, and although it hurt to be without him, I would agree, understanding that my son needed a father, needed his own father, in order to heal. Sam loved Alex, taught him, cared for him. Alex wanted to stay longer. One year extended to two, then two years extended to three. Alex filled out and grew to be a head taller than me. In our most recent picture together, he's looking down at me, a big smile on his face. With his father's help, he was becoming a man, growing into the person I knew he could be.

Through these weeks of waiting, Andy kept me company. We spent long mornings in the courtyard, drinking coffee as the sun warmed the flagstones, talking through everything that was happening, going over the events of the past weeks, trying to find solutions. As we talked, he would uncoil the garden hose and water the orange and lemon trees in their clay pots, then spray the rosemary and jasmine. I was not easy to be around on those mornings. I was by turns angry and sullen, teary and spiteful. And yet Andy was patient with me, generous with his affection, ready to cook lunch, willing to listen as I repeated myself. I could only think of what was happening in terms of story, and I was desperate to figure out the next chapter: What was Nikolai plotting? What would he do next? Andy heard all my speculations: that Nikolai would file for divorce in Bulgaria and never return (a tragedy) or, on the other side of the spectrum, change his mind, drive home, and want to reconcile (a comedy). But while Andy listened and offered advice, neither of us had any idea what to do. My stepfather couldn't help me sort through the tangle of my emotions. The confusion and the anger, the sickening sense of helplessness—these feelings were mine alone. I had to experience them and metabolize them myself. I was in it alone.

And so Andy had been, too, so many years before. I understood, as we puzzled over what to do, that Andy had been in the same state of confused despair during his divorce. *There's no easy way through it,* he said. *You just keep on moving. Time helps you see things more clearly.* He had been in a loveless marriage and, when he met my mother, his life pivoted. He had gone through the fallout of a nasty divorce—the shame of leaving his family, the pain of hurting his children, and the financial beating of alimony and child support—only to be hit with the rage and contempt of his twelve-year-old stepdaughter. Me.

"You know," Andy said one morning as we sat in the courtyard, "you were pretty hard on me and your mom when we went through this." He was right. I remembered how venomous I'd been. As a child, I had blamed him for my pain. I had snubbed him when he moved into our house, rejecting his affection, ridiculing his way of doing things, and reminding him that he wasn't my real father. My dad was wild and exciting and crazy; Andy was a normal, steady guy. I told him he didn't belong with us, that he should go back to his wife and kids. I rejected him—and his marriage to my mother—every chance I got. I'd tried to salve my wounds by destroying his happiness. I had needed to fight him; it was the only way I knew at the time.

Now, understanding what he went through, I felt admiration for him. How powerful his love had been, how strong his and my mother's commitment, to weather the likes of a little terror like me. Although Andy had not been perfect, and he and I had our share of fights, we had come a long way together. As Andy and I talked about our troubled past and came to some understanding of the damage we'd done each other, I felt a strange shifting in my relationship to him. Twenty years after I'd left home, we were reconciling as adults. I was thirty-eight years old and twice married, but I had finally left behind the petulant girl who blamed her parents for her pain. Now I was a woman who wanted to make amends.

Later, when he was back home in Wisconsin, Andy told me that his weeks at La Commanderie in April 2012 were some of the hardest of his life and that he left France feeling physically and psychologically traumatized. A large part of this, I imagine, was the way it dredged up memories of his divorce. But it also must have been difficult to watch me, who had always been such a fighter, taking such a beating. I had sunk into a state of stunned inaction. In the past I was anything but passive. For me, action—even the wrong action—was preferable to sitting around and waiting for a solution. But now, for these weeks of Easter vacation, I waited. I'd been blindsided. I hadn't anticipated such a show of force. I was surrounded. It was Nikolai's move.

In the final week of Easter vacation, I couldn't stand the waiting anymore. I had to get out of the house. Some mornings, I took solitary walks on the Roman road outside the village, walking along the flinty path to the Chapelle Saint-Nazaire, an ancient stone church with only a handful of narrow windows and an iron cross rising from the roof. I had never been inside the chapel— its medieval wooden door was always locked to visitors—but I imagined it dark and damp, filled with somber wooden chairs, a simple stone altar. One morning I woke before the sun rose, hiked to the chapel, and felt the first warmth of the day as I leaned against the stone wall. I tried the door, but it was locked, as usual. I felt the urge to pray, to ask the powers-that-be to help me. I remembered the pact I'd made in Maichin Dom, the vow I'd given to do my best for my family. It seemed so long ago, that promise. I had been trying to live up to it, to do what was right. I'd been given so much. We had come so far. I wondered if I could go back and ask for more. I needed clarity, just a brief moment when the clouds parted and I might see the way forward. I needed to understand that we would be fine, all of us, once we made it through this darkness.

Some afternoons I got into the car and just drove anywhere, stopping in the nearby villages of Junas or Calvisson, where I would have a coffee and read the *Midi Libre* at a café. Other times I would drive into the hills around Aubais, up into the vineyards of Pic Saint-Loup, driving fast, windows open. One morning after yet another unsuccessful attempt to call Nico, I was so frustrated that I got into my car, drove to the train station in Nîmes, bought a ticket to Paris, and was in Hadrien's bed by lunch. Andy promised to take care of Alex while I was away, and so I spent the night. I needed tenderness, a respite from worrying, someone to tell me that everything would be fine.

I felt deeply happy with Hadrien, but this happiness was shot through with self-doubt. How could I possibly start something new with a man now, as my marriage was ending? Wasn't it wrong to be happy in the middle of such a mess? I had left Sam and jumped into Nikolai's arms. Now I was jumping into Hadrien's bed, hoping his love could save me. I hadn't had time to be alone, time to find out who I was without a man in my life. I was too needy, too dependent, not strong enough for a relationship. I didn't want to use Hadrien's love as a Band-Aid and then, when I'd healed, go back to being the same person. I wanted to make a radical break with my old self. I wanted that old self to burn away and a new self to rise from the ashes. And so, as I left on the train back to Aubais, I decided it best to wait to see Hadrien again. I wouldn't escape to his bed until things were resolved at home. I would wait until I was whole again, ready and strong again, before coming back to Paris.

Andy and I drove Alex to school the day Easter vacation ended. We parked and then hunted around the playground, hoping to spot Nico among the children. When we saw that she wasn't there, we went to the *boulangerie* on the square and bought croissants. I picked at mine, playing with the buttery layers of pastry, trying to figure out what to do next. This was the final moment. If Nico wasn't in school today, the police would get involved.

When we went back to La Commanderie, the gray Citroën was parked in the courtyard. I glared at the car, with its shiny silver paint and black-tinted windows, the transporter of doom and destruction that had taken my girl away. Andy gave me a nervous look—*Better leave this matter to you*—and walked to the terrace, where he was installing tiles. The courtyard was empty, and so I went into the house, looking for Nico. Instead I found Yana in the kitchen, a pale-skinned, black-eyed woman with a sharp nose and bright red lipstick. She looked exhausted but somehow fierce. She had made four trans-European trips for her son in three weeks and would probably make another four if he asked her.

"Where's Nico?" I asked.

"I don't know," she said tersely, and left the room, as if being near me were too much for her to bear.

Nikolai stepped into the kitchen after she left. "What the fuck were the police doing here?"

"Where's Nico?" I asked, ignoring his question.

"I dropped her at school," he said. "And when I got home, I found a gendarme waiting for me at the front door."

Henri, I thought, my hero! Most likely he'd come to make sure Nico was back safe. "Henri was probably coming to see if you'd brought Nico back for school."

"Henri?" Nikolai said. "You know the gendarme's name? What, are you sleeping with the whole police force now, too?" He was trembling with rage. "Do you know what that guy said to me? He told me that I shouldn't have *scared* you and that he was going to be watching me to make sure I didn't do anything like that again."

"He's right," I said. "You *shouldn't* have scared me."

"Do you know how *embarrassing* this was for

326

me? My mother answered the door to find the police asking for me. She thought I was going to be *arrested.* The neighbors saw me being questioned. How could you do that to me?"

"How could *I* do this to *you?*" I said, astonished. I couldn't believe that he had just put me through hell and now *he* was yelling at *me* for embarrassing him in front of the neighbors. "How could *you* do this to *me?* And not only to me but to our kids! What is this that you told Alex, that he could *choose* to live with you in Bulgaria? And that Nico had chosen you? How do you think that made him feel?"

"I'm not going to lie to Alex. He has a right to know what's happening."

"Telling him to choose between his parents is *not* what is happening. We are going to have joint custody of Alex and Nico, which means equal time with both of them. They are not going to lose their family because of this."

Suddenly the doorbell rang from the rue Droite. We looked at each other, and with an almost imperceptible shift, a habit born out of years of putting up a front, we donned our public faces and walked to the door together, becoming, for just a moment, a normal husband and wife opening the front door. Henri stood on the stoop, looking concerned.

"*Bonjour,*" I said, stepping out from behind Nikolai.

"*Bonjour, madame,*" he said, looking over my shoulder at Nikolai, who had shrunk into the background, trying to hide. "I came earlier and had a talk with your husband."

"He told me," I said.

"Have you seen your daughter yet?"

"No," I said. "My husband took her to school this morning. I think she's fine."

"And you?" he said. Maybe he'd noticed how much weight I'd lost or how my hand trembled as I held the door. "Your husband is behaving? Are you safe here?"

I glanced over my shoulder at Nikolai, who had backed away, disappearing into the house. All his bluster vanished when confronted with authority.

"I'll be fine," I said. "Thanks for coming."

"You have my number," he said, giving me a kind look. "You let me know if there are more problems with your husband."

As I said good-bye, Henri stepped up, into the foyer, and called out to Nikolai, who was hiding around the corner. "*Au revoir, monsieur.*"

I stood outside Nico's school waiting and, at exactly five o'clock, she bounded out and into my arms, her whole expression one of happiness. I had a vision of her as a toddler, holding out her arms for me to pick her up and carry her. She was eight years old, too big for me to carry, but I grabbed hold of her anyway and hugged her tight, burying my face in her hair, feeling her wiggly, excited self in my arms.

"Nico!"

"Mama!"

"I missed you," I said, kissing her.

"Me, too!"

"You were gone so long. How was your trip?"

"Awesome!" she said, pulling away and hoisting her backpack over her shoulder. For Nico,nothing bad had happened. She'd been on vacation, simple as that. She had no idea what her father had done or what I'd been through. She had no idea that she was at the center of a strategic standoff. She was exactly the same little girl she'd been before she left—all confidence and energy—and I wondered why I'd thought the trip would have changed her, why I'd assumed that she would understand my pain and fear, as if they could be telepathically communicated to her. Thankfully, they weren't.

I took her by the hand, and we walked toward the car. At Chocolaterie Courtin we bought a sack of orangettes and shared them.

"What did you do on your trip?"

"We had McDonald's like ten times!" she said. "And Daddy bought me so many presents in Venice—my favorite is a glass merry-go-round! It is so cool, with all the horses made of different-colored glass. I'm scared to break it, though. It was expensive!"

"It sounds great," I said, calculating the cost of their trip, a good part of which was paid from our joint checking account. He was acting on his threat: If we didn't come to an agreement soon, he would spend everything we had. "You'll have to show it to me."

"It's at Grandma's house in Bulgaria. She's going to keep it until I come back. But my other presents are here."

"Other presents? What else is there?" The trip had been a full-on attempt to buy Nico's loyalty with fancy hotels and meals in restaurants and Murano glass merry-go-rounds.

"A jewelry box and a princess dress and some pretty shoes and . . ."

I stopped listening as she listed the gifts her father had bought her, holding back the impulse to inform her that this was one big buy-off. Her father was making her believe that every day with him would be a shower of ribbons and bows. He was giving her exactly what every little girl wants: a fairy tale she could believe in.

I squeezed her hand in mine. "Sweetie, we need to talk about some things."

"About Daddy?" Nico said.

"About Daddy and me. Do you know what is happening between us?"

Nico looked up at me with her huge eyes. "Daddy said that we're not going to live together anymore."

"Well," I said, keeping my tone of voice even, "your dad and I aren't going to live together anymore. But you and your brother are going to be together."

Nico looked at me a long moment, as if gathering her thoughts. "I told Daddy I would live with him."

"Whoever you live with, you're going to see both of us, and Alex, all the time. The only difference is that you'll change houses. Sometimes you'll be with your dad and sometimes with me. It means you'll have two bedrooms with twice as much stuff." I smiled at Nico, hoping that she could see the situation from that angle. Not a choice between her mom and dad, not a reduction but an expansion.

"But Daddy says he's leaving France."

"That's not for certain."

"Daddy said that if I go with him, we'll have a huge apartment just for us and I'll have my own room with a big bed and a TV on the wall that is just for me! And we'll have a puppy, a pug like Fly, but we won't name him Fly. And we'll live across from the Lycée Français, where there is a patisserie."

She said "patisserie" with a perfect French accent, like a native, and I felt a shiver of awe at how she had grown to be so different from me in the years we'd been in Aubais. She was so . . . *French*.

"Did your dad tell you all those things?"

She nodded, looking worried, as if I might spoil her good fortune.

"Whatever happens, everything is going to be fine," I said, not knowing if I said it for Nico's benefit or for my own. "Don't worry, okay?"

As I said this, her spine relaxed, a subtle muscular release, as if she'd been balancing a very heavy basket on the top of her head. *Don't worry.* She needed to hear those words, just like I did. "Daddy told me not to worry, too," she said at last.

"Well, he was right. There's nothing to worry about. We'll take care of everything."

And yet worry was eating me. The thought of living without her was too much to bear. My family—this constellation we'd formed together, these fixed relationships born of gravity—had become the basic structure of my existence. With its demise we would spin off into a new order, form new constellations, perhaps brighter, more stable, better than the original. It was the nature of time. It was the nature of family. But this death, this rebirth, was not something I was ready for just yet.

Maybe Nico detected something different in the way I'd touched her, some bit of desperation that she'd never felt before, because she pulled away and said, "Are you crying, Mama?"

"No, baby," I said, forcing myself to smile. I kissed her and pulled her close for a long moment. She was back, and she was not hurt, and that's all that mattered. "I'm just so glad you're home."

The Fortress

Andy left in early May, and we were alone in our ruined paradise.

Although it was beautiful outside, and the courtyard was alive with flowers and birdsong, a toxic energy seeped through the house, filling the rooms with a poisonous tension. We didn't know how to behave, now that we were enemies. And so we avoided each other. When I walked into a room, he turned on his heel and walked out. When he walked up the stairs, I closed myself in the bedroom to wait until he'd passed by. Sometimes this cat-and-mouse game became elaborate: I would sneak out a back door, or hide in a closet to avoid him. La Commanderie was big, but not big enough for the two of us.

If we ended up in the same room at the same time, we fought. When Andy was there with us, Nikolai had avoided fighting with me. He hated the idea of people witnessing our feud. But now we argued all the time. We fought about something his lawyer had said, or about something I'd said to Nico, or about something he or I had done years before that needed to be addressed *right then and there.*

My emotions shifted by the minute. One day I would feel bitter: *All those worthless, wasted years. All that effort to be happy together. What was the point of this marriage?* Another day I would feel guilt: *Look what I've done. I've hurt everyone. I've ruined everything.* Then I was the victim: *This is all his doing. He's ruined my life, and he's ruined the kids' lives, too.* Then I was angry, raging about the man who threatened to take the things I most cherished—children, friends, home. And in moments of clarity, I became remorseful, mourning the loss of my family, remembering the times Nikolai and I had been partners, when we'd been on the same side. In those moments I would feel complete and unmitigated sadness. All our shared memories, our love for Alex and Nico, the time spent with his family and with my family, our professional ups and downs—all of these experiences were *ours.* We had lived them together. And although I wanted the whole horrible mess of our marriage to be over and done with, part of me wanted the whole horrible mess to reverse itself, to rewind. I wanted go back to the beginning and live it all again. I wanted to be free of him, but I wanted to keep him, too.

This contradiction was at the heart of everything I did and everything I thought in those weeks. I couldn't accept the idea of losing my family, and so I continued onward as if I weren't. I didn't call the lawyer that Hadrien had recommended, and I didn't make plans to move out of

La Commanderie. We were splitting up, but nothing, nothing, was going to change.

I didn't realize how cracked this line of thinking seemed until my friend Gretta, a German woman who lived in a house off the rue Droite, stopped by one afternoon. She was married to a talented chef named Jules, who had made many dinners for Nikolai and me at their home. I invited Gretta to sit down at the outdoor table, in the shadow of the *micocoulier* tree. She lifted her infant son from a carrier on her chest and set him on the flagstones, letting him crawl after the cats, who regarded him with the same wariness they reserved for Fly. Gretta had a daughter Nico's age, and the girls played together after school and on the weekends. We'd become close in the past year, and I was sure that Nikolai had stopped by their place to tell Gretta and Jules about our problems.

When I returned with two cups of coffee, I noticed Gretta looking over the table, her brow furrowed. The table was littered with ashtrays and empty wine bottles, the remnants of Nikolai's evenings of drinking and chess playing. Lord had become a regular visitor, and the two of them were going through the wine cellar, drinking off the best bottles, cleaning out whatever Nikolai had not taken with him on his Easter trip.

I began to clean off the table. "Nikolai must have had friends over," I said.

Gretta stopped me. "Listen," she said. "I have

something to tell you, and you will probably not be very happy to hear it, but it is important that someone tell you what's happening."

"What's happening?" I said, as if I there were nothing at all out of the ordinary going on in my life, as if it were just another sunny afternoon in the Midi with two women having coffee in the shade. *Luxe, Calme et Volupté.*

"There are things that Nikolai is saying about you," she said, giving me a serious look. "In the village."

The tone of her voice chilled me. "Nikolai has been at your place?"

"He came three times in the last week," she said. "He stays up drinking with Jules." She looked uncomfortable but continued. "I'm not going to repeat the details, honey, but he's saying things about you that strike me as . . . well, they just don't *seem* like you. Honestly, I don't recognize the woman he's talking about." She bent over and wiped her son's nose. "I know what it's like to have people gossip about me—we live in a small town, after all, and people always talk—but those people are not my husband."

"What is he saying?" I asked.

She bit her lip. "It is like you're the devil or something—the most evil woman in the world. He comes to our place and starts complaining about you and goes on about how you are mentally sick, an alcoholic, suicidal. He talks about how you've ruined his life. He says things about you that are totally unbelievable."

"Like what?" I said, feeling my stomach clench. I had some clue about what he was saying, but I wanted to hear *her* say it.

"About your *character,* darling. About your abilities as a mother. He says you have a drug problem that keeps you from being a good wife. He says you're frigid, but then he turns around and says that you are a slut. He isn't making much sense."

"I must be both," I said, sarcastic. "A frigid slut."

"I don't believe what he says anyway. I know you, and I'm not blind: I can see the truth for myself." She looked at me a moment, as if trying to decide something. "But you know, if he keeps doing this routine around the village, people are going to start listening to him."

"He's angry," I said. "He's trying to hurt me. Isn't it obvious?"

She looked at me and raised an eyebrow. "He's making his stories pretty believable."

I wasn't sure I wanted to know, but I asked anyway. "How?"

"Last night he came to our house and told us that you had a history of having affairs. When I told him I didn't believe him, he took out a piece of paper. It was an e-mail you wrote to a man named Jack. I read it. It looks pretty bad for you, darling."

"That is an old e-mail," I said, realizing suddenly that Nikolai had been planning this. He'd saved the e-mail so that he could use it against me one day, and I had to admit he'd used it to great effect. Although the incident with Jack had been one night of partying, Nikolai had turned it into a full-fledged duplicitous affair. "That happened years ago," I said lamely. "And it wasn't actually *an affair.* It was just a stupid fling."

"And this new guy?" she asked, referring to Hadrien.

"That's a different story," I said. "I met him with Nikolai when we were in Paris in March."

"Anyway, it doesn't matter. People have new relationships. It's natural. But he's saying that you've been sneaking around on him for your entire marriage."

"He doesn't just want to divorce me. He wants to humiliate me. He wants to make sure that I can't go anywhere in this village again."

I put my head on the table and closed my eyes. It was one thing for the village to know we were splitting up, but it was another for people to believe I was a bipolar, alcoholic, suicidal nympho. I was so mortified that I wanted to crawl into bed and stay there for a week. I had always been sensitive about what other people thought of me. Consciously or unconsciously, I'd stayed within irreproachable feminine boundaries: the good wife, the good mother, pretty but not tasteless, sexy but not flamboyant, in control but not controlling. I shouldn't have cared if people judged me, but I did care, especially when the information they had was so one-sided. Surely people in the village understood that a love story is a duet. Sometimes in sync, sometimes out of rhythm, but there are always two voices. There was Nikolai's story, and of course there was mine.

"I didn't come here to upset you," Gretta said, rubbing my hand. "I'm here, darling, because I want to tell you that you need to wake up. I know you want to pretend this isn't happening. It's only natural, but you need to fight back."

"How?" I said.

"Do you have a lawyer?" she asked.

I shook my head. Although Hadrien had been urging me to call the lawyer he'd found, I hadn't been able to actually dial the number. I was stuck, frozen, unable to move forward to do anything that would make the situation real.

"So you must call a lawyer *today,*" she said. "As soon as I leave. You shouldn't have to go through this by yourself. Get help. You aren't the only one who has had a bad breakup."

Gretta was right. I needed to defend myself. I needed to stop living in Neverland and get help.

"This is a small place," she said. "Everyone knows everything. Even if you don't say a word, they know."

"Believe me, I see that."

"And people are always harder, more judgmental, with women. A man can do almost anything and get away with it. But a woman? Never. If you don't defend yourself, they'll burn you at the stake."

I wasn't spending time out in the village, but I wasn't completely alone either. After Andy left, I spoke to my mom on the phone many times each week. I also called Diana in London and my friend Laura, who lived in New York City. These women had been through divorces—Diana was still going through her divorce, and Laura had been divorced ten years before. Together they gave advice and support that kept me from sinking even deeper into isolation. Laura was a lawyer, a mother of two, and she understood exactly what it felt like to be in my shoes. Laura's ex-husband had suffered mental-health issues, and she stressed that these problems had only become worse during their divorce. "There is no rational way to discuss things with a man like that," she'd said. "It's black or white. You're his perfect goddess or you're his worst enemy. A narcissistic personality makes everything into a personal attack. When he feels you've turned on him, he'll go for blood. You could offer him every last dime you have, you could give him full custody of your kids, and he'll want more, because it isn't about finding a solution—it's about his ego."

Diana phoned me from London to tell me she

had consulted her psychic, Yolanda, about my situation. Diana had consulted Yolanda in the past about her own divorce, and had told me that the woman had an uncanny ability to see these kinds of situations clearly. Diana gave Yolanda the basic information about me and Nikolai—birthdays, the fact that we had a child, and that we were having relationship troubles. I had never consulted a psychic before, but at that point I was interested in hearing anything that might help me to understand what to do next. Yolanda sent the following assessment of the situation:

> The meeting in Time and Space between Danielle and Nikolai happened only so that they could create the child.
>
> At this point they do not have a common path together. If they manage to achieve a peaceful existence and do not get divorced and everyone has their own private life, that would be fine. If not, they will be better off apart. (That is if they are formally married.) If they are not married, they are practically not together. If at this point they manage to get over their EGOs, they will give the child a chance to go very far. The child is a gift from God—a soul which has come into this world for art, for Love. The child is overly sensitive, and there is a danger that if at the moment they

do not manage to get over themselves, they might put her into such a state of stress that she will shut down. The child has very abstract thinking, and with parents, between whom there is peace, love and harmony, she could show the world what she is capable of. Of course, I write all this with an "if."

At this point they really do not have a common path together, and splitting up would lead to a calm environment. If the child has not been christened, she should get christened. The bond between the child and the father is very strong. Why hasn't the child taken the family name of the father? I am just curious.

Neither you nor I could give advice to Danielle. She chooses what to do.

As a whole, if they can survive 2012 and 2013 without divorcing and to live together in peace, from 2014 they can get close again. The choice is theirs.

Diana and Laura were very different women, but they both urged me to get the financial situation under control. Nikolai and I had joint bank accounts, we owned the house together, and all our assets were mixed. Beginning with his trip to Bulgaria by way of Venice, he was burning through a lot of cash.

My mom was worried about money, too, but she was more concerned about the living arrangement. "Has he moved out yet?" she would ask when she called from the States. She had been getting updates about the situation from Andy when he was still in Aubais, and she knew how emotionally tense the breakup had become. "It's clear to me," she said during one of our calls, "that one of you will need to leave that house. Like *now*."

"His lawyer told him that if he leaves, I can take legal possession of the house," I said. "So he says he won't go."

A few years back, a childhood friend had been killed by her husband during an argument. He'd hit her over the head with a lamp. She died of head trauma, and the husband went to jail. This was the unspoken benchmark of how bad things could get.

"Then you need to get out of there," she said. "It's not safe."

"But the kids are here. I can't abandon them during this. And if I leave, it's the same thing: He has possession of the house."

"So you're both squatting?"

"We're both squatting."

"Well, better safe than sorry," she said, worry filling her voice. "People go out of their minds during a divorce. You need to make a clear separation. If you're alone together in that house, anything could happen."

• • •

Not long after Andy left, our separate domains of La Commanderie solidified into two distinct territories. Nikolai's territory comprised the entire first floor: his office, my office, the window-lined salon with the piano, the downstairs kitchen, and the dining room. Mine was the second floor, with the kids' rooms, the attic playroom, the master bedroom, and the makeshift upstairs kitchen. Although the kids roamed between the floors and had access to the courtyard whenever they wished, I didn't go to the first floor if I could help it. I used a back stairway that led directly to the garden to get outside, and I only went to the courtyard when I was certain that Nikolai was gone.

One afternoon I decided to clear out all of Nikolai's belongings from the second floor. I set about removing his clothes from our closet and packing them in a duffel bag. As I folded his cotton dress shirts into a crisp pile, I noted that I'd chosen almost all these shirts. I remembered buying the purple-and-black-striped one in Paris the year before. I loved shopping in Paris, and I'd had fun buying it. I had worried over the size and the fabric, wondering if the color would be right for him. I realized, as I threw the shirts in the duffel bag, that he hadn't actually worn many of them. Lots of them still had the price tags attached. I had liked the shirt with the purple and black stripes, but maybe it hadn't been his style.

I grabbed a stack of jeans and threw them into the bag. The Vilebrequin swim trunks I'd bought on clearance, all his socks—matched or mis-matched—I dumped in. T-shirts. Underwear (boxers and briefs), sweatshirts—I removed every last piece of clothing that was in our closet until his half was empty. I pushed my clothes over to his side, spreading them out, letting them luxuriate in all the space. It was so strange, so unnatural, having such an empty closet.

The duffel bag was heavy, as if I'd zipped a cadaver inside. I dragged it down the hallway to the stairs. I passed the Paris-Lyon door, descending the stone steps, letting the bag thud as I went. The steps were worn to a gloss from hundreds of years of feet passing up and down, and although I had walked them many times, I was always careful not to slip, especially after I'd fallen when Nico was in Bulgaria. I knew from experience that it was a long, hard drop to the bottom.

I'd planned to leave the bag outside Nikolai's office door and go back upstairs, quick and quiet, before he had the chance to come out. But as I dropped it, something strange caught my eye. There, carved into the wood of his office door, was a series of symbols:

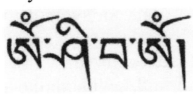

I studied them, trying to recognize the strange shapes. They were not letters or even pictures, but a strange script I couldn't read. I looked at it sideways, back to front. Suddenly I understood: These were Tibetan words. I had seen such symbols in the Buddhist texts Nikolai had on his altar and in the books in his office. I squinted at the symbols, wishing I could understand their meaning. Maybe they were some kind of prayer, or wish, or mantra. I couldn't know for sure, as I didn't understand Tibetan and had no access to a Tibetan dictionary.

Suddenly the door swung open and Nikolai stood before me. He looked as if he hadn't slept for days—his black hair stuck up in all directions, and his face was pale and puffy. He had dark circles under his eyes. He reeked of smoke and sweat. I glanced over his shoulder. There were bottles of wine everywhere, ashtrays overflowing with pipe tobacco, books and papers spread on the floor. There were pillows and blankets on his couch and a pile of dirty clothes thrown in a corner.

"What do you want?" he said, glancing down at the duffel bag.

I pushed it to him—*These belong to you*—and pointed to the carved symbols on the door. "What's that?"

He stared at me, confused.

"The door," I said. "What in the hell is that?"

346

"What does it look like?"

"Vandalism."

"It's not vandalism," he said, his nostrils flaring. "It's protection."

"Protection from what?"

"From you."

"Do you think I'm going to break down your door?" I asked.

"Protection from your psychic attacks."

I considered this phrase a moment. *Psychic attacks*. Nikolai was telling me that he'd carved a Buddhist mantra into the door of his office to protect himself from my psychic attacks.

"I don't even know what's involved in a psychic attack," I said.

"You should. You do it all the time," he said. "Even when you don't realize it. Your mind creates the attack, and I feel it in the air."

"Like pheromones?" I asked.

He started to close the door. I put my foot in the way. I wasn't done yet.

"This is an *antique* door," I said. "You can't just ruin it like this."

"Does it look like I care about the fucking door?" he replied, bending to pick up the duffel bag. It was true. He didn't look like he cared about the door. He didn't look like he cared if he carved up everything we owned, or if he emptied our bank account, or fucked up our kids, or destroyed all our friendships. He didn't care if he dragged himself in the mud, so long as I was dirtier at the end of the struggle.

Nikolai was gone—the Citroën was not parked in the courtyard, and his office door was locked shut—when I rounded up the kids. "Who wants to go to Sommières for ice cream?" I yelled down the hall. They emerged from their bedrooms. Alex put on his shoes and seemed ready to go, but Nico seemed uncertain. Since they had returned from Bulgaria, Nikolai had a habit of keeping Nico under his watch at all times. I couldn't know for sure, but I suspected that he asked her to report to him all her actions when she was with me, as if I might do exactly what he had done: Steal her away when he wasn't looking. The thought had crossed my mind. I could load both kids and Fly into the car, drive away from Aubais, and never look back.

But that wasn't the plan. Today we were only going for ice cream. Alex tucked a book under his arm, and Nico slipped on some sandals, and together they followed me out to the car. But when I went to open the gate, it wouldn't budge. The gate was heavy, and I'd always had some trouble with it, but now it wouldn't move no matter how hard I pulled. I tried again, putting my weight into it, but it didn't slide an inch. I was about to ask Alex to help when I saw something stuck under the bottom of the gate: There was a board wedged into the groove between the gate and the ground. Someone—it wasn't too hard to guess who—had worked it under, jamming the door closed. I squatted down and began working the wood out, tugging and prying at it, mumbling, "Does that motherfucker really think he can block me in the house with a piece of wood? I'm not that easy to lock up." A splinter slid under my fingernail, and I scraped my knuckles on the gravel, but I managed to tug the board free and toss it aside. *Freedom,* I thought as I unlatched the gate, lugging the heavy doors open.

But as the door swung back, I saw a streak of silver glinting in the afternoon sun: It was the Citroën, parked in front of the gate, blocking my car from leaving. I couldn't take the kids to Sommières for ice cream if I couldn't drive through the gate. Absolute pin.

I looked at the car for a long moment. My mother's Toyota Celica had been the exact same shade of silver. I remembered the time, just after my parents split up, when my father had yanked out the spark plugs of my mother's Toyota. It had been the dead of winter, the streets covered with snow, the worst conditions in which to be carless in Wisconsin. *I paid for that car!* my father had yelled, shaking the spark plugs in his fist. *I'll be damned if you'll drive it!* My mother said nothing, but she turned and walked off into the snowstorm, disappearing in a white haze.

"Why did Dad park the car there?" Alex asked, scrunching up his nose as if trying to solve a bizarre riddle.

"I'm not sure," I said, leaving the gate open and walking into the downstairs kitchen, enemy territory, where I pulled out a box of Petit Écolier cookies from a drawer. I'd wanted to talk to them over ice cream, but milk and cookies would have to do. I put the cookies on a plate and poured out two glasses of milk.

"Sit down a minute, guys," I said.

Nico took a cookie and said, "Are we going to have another one of your *talks?*"

"Are there so many?"

"Like *so* many," she grumbled, biting into the cookie. They were her favorite, and we always had a box or two in the cupboard.

"All the time," Alex agreed. "You're always asking how we're *feeling.*"

I hadn't realized I'd been doing that, but now that they mentioned it, I could see I'd been checking in with them about their feelings a lot more than usual, like every day.

"It's a good question to ask," I countered. "It's important to be able to talk about how you feel."

"I *feel* like going back upstairs to play Sims," Alex said.

"Actually," I said, "I just want all three of us to be able to talk to one another."

350

Nico and Alex exchanged an *Oh, my God, Mom* look.

"I know this isn't easy. You're brother and sister," I said. "You two need to stick together."

"Actually," Nico said, "Alex is not my *real* brother."

I stared at her, stupefied. We'd never made this distinction in the past, and Nico had never said anything even remotely like that before.

Alex looked hurt. "I am *too* your real brother," he said.

"My dad is not your dad, and so you're not my *real* brother," Nico said. "You are my *half* brother."

I couldn't help but wonder if this was Nikolai's doing, his new strategy. Divide and conquer. If he could sever the connection between Nico and her brother, he could take her more easily. It would be easier for her to leave her brother behind. It seemed to me that he was ripping apart the seams of our family, stitch by stitch, until all connections were gone.

"Do you know, Nico," I said, "when you were a newborn baby, Alex was one of the first people to hold you after we came home from the hospital. I have a picture of him with you in his arms. And do you remember who helped you learn to ride your bike? It was Alex. And who shared a room with you in Providence, before we came to France? Alex again. He's always been with you, Nico. That makes him your real brother."

"What if I told you that you're not my sister, Nico?" Alex said, and the pain in his voice shot through me. She had really hurt him. "How would you feel then?"

Nico gave Alex and me a confused look.

"The people who love you and who are here for you are your family," I said. "That's what's important."

Also important was that I didn't re-create my past in the present. I found myself comparing my divorce with my parents' divorce more and more, trying to tease out lessons and wisdom from what I'd witnessed as a child. I didn't want to repeat their mistakes. When my parents separated, it felt like being pulled apart, stretched between my mother and my father until my ligaments snapped and my muscles ripped and my limbs tore. After the divorce I had collected my damaged self and stitched her back together, but I was always weak at the scars. I didn't want that to happen to Alex and Nico. I would do anything to protect them. Even if it meant giving them up.

While their father was living downstairs, and our life was veering off into the strangest of territories, I tried to make things seem as normal as possible for Alex and Nico. I took refuge in our routines, the ones I had worked so hard to establish. Every day they sat at the upstairs kitchen table and finished their homework, ate *le goûter*, and read *Le Petit Quotidien*. Every night I made sure they had baths and kisses at bedtime. We played board games and read stories as Fly, our stubby guardian, sat by the Paris-Lyon door, his ears prickling up every time he heard something in the stairwell.

Alex and Nico needed a normal life, and a normal life meant that there could be no crying in front of them, no speaking on the phone about the divorce within their hearing, no bad-mouthing Nikolai in front of them. Normal meant keeping up appearances—keeping myself clean, well dressed, and functioning on a basic level—while in reality I felt incapable of getting out of bed every morning. Normal meant no phone calls with Hadrien when the kids were around, no mention of Hadrien, not even the slightest hint that there was someone in the world named Hadrien. Normal meant being strong for them when I barely had the strength to keep myself going.

The Saturday afternoon in the fourth week of the standoff, I'd shut myself into the bedroom and was talking to Hadrien. Nico and Alex were out in the courtyard playing Ping-Pong, and so I thought it was safe to give Hadrien a call. We spoke every day, often for hours at a time. He called late at night, after the kids had gone to bed, and I would be hurled into another dimension, one of understanding and friendship, one filled with jokes and tenderness. We talked about everything and began to know each other more deeply. I discovered in these long conversations that he was caring and emotionally articulate. He could voice what he felt and help me express what I felt, too. But above all he was warm. And this warmth was what I needed after my long, frozen marriage.

Normally I would have waited until after the kids went to bed, but we had something important to discuss. Hadrien had called my lawyer for an update. I had finally hired a lawyer in Montpellier, and as my French was not good enough to allow me to understand all the legal language, Hadrien had begun to translate the finer points of the negotiations as they progressed. What I wanted remained the same: for everyone to stay in Aubais, or at least in the general area, so that Alex and Nico could live with both parents, keep their friends and their school. Nikolai didn't want to stay in France. At first he said he wanted to move to Bulgaria. Then he told me he was planning to move back to Providence. Then he changed his mind again. Now he planned to go to Sofia, as originally planned. He wanted a lump-sum payout for his part of the house, plus alimony and child support.

Recently Nico had come to me to say she wanted to live with her dad. He had already promised her a big room in an apartment by a *patisserie*, and a dog like Fly, and a wide-screen

TV, but now he was taking a new approach. "Daddy says he can't live without me," she said, her eyes wide with concern. "You have Alex. If I don't go with him, he won't have anyone." Nico was nine years old, and she should have been spared this kind of emotional blackmail, but there she was, telling me her father wouldn't make it without her.

I knew firsthand how powerful, how magnetic, the allure of a wounded parent could be to a child. My father had been deeply hurt by my mother, and the twelve-year-old Danielle had made a calculation similar to the one Nico was making: My dad needed me more than my mom did. It hadn't occurred me to that my mother had a different way of suffering, that she hid her pain from me. My father had put on a bigger show, and he had won my sympathy. Now, years later, my daughter had been put in the same position.

"Nico says she wants to live with her dad," I said to Hadrien.

"Do you think that's best for her?"

"No," I said. "Of course not. He isn't equipped to care for her. But what choice do I have? Drag her through a custody trial? It's too much for anyone, let alone a little girl. What a nightmare."

"Well," Hadrien said, "your lawyer thinks you should give him what he wants financially. And if you let Nico go with him, he's ready to accept a buyout of the house. It is important to note that a custody agreement can be overturned. The financial agreement, however, cannot."

"So," I said, thinking this over, "if I agree to his terms and let Nico go to Bulgaria now, I can come back and reopen the custody case later?"

"Yes," he said. "And you will have stopped him from destroying you financially. There's always the option of going back for Nico later."

Suddenly I heard something push against the bedroom door. I walked over and opened it. Nico jumped, her big brown eyes going wide with wonder. "Mama!" she said. "You scared me!"

"Call you later," I said to Hadrien, and disconnected my call as I steered Nico inside my bedroom. "Hey there," I said. "Were you waiting for me?"

"Yes," she said. She looked at the floor, and she held herself very straight, very rigid, as if she were preparing to dive into a deep, cold swimming pool. I'd noticed that her posture changed when she was with Alex and me. She became stiff, unnatural. My exuberant little girl would become deliberate, careful, as if her words were memorized, her gestures rehearsed. Maybe it was the strain of the divorce. I didn't know. I only knew that Nico was not the same child she'd been two months before.

"Were you waiting for me a long time?" I asked, wondering how much she'd heard.

Nico nodded, recondite, but didn't say anything.

"Why didn't you just knock?"

"I don't know," she said, shrugging. She sat on the edge of my bed.

"I was on the phone," I said, sitting next to her. "Did you hear me?"

She looked at me, wide-eyed, and shook her head. Then, realizing that she'd been caught, said, "Well, a little."

"Did your dad send you up here to listen to me?" I asked.

She shook her head again, with less conviction. I was sure she'd heard much more than a little, and I had to wonder if Nikolai had sent her spying at my door.

"It's okay," I said. "I won't get mad if you tell me."

She looked up at me, and I knew I could push her to tell me everything that was going on behind the death-mantra door. I knew, with just the right words and just the right looks, with a few promises and hugs, I could extract the enemy plan. She wanted to please me, just as she wanted to please her father. But could I go that far? Could I use my child as an instrument of war? Was anything in the world worth that?

"No," Nico said. "Daddy didn't send me."

I took her in my arms and hugged her. Her father and I had always been the ones there to keep her safe. But now it wasn't outside forces that threatened her. Now I needed to protect her from us.

The spells that had begun with the burning of my hair on his altar and progressed to the Tibetan mantra knifed into his door continued during our standoff. I would look at my phone and find messages like THE GYPSIES WILL HAVE YOUR SOUL! and I WILL MAKE SURE YOU ROT IN HELL FOR ETERNITY! I would find, interspersed between these messages in English, the Tibetan symbols that Nikolai had carved into his door:

When these symbols first appeared on his door, I had no way to understand them. But now Nikolai sent them to me in a digital format, and I could translate them for the first time. Using my iPhone, I copied the symbols from the text message and pasted the phrase into an online Tibetan dictionary. The definition that came up was: "The seed syllable for the Body of all Buddhas. Die, lifeless, dead, deceased, depart, expire, passed, appeasing, death, quietude." Maybe these symbols could have been interpreted in a number of ways, but to me they were nothing less than a message of death and destruction. They were threats, death threats, curses and dark spells, incantations for my death. He wanted me to die, to become lifeless, to decease, to expire. He wanted me dead.

Every time one of these threatening messages came to me, I went into a tailspin. Had he actually paid Gypsies to put a curse on me? I remembered what he'd told me in Bulgaria—that people often got revenge by hiring Gypsies to cast spells. What did it mean that he would make sure I rotted in hell for eternity? Were these curses something he'd learned in India? What could they do to me? What if it were more than a curse? Maybe he was sending these threats with a more literal intention. Maybe he was planning to kill me himself.

I went to my computer and began searching for statistics, hoping to calm myself down. There was nothing to worry about, I told myself. People got divorced all the time without actually murdering each other. My parents hadn't killed each other. In fact, they'd never touched each other, just yelled a lot. I reminded myself that Nikolai and I were both educated human beings, both with master's degrees, both with many books published, the parents of small children. We were the type of people who used words to solve our problems, not the type of people out to slaughter each other.

But what I found only served to make me more anxious. According to the Web site of the Department of Justice, around 30 percent of women murdered each year are murdered by a husband or boyfriend. One-third of all women murdered! Men, it turned out, were murdered by their wives or girlfriends around 4 percent of the time. One man out of twenty-five! According to these numbers, Nikolai was much more likely to murder me than I was to murder him.

But statistics could not describe us. We had never believed we were like other couples. That was why we'd fallen so hard for each other to begin with. We believed we were special. We didn't need to play by the rules. We made our own rules. We were reckless, hurting the people we loved—Z and Sam and Rada and Alex and Nico—to get what we wanted. I had always believed we were exceptional, but now I saw that we were just your run-of-the-mill egotistical assholes.

Late one night, after the kids were asleep and before I called Hadrien for our nightly talk, I ran a bath, undressed, and sank deep into the hot water. It was the only time of the day that I felt removed from the battle, when I put down my shield. I turned the lights off and lit a candle in a corner, letting it cast a low and inconsistent glow across the porcelain tub, the stone floor, the large, liquid mirrors. Running my fingers over my body, I felt the bones jutting through the skin, sharp and unnatural. One foot floated up, rising like an iceberg in a sea, then the other foot. The big nail of my right toe hung askew, loose and blue. Two small nails on my left foot had already fallen off. I didn't know if I'd stubbed my toes or if stress and malnutrition had caused them to fall off, but my toenails were peeling away, as if they no longer wished to remain part of my feet.

After my bath I looked in the mirror and saw the woman I'd become in the past weeks. There were two deep moons of blue under my eyes. My skin was pale, parchment white, nearly transparent. I was sleep-deprived, underweight, and frazzled. Later, after I'd left the fortress, I had a series of blood tests at the Georges-Pompidou Hospital in Paris and found that I had become severely anemic. I would take iron supplements, start sleeping through the night, and eventually my strength would return. But at the time I didn't believe that the transformation arose from a physical problem. I believed it was a spiritual one. The toenails, the dizzy spells, the bruises, the thinning hair—these were signs that I was under psychic attack. The words "die, lifeless, dead, deceased, depart, expire, passed, appeasing, death, quietude" worked their way into my consciousness, and I found myself whispering them, repeating them, as if praying. Praying for my own death. I was sinking under the weight of the curse, growing weaker every day, withering away under his black magic. Of course the spell had no objective power. Its only power was in its ability to work its way into my head and infect my thinking, to make me believe that it existed, to spook me. If I didn't believe in its power, it would disappear in a puff of smoke.

But in the bath I didn't want to think about curses and spells. I just wanted to float in the warm water and imagine that I was far away from the fortress, far away from my life and the seemingly insoluble problems that lay ahead. Far away from the quickly unfolding divorce and all the back-and-forth between his lawyer and my lawyer as they negotiated an agreement under Article 230 of the French Civil Code, divorce by mutual consent, *divorce amiable.* Far from the guilt I felt about what I was doing to Alex and Nico. Far from the judgment and condemnation of people—Lord and Lulu and Jules and Yana and Ivan and everyone else—who didn't understand that I had been pushing a boulder up a hill for years and who now, as it rolled back and flattened me, blamed me for the reverse momentum.

I didn't want to think about any of that. I wanted to think about Hadrien, the man who made me laugh, the person whose voice helped me forget everything. He was clean of this mess. He had never been to the fortress, had never walked over the cracked tile in the kitchen. Had never seen ghosts. He didn't even believe in ghosts, and—come to think of it—neither had I until I'd stepped into this house. He was sane. He was kind. He was free of this poisonous place.

I sank deeper into the water, the heat lapping at my chin. The room was still, tranquil. I put a washcloth over my eyes and leaned back against the cool porcelain, rubbing the knots out of my neck. My mind drifted through the house. I imagined each room, envisioning the kids' rooms, the attic playroom, the piano in the salon, the Paris-Lyon door, the stone stairwell with its steps as smooth as river rocks. I saw myself walking down the steps. My feet were bare and, suddenly a hundred little hands slipped out from the darkness, tiny translucent fingers straining to grasp my ankles as I walked. They were trying to grab me, to trip me, so I would tumble down, down into the shadows.

A strange sensation, cool as a breeze, swept over my skin. The mistral, which often slipped through the edges of the old casement windows and cut through the steamy air, wasn't blowing. No, the night was still and tranquil. It was something else, a presence, a consciousness lurking in the ether. I opened one eye and saw a leg. I opened an eye a little more and saw a hand. Opening both eyes, I found Nikolai standing above the bathtub, gazing down at me, his black clothes cut from shadow, the whites of his eyes glowing in the candlelight.

I gasped, terrified, and sat up. I clutched my knees to my chest, covering my body, sending a wave of water splashing over the edge of the bathtub. How long he'd been there, staring at me as I floated in the bath, I didn't know. It could have been thirty seconds or five minutes.

"What are you doing in here?" I asked, holding my legs tighter to my chest.

Caught in the candlelight like an otherworldly creature, Nikolai stared at me. "I wanted to talk to you," he said, his voice gentle, sweet. It sounded like the voice of the man I'd met long ago. "Can we talk?"

"What in the hell are you doing?"

"You're so beautiful," he said. His expression was pained. He found me beautiful, and this hurt him. "I wanted to tell you that."

"You can't just come in here when I'm in the bath!"

"You're my wife."

"Get out!" I screamed, splashing water at him. "Get out of here. Now!"

After Nikolai left the bathroom, I wrapped myself in a towel, walked to the hallway, and locked the Paris-Lyon door between the first and second floors. Each night after, I would repeat this gesture, fastening the lock on the door, securing my territory. The Paris-Lyon door became our new border, a definitive point of entry to our respective jurisdictions. I was in Paris. He was in Lyon.

Each night after the second floor was locked securely, I made the rounds, checking that the windows were latched, turning off the lights in the living room, turning on the night-light in the hallway, kissing Alex and Nico a second time, and adding more water to Fly's bowl. It was a nightly ritual, like scouting the perimeter of a campsite to make sure the wolves were at bay.

After the surprise visit during my bath, I taped my scorpion protection mandala to my bedroom door and put the *mala* mirror in the hallway, between the kids' doors. I had no idea how to use the *mala*, and so I hung it at eye level, so as to check my teeth or my hair should the need arise. The *mala* refracted light across the stone floor, sending wavering white disks over our feet when we walked downstairs. A mystical disco ball.

Although Nikolai had given me these gifts months before, I had never taken the time to learn what they were meant to do. My astrological sign is Scorpio, which is probably why he'd given me the scorpion protection mandala, but I'd never understood the symbolism of a scorpion. One afternoon before the kids came home from school, I looked it up online and found that the main symbol of the scorpion is defense. A Web page about animal symbolism described the scorpion physique as threatening and tough, with its hard, protective exoskeleton meant for attack. The page went on to describe the scorpion method of defense: It holds its stinger high and arched, ready to strike. Another Web site suggested that the essence of the scorpion is like a ninja in black, swaying its tail, silent in its approach, striking quickly and decisively. After I read this, I felt a shot of confidence every time I walked past my scorpion protection mandala. I was a badass scorpion ninja warrior, ready to sting.

But despite my tough exoskeleton, I was taking a beating. Earlier that afternoon I'd fainted on the stairwell. I was climbing the steps, and suddenly everything around me began to drain away. I felt my fingers slip along the smooth wooden banister, a slow, sweeping release, and then I hit the floor. I woke a few seconds later with Nico screaming my name, standing over me, afraid. Nikolai heard the commotion, stepped out of his office, glanced at me lying on the floor, turned, and walked away, leaving Nico to help me stand up. I spent a long time with her afterward, assuring her that I was okay.

And I was. Sort of. By nightfall I was sore everywhere, and a new bruise spread over my shoulder. I collapsed into bed, exhausted and stiff. Turning on my lamp, I picked up a book from the stack near my bed. I tried to concentrate on the words on the page, but they seemed to move and bend, dancing away before I could read them. I willed myself to concentrate. Reading was freedom. It allowed me to imagine I was someone else, a character in some other story than my own. It was my nightly escape. And so I fixed the letters with my eyes, reading the same sentence three times without retaining the meaning before giving up and putting the book down.

I turned the light off, and the room swept away, leaving only the faint outline of a chair, a glint of curtain, a nightstand. Suddenly Fly ran to the side of my bed and barked. His ears stood alert, and his curly tail had gone straight. Something wasn't right.

I slid out of bed and walked barefoot to the bathroom, to check the window. It was secure, and so I walked out into the hallway, my feet slipping on the cool stone. It was after midnight, dark and quiet. Nothing seemed to be wrong—there was not a sound coming from Alex's and Nico's rooms—and yet Fly was pacing around frantic. I bent to scratch the scruff of his neck, trying to calm him down, when suddenly a shadow passed over me, fluttering upon the floor like a black curtain. I looked up, and the shadow coalesced into a tall, dark figure wavering behind the glass door. My heart leaped to my throat. This phantom being, this black shadow standing on the other side of the Paris-Lyon door, staring at me with fixed eyes, was my husband. How long he'd been there and what he wanted, I didn't know, but I understood one thing: No matter how well I barricaded myself upstairs, no matter what divisions I made between us, he was not going to leave me alone. I met his gaze and held it for a long moment. He didn't blink; he didn't turn away. His expression was uninflected. He stared at me with the frightening neutrality of the walking dead.

• • •

I lay in bed, anxiety pulsing through me. I waited, expecting Nikolai to materialize from the darkness, to hover like a bat in the dark over my bed, watching me as I slept. But I couldn't sleep. I lay awake, going in circles in my head about what in the hell was going on. Why had he been there, standing at the Paris-Lyon door, watching? Had he been there for a long time, or had he just walked up seconds before? Had he been in a trance, sleepwalking, high on valerian tea? Was he trying to get past the door or just observe us? He'd stood there watching me. Our eyes locked for thirty seconds or so before he turned and floated back down the stairs, silent, gray as a zombie.

Finally, after an hour of such questioning, I crawled out of bed and walked through the rooms of the second floor, trying to bring myself down, trying to reassure myself that I wasn't in a horror novel: *This man is your husband. He is not a zombie. He is not a vampire, not a killer, not a ghost. This is a man, not a monster. A man.*

I went to the Paris-Lyon door and unlatched the lock. A depth opened below me, a cavern of emptiness, a cascade of thick space in the darkness. I grasped the slippery wooden banister, guiding myself down the steps, down into the dark. I wasn't going to turn on the lights. It might call someone, or *something,* to the stairwell, and I wanted to be alone.

The stone chilled my bare feet as I stepped into the hallway on the first floor. Everything was still. No light shone from under Nikolai's office door. He was asleep, or maybe awake in the darkness. I tiptoed past the Death-Mantra Door, walking softly through the salon. Moonlight shone through the windows, over the piano, pooling on the gray floor. Wading through the shadows, I made my way into the kitchen, to the oldest part of La Commanderie, where the thirteenth-century wall rose over the trapdoor. I should have been afraid, but there was nothing at all to fear, and so I knelt on the cool marble floor and lay down over the trapdoor, my cheek against the broken tile. "Come back," I whispered, hoping the woman in blue would hear me. I needed the sense of calm, the comfort, she had promised. I needed her guidance. "Come back. Come back." But there was no stirring in the air, not the least sign of her existence. There was nothing at all except my voice, whispering.

Later, in my bed, I slept fitfully, my mind filled with terrors. I floated in and out of a place where pictures blossomed like poisonous flowers behind my eyes. I stood with Gretta at the center of the village as a woman was led to a pyre. The villagers circled, waiting, and suddenly there was music and dancing. *C'est la Fête Votive d'Aubais*! Everyone gathered together to watch the running of the bulls. There was smoke and the smell of tar. A jester called out to the crowd, *Back to your houses, the plague, the plague!* And then the baby appeared, walking timorously over the roof tiles toward the edge. One leg, then the next, it strained onward to its end. There was nothing I could do to stop it. Nothing at all.

I woke the next morning, a blanket of light streaming over the bed. I hadn't slept much, and I was exhausted and disoriented, the world of my mind spilling forth into the real world, the two bleeding together, liquescent realities. Where was I? In a dream? In a story? I tried to put all the pieces back together again: *You are locked in the top floor of your house, waiting for your husband to leave, holding out to keep your home and your kids, holding out for some kind of agreement. This is just a bad dream. It will disappear when you open your eyes and wake.*

On school mornings I pulled myself out of bed and made the kids breakfast. I would make French toast or crepes filled with Nutella, putting everything out on the table before I woke them. They would sleepwalk to breakfast and become conscious halfway through their first crepe, the sugar kicking into their systems. By the second crepe, they would be telling me what was planned at school that day. Fly would be wagging his tail and waiting for one of them to throw his toy squirrel. I would make a second latte at the

Nespresso machine. It was times like these, when my children were happy and energetic, that I felt the most unsettled: How, in the middle of this cataclysm, could everything seem so *normal?*

On one such morning, I made the crepe batter—two eggs, flour, milk, and a pinch of salt—and then set the table. I'd just put the orange juice on the table when I looked out the window at the courtyard. Fly and the cats were roaming under the *micocoulier,* but there was something else that caught my eye. Parked near the Citroën sat Jett's blue Peugeot. I was so surprised that I opened the window and looked closer, as if to verify that it wasn't a hallucination. Jett's car was never on our property anymore. We had virtually stopped talking in the past six months. She hadn't called me back earlier in the week when I'd phoned. In fact, during our last conversation she told me that I shouldn't call to discuss Nikolai with her, that she wanted to remain neutral. She said she was staying out of our war. But there was her car, right there.

Nikolai had people at the house all the time. Once when I made the mistake of venturing out into the courtyard during aperitif hour, Lord confronted me about the fact that I had filed a report at the gendarmerie. Apparently my complaint had been read aloud at the *mairie,* at some sort of local council meeting, and everyone in the village knew the details of Nico's time in

Venice and Bulgaria. "Shameless," Lord said, shaking his head. "To embarrass your husband in public in such a manner. Utterly shameless." I understood what he was saying. He believed that I should keep quiet about what was happening. He believed that I should keep up appearances and pretend that everything was fine. I knew that this was the way things were done in many marriages, because that was how things had been done in mine for the past decade. But I wasn't interested in appearances. Trying to shame me into silence and secrecy.wasn't going to work. Not any more. I told Lord to go to hell and walked back into the house.

There had been a party in the courtyard the night before, but I hadn't known that Jett had been there. I wiped my hands on a dish towel and walked down the hallway, past the Paris-Lyon door, down the stairs, to the first floor, Nikolai's turf. There were voices coming from Nikolai's office, low whispers, and the thought entered my mind that there had been something strange, something a little too familiar, about Nikolai and Jett over the past year. Since I'd been away for my book tour, actually. I remembered a weird moment the previous fall when Nikolai had told me he didn't want Jett coming to the house anymore because she was "too desperate"—or was it that her pheromones were too strong? I could hardly recall. Of course. *Too many pheromones.* Overwhelming.

I knocked twice on the death mantra and turned the doorknob, fully expecting it to be locked, but it wasn't: The door opened a crack, just enough for me to see a nude Nikolai as he lunged at the door, slamming it shut in my face.

I knocked again, and for some reason—probably shock creating a short circuit in my brain—the only thing to come out of my mouth was this totally absurd sentence: "Can you two keep it down? I'm trying to make the kids breakfast!"

After some scrambling and urgent whispering, the door was flung open and they shot out like bulls in a rodeo. Nikolai shoved me backward, and Jett ran from the office down the hall, Nikolai scurrying after her, slamming the door to the salon shut and locking it. *Click.*

I pulled myself up from the floor, stunned. It took a minute or two—as much time as it took me to get back upstairs—before I realized that I had just found my not-yet-ex-husband naked, in his office, with my so-called friend. I expected as much from Nikolai, especially now that we were officially separated, but *Jett?* How many afternoons had we drunk wine and bitched about men together? How many times had she encouraged me to leave Nikolai so that I could be free?

I was going over in my mind what had just happened, as if double-checking the numbers of some complicated algebraic equation: I heard them, then I knocked, then I saw him *naked,* and then I informed them that they needed to be quiet because I was making breakfast. This calm, mathematical approach was a cover, a kind of shock-absorbent cloak that I put on to buffer me from the explosive core of red-hot pain and anger that was rising through me.

Back upstairs, the kids were waking. "Good morning, sunshine," I said to Alex, trying to put on my best happy-mommy face while feeling that I'd been punched in the gut.

"What was all that noise?" Alex asked. He usually woke early and probably had been awake when I was making the crepe batter.

"Just your dad locking the doors again," I said. "You want crepes?"

"Yeah!" Nico called from her room, where she'd been listening. "With Nutella!"

"And whipped cream."

"Let's see what we've got," I said.

I made the crepes and began serving them when the full extent of my anger hit me: My friend is in my husband's—okay, my *estranged* husband's—bed, and I am *making crepes?* What was wrong with me? I needed to go back there and get that woman out of my house.

But when I went downstairs, the door to the hallway had been locked. Nikolai must have bolted it from the other side. And so I marched up the stairs, back through the Paris-Lyon door, through the kitchen, passing the kids—*Brush your teeth when you finish with your crepes*—stomped out the back door to the terrace, took the exterior staircase down into the courtyard—which was littered with empty wine bottles from Nikolai's soiree the night before—to the table under the *micocoulier* tree, where Jett and Nikolai were drinking coffee and smoking.

They looked painfully hungover, their clothes wrinkled, the buttons done up the wrong way. The rage I'd felt just moments before drained away. I felt a sudden urge to sit down and have a cup of coffee with them. Despite the fact that I hated them at that moment and wanted to kill them both, I had once liked, even loved, these people. Considering that I was falling in love with Hadrien and wanted to sign a reasonable divorce settlement with Nikolai, I might even have welcomed the whole arrangement. I wanted my husband out of the house, and this was one way to do it. But as I walked up to them, Jett lifted her liquid black eyes and said, "Did you come to make us breakfast, too, darling?"

That, for me, was it. All my cloaked anger rushed forth. I folded my arms across my chest and said, "Get the hell out of my house, you fucking whore!"

Nikolai and Jett stared at me, stunned.

I turned to Nikolai. "How could you sleep with *this woman* with our children upstairs?"

Nikolai stared at me, his mouth agape. He

stammered for a moment before saying, "I was sick last night, and she stayed to help me."

"Stayed to help you?" I said. "Help you with what?"

"He was having a panic attack," Jett said.

"Nothing happened," Nikolai added.

"Ha!" I said, my voice rising. "Jett the nurse! Do you know the same Jett that I know? I suppose you've been doing this nurse routine the whole time."

"Danielle," Jett said, her voice condescending, *"please."*

I gave Jett a look, and the look said, *Shut up or I'll rip that lascivious tongue from your mouth.* "I suppose you've told him everything I've told you over the years. How perfect. Two spies in bed together!"

Jett started shaking her head. "I didn't tell him anything—"

"I told you to *get out of my house!*" I screamed, and Jett half stumbled from her chair. They were really, truly, pathetically hungover. It must have been some night.

"You know what? Actually, bring *him* with you. You can have him," I added as she started to walk away. "Because I don't want him. *I am having the most fantastic sex I have ever had in my life!*"

Nikolai stood up, knocking his chair over. "So you admit it!"

"Yes, I admit it, I have slept with Hadrien, and he is *fabulous* in bed," I said. *"Incroyable."*

Nikolai looked at me, his face growing redder by the second.

The public acknowledgment, sotto voce, that I was having amazing sex after years of a nearly celibate marriage was so liberating, so freeing, that I said it again, rephrased. *"I had no idea sex could be so good!"*

"You fucking bitch!" he screamed. "Don't you think you've done enough to ruin my life already?"

"Get out of here!" I shouted, pointing to the blue gate. "Out!"

"Demon!" he screamed, coming at me, his face beet red as he pushed me backward. Jett, who had edged closer to Nikolai, made a grab for him and pulled him back.

"Come on, Nikolai," she said, taking him by the arm and steering him away. "Calm down. Let's go. Calm down."

Nikolai stared at me as Jett escorted him to her car. And as he left, his eyes fixed upon me with pure hatred, I could have sworn I heard him whispering the death threat he'd carved into his door, the mantra he'd texted me: *"Death, decease, terminate, extinguish, die."*

After Nikolai and Jett had gone, I collapsed into a lawn chair. The confrontation left me utterly exhausted. For half an hour, I couldn't move, and so I stared into the courtyard, at the roses in bloom, the waxy gloss of the oleander's flowers, the huge dead cypress tree with its resident crows circling. The whole courtyard was blooming with flowers. The jasmine vines were a mess of tangled fragrance, the smell of rosemary hot in the air. It was paradise, the same paradise that had drawn me to the village to begin with. I couldn't help but remember our first day in Aubais, and how I had fallen so deeply in love with the sounds and smells and colors of our village. It hadn't been just the beauty of the place, but the promise of what we could become there that had so moved me. I loved it still, loved it the way one loves a prized childhood memory, one that has been slowly warped by the act of growing up.

I didn't have many close friendships at that point in my life, partially because I'd moved around so much and partially because I spent my free time with my husband and children. But when I made a friend, I cherished that friendship, and truly cared about that person. Jett was one such friend, and I had liked her despite her flaws. I had liked her when she gave me the wrong advice and when she was judgmental about my life. There'd been many reasons to be critical of Jett, but I hadn't been. I had trusted her. Jett was my closest friend in Aubais, and her betrayal cut deep.

Eventually Alex and Nico came downstairs, their

backpacks on, ready to go to school, but I told them to go back upstairs and play, that they were staying home. "Today," I said magnanimously, "is a free day." Alex and Nico looked at me in astonishment. Never in the history of their school experience had I said such words. But the day a woman finds her husband—*estranged husband*—in bed with her friend is an instant holiday for everyone. "Go play!" I said, and when they stared at me as if I'd gone mad, they were not far from the mark.

When I finally left the lawn chair, I found my phone and composed the following text message: AS YOU PROBABLY KNOW, NIKOLAI AND I ARE GETTING DIVORCED. IT IS NOW CLEAR TO ME WHY: I JUST FOUND HIM IN BED WITH MY FRIEND JETT. I then sent this message to all our friends in the village and beyond, friends I hadn't spoken to in months, friends who might or might not have known that Nikolai and I were having trouble at all, let alone getting divorced.

I sent it out and waited for responses to roll in, the waves of support and sympathy, the indignation. Never mind that my message was total nonsense: Nikolai and Jett could have been sleeping together for months, but that wouldn't have been the cause of our divorce, just as Hadrien wasn't the cause. *We* were the cause of our divorce. Our pride and stupidity. Our selfishness and egotism. It was our fault. We'd been building walls to keep the world out, but we were our own worst enemies.

I checked my phone, looking for responses to my text. Surely this information would bring everyone back to my side. Soon they would stop by the house to see if I was okay, and my friends would hug me, and we would laugh and cry together at the horrors I'd been through these past weeks. They would understand that I'd been wronged. I would be vindicated.

The first message to come back was from Lulu. It was short and to the point: JETT? I DON'T BELIEVE IT FOR ONE SECOND.

I read the message again. *She didn't believe it?* What, did she need pictures of his naked ass? Well, I didn't really believe it either, and I had actually witnessed it, so I couldn't blame her for doubting. I wrote back, BELIEVE IT. I JUST WALKED IN ON THEM.

I would have written a more extensive response to Lulu, but another text came in from a female friend, an artist who had been through a difficult breakup some years before. She wrote the comforting: ☹.

I sent a quick text to Hadrien, who had heard about Jett during our phone conversations, saying, JUST FOUND NIKOLAI IN BED WITH JETT. He responded, LOL. AT LEAST IT WASN'T THE BABYSITTER.

The babysitter. That was someone I had not

included on the group text message. I took out my phone and was retyping the message, customizing it for Sveti, when it struck me how ridiculous this whole thing had become. I had just sent an electronic newsblast about Nikolai's sexual activities to all our friends, people who could not have cared less about what Nikolai or I do in the bedroom. I was doing exactly the same thing that Nikolai had been doing to me for weeks—using our friends as ammunition for our battle. It was a mistake, a big mistake. I'd written the text in a rage, and I regretted it. I'd written the text in weakness and fury. I'd tried to embarrass Jett and attack Nikolai, and in so doing I'd made myself into exactly the kind of person I didn't want to become.

In the beginning, when we'd discussed the separation over our bottle of Bollinger 2002, I'd wanted an honorable separation, one in which we admitted that we'd failed but acknowledged the fact that we'd tried to build something beautiful and meaningful. I'd wanted to keep the idea of our efforts—our noble and outsize and romantic and ridiculous attempt at love—safe. I'd wanted to separate as friends and go on with our lives in dignity. And while Nikolai's behavior over the past weeks had hurt me, I had been determined to stay above it: I was not going to stoop to his level. I had intended to walk with my head held high. But now there I was, in the mud with him, thrashing and sinking in the filth.

• • •

The rest of the day slipped by me in a haze. I lay in bed, thinking and staring at the ceiling, going into a spiral of anger and self-recrimination. I wanted to get out of bed but couldn't move. A weight pressed on my chest, pinning me to the mattress. My limbs were heavy, filled with lead. The thought of facing the outside world was too overwhelming to imagine. The weight on my chest became heavier and heavier. It was a stone, fixing me in place as the dirt rained down, cold and hard, covering my legs and arms, my face. Soon I would be hidden. Soon I would be buried alive.

Looking out the window, I saw that the sky was already growing dark. I'd spent the entire day stewing in my own acid, dissolving in the wash of anger and shame and guilt. The worst part was that kids had surely heard us fighting. They had probably witnessed me screaming at Nikolai and Jett and the two of them leaving together. No doubt they'd heard me crying in my room after sending the text message and heard the crash when I'd thrown my phone at the wall. I wanted to justify my childish actions, to blame Nikolai or Jett for them, to find some excuse for what I was doing to Alex and Nico. But I knew, even then, that I was hurting them. My actions had consequences. They were not subject to revision. And this knowledge made me feel more worthless than I'd ever felt before.

If only it had been possible for the ghost of my future self to appear in that darkening room and kneel at the side of the bed to comfort me. She would have stroked my hair and whispered in my ear that everything would be okay. She would tell me that it was not too late to salvage my life, that Alex and Nico would be fine, and I would be fine, too. But maybe I did hear some hint of my future self, just a whisper through the layers of time, because even at that weak, dark moment I was grasping for her, longing for what she would teach me. I would fight to find her, this woman of the future who had burned away the layers of self-pity and delusion until just the blackened, roasted marrow remained. One day I would meet that woman, and we would embrace as sisters who had descended to hell and emerged new.

By the time Nikolai came upstairs later that day, I had worked myself into a state of despair. He knocked on the Paris-Lyon door, calling my name. I pulled myself out of bed and unlatched the chain lock, so we stood together at the doorframe, he on one side, me on the other. He wore the same clothes he'd had on that morning, the wrinkled T-shirt and the black jeans and sandals. He looked every bit as hungover as he'd been when he left, only now he wasn't screaming and cursing me. Now he was calm. He smiled weakly. "I'd like to talk to you."

"Talk?" I said, looking up at him, not quite able to trust the gentle tone of his voice. It was the exact opposite of the cacophony of emotions banging in my brain, the atonal noise of self-recrimination and anger. "Talk about what?"

He shoved his hands into his pockets. "This standoff needs to end."

It needs to end. The phrase swirled in my mind. My thoughts were growing circular and frenetic, until they seemed less my thoughts than an echo in the house. *It needs to end.*

"We need to end this," he said.

Yes, we need to end this. His voice was hypnotic, soft as a whisper. Had he actually spoken? Or had I imagined his voice telling me that this needs to end? *It's karma. It isn't even our choice. We've been waiting many lifetimes for this chance.*

"Danielle," he said. "Do you hear me? We need to end this. We need to sign an agreement."

Something in my brain snapped. I said, "How is this *ever* going to end?"

"We need to make an agreement," he said. "Now. Here."

"Tell me—does it look like we're ever going to agree about anything?"

He gave me a tender look, one that reminded me of the Nikolai I'd known ten years before, the pleading, vulnerable Nikolai. The Nikolai who had begged me never to leave him. "I don't know what you're holding out for," he said. "I mean, even if you get what you want—and you stay here in the house with Nico and Alex and I leave—how are you going to manage by yourself? This is a medieval village. It isn't easy to be alone here. You've lost all your friends. You can't even open the gate without help, let alone manage this house."

I began to laugh, a sick and twisted laugh, as if I'd been inhabited by a demonic spirit. "Do you actually think you're such an enormous help to me? You're even less helpful than Sveti. If Sveti works twenty-five hours a week, that will be way more assistance than I'm getting from you. I'm going to be just fine."

"But Sveti won't work for you," he said, and it seemed to me that his eyes filled with a joyful glimmer, as if he'd been waiting for just the right moment to tell me.

"What do you mean?" I said, leaning against the Paris-Lyon door, in need, suddenly, of its support. "Sveti's going to stay on and help me."

"She didn't tell you?"

"Tell me what?" I said, my stomach sinking.

"I'm sorry," he said with fake contrition. "But she told me last weekend that she wasn't going to be working here anymore. She doesn't want to be in France after the divorce. She said it was too sad to see kids suffer through this kind of thing."

I stared at Nikolai, speechless. For some

illogical reason, Sveti had become the linchpin of my plan to stay in France. In my mind I could lose my husband and still manage my life there if I had help from a strong, competent woman like Sveti. For some reason the possibility of finding someone else to help me was unthinkable. In my unbalanced state of mind, I had fixated on Sveti. In truth my feelings had nothing to do with the nanny, but at that moment, in that state of agitation, Sveti's abandonment was all I could see. I needed her, and only her, or everything would fall apart.

"Are you telling me Sveti quit?" I was losing control, and words came out as one astonished proclamation.

Nikolai nodded.

"How could she quit *now?* This is when I need her the most. She knows that I can't stay here alone without her!"

"She's decided to go back to Bulgaria with me," he said, a smug look crossing his face. Or was it a compassionate look? I was so twisted up, so trapped in my head, that I couldn't tell the difference anymore.

"What is she going to do in Bulgaria with you?" I asked.

"I'll need her help with Nico."

"But you're not going to have Nico," I said. "Nico is going to be here!"

"My parents hired Sveti," he said, looking at

me with contempt (or was it concern?). "She's Bulgarian. You can't even speak to her. Did you really think she would stay here with you?"

Something about the way Nikolai said this, in combination with the noxious emotional fumes of my day, ignited in me. "You stole her!" I shrieked. "You fucking stole Sveti! You *know* I can't make it without her, and you convinced her to leave!" I was incensed, illogical, all the emotions I had battled to hold back spilling forth. For the first time in all the weeks we'd been fighting, I burst into tears in front of Nikolai, big gulping sobs. "How could you do this to me? How could you fucking steal the babysitter?"

"Wait a minute," he said. "Hold on, I didn't *steal*—"

"This is all part of your master plan, isn't it?"

"Master plan?"

"To take everything piece by piece. To rip away my entire life until I have nothing, *nothing* left!"

"Danielle, I—"

"What else do you want from me?" I shrieked. "You've brainwashed my daughter, you've stolen all my friends, you've taken over the house. You've spent our savings. You drank my wine. You're waging a smear campaign against me. What else do you want, Nikolai? Do you want my limbs, too? My arms? Maybe a few fingers?" I thrust my hand into his face, as if offering the fingers to him. "Take them! I don't need them anymore." I was working myself into a frenzy, going up and up and up, raising the tone of my voice until I was the mezzo-soprano of an Italian opera, screeching with pain and betrayal. "Tell me: What else do you want now that you've stolen Sveti?"

Nikolai started to back down the staircase, slowly, gingerly, regarding me with the frightened look of an animal at the end of a rifle.

"Congratulations! You set out to destroy my life, and now you've done it."

"Hold on," he said. "Just hold on a minute."

"You really want to *win* this game of chess?" I walked to the edge of the staircase and flung one leg over the slippery wooden banister railing, feeling the pull of gravity under me. The drop was deep, onto stone, a long, hard fall. "Why don't we get this whole thing over with right now!"

"Danielle," Nikolai said, taking another step backward on the stairs. "Calm down."

"And one day when our kids ask what happened to their mother, you can tell them that you drove me to this, you drove me to kill myself. *Is that what you really want? To kill me?*"

"No," he said, still backing down the staircase. "I don't want that. Just calm down."

I threw my other leg over the slippery balustrade and felt, suddenly, a weightlessness, the vertiginous sensation of being a bird perched on the ledge of a skyscraper. I could just let go. I could do it. I didn't even have to think about it. It would be as easy as relaxing, letting my muscles retract. Easy. Easier than crawling back over the railing. Easier than facing Nikolai. Easy.

Nikolai rushed forward, grabbed me by the shoulders, and pulled me backward, onto the floor. We lay there locked in a tense embrace, his arms around me, and for a moment I thought he would lean over and kiss me. The monster would die. The princess would awake. Instead he pulled away, gently, and walked down the stairs. I heard the door slam as he left. I lay there broken, almost wishing that I had in fact jumped.

The White Queen

After what happened on the stairs, I called Hadrien. For the first time in the two months that we had known each other, I couldn't get through to him. I left a message and then sent him a text: CALL ME. Fifteen minutes later he called back. There was noise in the background, and I realized he was at a bar in Paris, one of those exotic places that free people frequented. He was probably with friends, doing all the things that normal people do when they're not going insane in a thirteenth-century fortress.

I explained what had happened in the stairwell, how I was scared to stay at the house any longer, how desperate I felt to stop the fighting, how sick and alone I felt. It had all gone too far. And, worst of all, I didn't trust myself anymore.

"I wish Andy were still here," I said.

"Wait," Hadrien said. "When Andy was there, Nikolai didn't harass you?"

"He's smart enough to behave himself when someone else is around."

"I think I have an idea," Hadrien said.

"What kind of idea?"

"A plan," he said. "I know that you think you need to stay and hold your ground, but it's clear that this approach is not going to work. You need to do the opposite. You need to leave."

"But what about Alex and Nico?" I said. "I can't leave them here."

"Bring them with you," he said. "Take them out of there."

The idea was so simple when he said it, but when I tried to work out the logistics, it seemed impossible. "But how? He won't let me leave with them."

"I'm coming down there to break you out."

I started laughing, and it felt so good, so normal. This is who I was, not that crazy person in the stairwell. "You're planning a jailbreak?"

"Listen, it sounds crazy, but I think I know a way to get you and the kids out of there."

"Out?" I said. It was what I most wanted, to leave the fortress with the kids, to go somewhere safe and calm. I could hardly imagine such an idea. "Where are we going to go?"

"With me," he said. "I'm going to get you out of there. I promise."

I met Hadrien at the train station the next morning after the kids had gone to school. For the past weeks, Hadrien's voice had become a lifeline to me, and I knew its every nuance and register, how high or low it pitched, how he sounded when he whispered or laughed. But his body was another story. It had been many weeks since I'd been alone with the flesh-and-blood Hadrien. He was taller than I remembered, healthy, strong, and well rested, while I was pale, thin, and skittish. He took me in his arms and kissed me, as if he didn't notice that I was a shadow of the woman he had met in Paris.

Seeing Hadrien made it clear how damaged I was, and not only because of the anemia. After two failed marriages, I wasn't sure how to go forward in a new relationship, especially with a man who was so unscathed. Yes, he'd had a bad breakup of his own, and he was in some ways more mature than me, but I was a mess. I couldn't imagine being good for him. He offered noble, selfless love, and I wasn't sure I had any right to accept it. Didn't he deserve someone without my history of failure, a healthy woman with a clean, unsullied past? I wasn't sure I could venture another close relationship, and I was absolutely certain I couldn't be with a man who depended upon me for his happiness.

In the years after we met, Hadrien and I would stay together, but I would need a lot of time before I was ready to give myself fully to a relationship. He didn't rush me. There would be long stretches of time when we were apart, months when he was in France and I in the United States. In these periods without him, I learned what it meant to be alone. I grew to be a person who cherished freedom, who looked forward to a solitary weekend or a vacation with Alex and Nico, no man in sight. When Hadrien and I were together, I honored my need to be a singular person in relation to another singular person. Gone was the fusion-bound love of my marriage. Gone the suffocating dependence. We kept our finances separate; our friends were often different. I realized I couldn't be happy in a relationship unless I was happy alone first. It seemed like such a simple idea, but it had taken me a long time to learn it. Yet once I did, I became stronger, more realistic about my needs. There was no room for artifice. I wanted only what was essential: honesty, trust, and respect. I could no longer tolerate anything that was not love. And because of this new way of understanding love, I could build a future on solid ground.

"What happened to you?" Hadrien asked, looking me over with care. He ran a finger over the fresh bruises on my arm and shoulder.

"I think those are from falling down the stairs," I replied. "The second time."

"One or two bruises, maybe," he said. "Not this many."

I'd forgotten how bad I looked, with my dark circles and my thinning hair.

Hadrien turned an arm over, inspecting the bruises more closely. "Is he hitting you?"

"He's attacking me with his thoughts," I said, without stopping to think of just how crazy this would sound to a sane person like Hadrien. "He's performing *psychic attacks* on me. All his hate is working into my body and eating me from the inside, like cancer."

He looked doubtful, then worried. "You need to see a doctor."

"I don't know if I'm going to be able to recover from this."

"Of course you will," he said. "But first we need to get you out of here."

"You told me you have an idea." I was ready to hear his plan. I couldn't think of anything that would work, and I'd been trying to figure it out for weeks.

"Come on," he said, taking my hand. "Let's sit down."

We walked to a café and sat on the terrace, looking at Nîmes's ancient Roman amphitheater, where we ordered two cafés au lait. "At first," Hadrien said, "I thought I would come in there and escort you out, but that would have been difficult alone, and so I asked a few friends of mine if they would come with me, and they agreed, but then I realized it could get violent, and too scary for your kids. And so I began to think of other ways, ways that were not so . . . obvious." He leaned over the table. "You said that he changed his behavior when your father was at the house?"

I nodded. "He was still angry when Andy was

there, but he tried to hide the worst of his behavior. He doesn't want a confrontation, especially with another man."

"He wants to push you into signing the agreement, but he doesn't want witnesses. He doesn't want anyone to know that he's bullying you."

"Well, it's more complicated than that," I said. "Since the separation Nico has said that her brother isn't really her brother, and that she's part of a family of vampires with special powers, and that she should live in Bulgaria because she's going to have her own dog, flat-screen TV, and private *patisserie.* Alex hates being around us so much that he's practically living in the attic. The stakes are higher than just my mental health."

"So what if you have someone else there, to witness what's happening?"

"Are you suggesting that you move in?" For a moment I imagined me, the kids, and my young Parisian boyfriend all living upstairs, guarded by our ferocious pug, Fly.

"Not me," he said, smiling his beautiful smile, the one that seemed to eclipse everything around him. "Someone else. Someone older, someone powerful and—most important—authoritative, so Nikolai feels that his behavior is being watched."

I turned the idea over in my mind. He was right. I could actually get through this with someone there to help shield me. If Andy—or someone like Andy—came to the house, Nikolai wouldn't have the courage to be so aggressive. He might even call his parents, and they would swoop in and carry him away to Bulgaria. He might disappear. The kids and I would be free. The standoff would be over.

"It's a great idea," I said, taking the last sip of my coffee. "But who?"

Hadrien's mother, Eve, arrived on the next train. We walked back to the station to pick her up and found her waiting on the platform. Dressed in a classic jacket and pantsuit, her blond hair short and styled, Eve was sophisticated in the way I'd imagined all Frenchwomen were sophisticated. I tried to imagine her walking through our village, with her leather bag and her chic haircut, and I had to smile. She would stick out as much as, even more than, I did.

"*Bonjour*," she said, kissing her son and then me. She looked me over, her blue eyes narrowed, taking in her son's new girlfriend. I tried to imagine what she saw: a sickly, bruised woman of thirty-eight with straw-dry hair and purple rings under her eyes. This was the woman who had stolen her beautiful son's heart.

Hadrien threw Eve's small rolling suitcase into the back of my car, and we drove to the center of Nîmes, near the market, where we parked and went to a restaurant for lunch. Eve asked questions in rapid, elegant French: How did I come to live in France, and what was my background, and what was my profession, and how old were my children, and wasn't it hard to be so far from the United States? I tried my best to explain everything that was happening, sketching the big picture in my imprecise French: bad marriage, angry husband, big old haunted house, can't leave without my children.

"This is what I propose," Hadrien explained. Eve would accompany me home and stand witness. Nikolai, of course, would have no idea that Eve was Hadrien's mother. He would think, when I brought Eve to the house, that she was just a friend visiting from Paris. I would tell him that she was a work acquaintance and that she was in the area and so I'd invited her to stay for a night or two. My French editor had done the same thing the summer before, so it was not outside the realm of possibility. If I looked at it from Nikolai's point of view, I could see that bringing my boyfriend's mother to our house would be an awful betrayal. It was sneaky and went against my original intentions of being dignified and cordial. But at that point I had no choice. My reserves of strength—mentally and physically—were gone. After what had happened in the stairwell, I was afraid of what would happen if our bitter holdout continued. For my own sanity, and for the safety of my children, I had to leave that house. And I wasn't leaving without Alex and

Nico. If bringing Eve into our feud would get me out of there, I was ready to give it a try. And besides, everything had been fair game for Nikolai—our friends, our kids, our money. It was time for me to take a stand.

Sensing that I had doubts, Hadrien switched to English, a language Eve couldn't understand. "What is it?" he asked. "Is something wrong?"

"Does your mom know the mess she's getting involved in?" I said. "We're on the verge of killing each other in there. I don't think she realizes how tense it is."

"I explained everything this morning," he said. "She understands."

"I doubt that," I said. "It is seriously horrible at my house."

"*Qu'est-ce qu'il y a?*" Eve asked.

"*Ce n'est rien, Maman,*" Hadrien replied. He turned back to me and said in English. "You don't understand. She *wants* to help you. She went through a bad divorce before she met my father. My older brother is actually my half brother, and she had to work out custody problems with his father. She understands how hard this is; she sees a lot of herself in your situation. When I told her what was happening, she felt very strongly that she needed to help you."

"*Français, s'il vous plait,*" Eve said. "*Est-ce qu'il y a un problème?*"

"Are you sure you want to get involved in this?" I asked Eve, switching back to French.

She looked at me a long moment and said, "I am doing this for you, but I am doing this most of all for my son. He called me late last night and said, 'Can you buy a train ticket to Nîmes for the morning? I need your help.' He had mentioned you to his father and me a month ago. I knew he was involved with you, but now—after he asked for my help—I see he loves you, and real love is a rare and precious thing. It is something we must fight for. You're in a bad situation. *Bon.* It can happen to the best people. Let me help get you out of it."

Eve used the *vous* form of "you," meaning "both of you." She wanted to help Hadrien and me, together.

I didn't know how it was that I deserved her help, but I knew right then and there that Eve was a tough woman, a queen ready to fight. Her help was a gift, one that came to me from the ether, and I must accept it. As she finished her dessert and asked for the check, I couldn't help but wonder if I would be strong enough to do what Eve was doing now. In the future, when Alex or Nico needed me, would I be brave enough to go in fighting? Would I evolve from a bumbling princess to a powerful queen? I hoped so.

"This is the plan that Hadrien worked out," she said as we walked out to the car. "I will come with you to the children's school at five o'clock."

"He'll be there," I said, realizing even as I said it that I was making a fist, clenching my teeth. My whole body had gone tense at the thought of seeing Nikolai.

"*Bon*," she replied. "You will introduce me to him. You tell him that I am an editor friend from Paris. This is not a lie. I *am* an editor, and I *do* live in Paris, and we are now friends. I will say that I wanted to see your home and to spend some time with you. All true. Then we go back to the house, where at some point in the evening I will invite you and the children to come with me to Paris for the weekend."

"Nikolai will never let me go to Paris for the weekend," I said. "Not with both kids."

"I will make the invitation in front of your husband," Eve said. "And you will accept the invitation in front of your husband. It will be a *fait accompli*. We will buy the train tickets online, and it will be settled. He will have no choice but to allow you to leave, or to argue with me about it."

"And if he doesn't let me leave with Alex and Nico?"

"I will suggest that we call the police, as it is surely illegal to hold a woman and her children captive in her own house."

"I'm not sure," I said, although I knew two

things: Nikolai hated the gendarmerie, and he lost his bluster in front of a witness.

"I can be very persuasive," she said. "I think he will agree to my invitation."

Hadrien leaned back in his chair. "It's our Trojan horse. You bring a harmless editor into your home, but she is not harmless—she is actually the weapon who will help you win the war."

I was hesitant about introducing Eve to my children, as it meant giving them the same half-truths about her identity I would be giving Nikolai, but I was absolutely certain that they should have no contact with Hadrien. Whatever he was to me at that point—lover, savior, reality check, knight in shining armor—it wasn't the right time to introduce him to my kids. I wouldn't have been able to explain who he was or what he was doing in our lives, and I didn't want to lie to them. Someday they would know Hadrien, but not now, not yet. They weren't old enough to understand what had happened. They couldn't fathom that Hadrien was like a lighthouse: He had not caused the storm, but once I found him, I could finally see how to steer out of it. And so we dropped him off at a hotel in Sommières while Eve and I went to the kids' school together.

It was a party of four waiting for Nico and Alex at the school in Sommières: Nikolai and Sveti, Eve and I. Although it was warm and sunny, the flowers blooming and the wind mild, Nikolai wore all black—black trench coat, black boots, black jeans, and his black porkpie hat. A rush of adrenaline spiked through my system upon seeing him. It was an animal reaction now, an instinct, what a cat must feel upon seeing a dog. I couldn't help it. Fear lived in my muscles, in my skeleton, in my spine. When I saw him, I saw the bat hovering over me in my sleep, gliding down slowly, slowly onto my face, the soft wings brushing my cheeks, the teeth against my neck. I saw his pale, ghostly face behind the Paris-Lyon glass. I wanted to go back to the car and drive away.

"That is your husband?" Eve whispered in my ear.

"He comes every afternoon, to pick up our daughter."

"And your son?" Eve said, a dark look crossing her features. "He comes for him, too?"

"No, he leaves Alex to me," I said. "I come here to get Alex. Nikolai is only interested in Nico now."

"*Le pauvre*," Eve said, biting her lip, and for the first time that afternoon I saw some reflection of her own divorce in her actions, the memories of her own traumatic split resurfacing.

Nikolai stared a moment, trying to place Eve. We walked up to him, and I introduced them in French, telling Nikolai that Eve was an editor from Paris. Eve looked him over, as if assessing a particularly inelegant sentence, not quite sure how to correct him. They kissed on each cheek, in the French style, although it was clear that Nikolai wanted to have nothing to do with her.

"Editor from Paris?" Nikolai said to me in English, looking at first confused, then suspicious. "You never mentioned an editor named Eve before."

"Maybe not," I said, shifting my weight from one foot to the other, feeling like an insecure teenager. "But she's in the area, and I suggested she stay with us. It's just one night. She'll leave tomorrow."

As Eve had pointed out, none of this was false. Yet of course it wasn't exactly true either.

"Thank you for having me at your home," Eve said in French, and Nikolai—who would not meet her gaze, who was wary of this outsider coming into our personal hell—only nodded, his eyes on the school door, as if Eve and I were not there at all.

Nico bounded out of the school, her backpack hanging from her shoulder, her long brown hair tied in a loose braid. When she saw our small group, she stopped short, surprised, looked from one parent to the other, unsure of what to do. Until then I'd tried to avoid conflict by letting Nikolai pick Nico up from school. The last thing I had wanted was to have a tug-of-war over our daughter in the schoolyard. But now we were both there, waiting, and Nico was faced with a choice—did she go with her mother or her father? Where were her loyalties? What did we expect of her? Eve, perhaps sensing this, stepped in front of Nikolai and me and greeted Nico with a big warm, *"Bonjour, mademoiselle*! You must be Nico! I've heard so much about you."

From that moment on, Eve was in charge. She maneuvered around Nikolai, talking merrily as she steered Nico toward my car. With a crisp wave, she told Nikolai we would see him back at the house, and when he tried to object, she ignored him. I found Alex and waved him over. He climbed into the backseat next to Nico, and suddenly I was with both my children again, the three of us together, outside the blue iron gate of La Commanderie. I hadn't expected to feel such an intense emotional response, but tears came to my eyes as I fastened my seat belt. I felt a rush of hope. It had been weeks since Nico and Alex and I had been together outside the fortress wall. It had been weeks of tension and fear and nightmares. But we were together now, in my car with the radio on, the light pouring through the windows. It felt like seeing the sun after weeks of rain, or eating a huge meal after a long fast. My children were both there, in the backseat of my car, together with me again. Eve would invite us to Paris, and we would leave Aubais. We would get through this dark fairy tale. We would arrive on the other side of the forest, happy and whole. The future opened up suddenly, like an endless ocean glittering under the Languedoc sun.

I took the long way back to Aubais, driving slowly over country roads, rolling past vineyards and olive groves, the sky bright and cloudless. We stopped by a farm stand, and I bought two huge bags of cherries, black and sweet, to take home for *le goûter.* I took deep breaths of fresh air, the oxygen tingling in my lungs like hope. For the first time in weeks, I could breathe. I hadn't felt the sun in ages. I'd been inside the dark stone walls of the fortress for so long that I'd forgotten the outside world, the bursting, fecund beauty of the south of France.

Nikolai was already in the courtyard when we returned. He'd set up his chessboard on the table under the *micocoulier* tree and was going through his moves. A bottle of wine and some wine-glasses sat nearby. I led Eve and the kids upstairs, where I sat Alex and Nico down at the table for our daily ritual of unpacking the backpacks, reading *Le Petit Quotidien*, doing homework and having *le goûter.* Eve pulled up a chair and sat between Alex and Nico, helping Alex with his impossible verb conjugations and Nico with her math. After washing the cherries and putting them in a bowl on the table, I opened the windows that gave over the courtyard, letting in sunshine and warm air. From where we sat, we could see Nikolai, phone in one hand and chess pieces in the other.

Stepping away from the kitchen, I checked my phone. Hadrien had sent me a text message. He was still at the hotel in Sommières and wanted to know what was happening. I replied, WE'RE HOME. EVERYTHING IS FINE SO FAR.

He texted back, BE STRONG.

Suddenly the landline telephone rang. Nico jumped up and answered.

"Yessss," she said, turning her big brown eyes toward Alex and me. Someone said something on the other end, and she hung up. "That was Daddy," she said. "He wants to talk to me."

"You're doing your homework now," I objected. "He can talk to you later."

"He told me to come now," she said, ignoring what I'd told her and running out of the room. "I'll be right back."

I glanced out the window and saw Nikolai staring up at us.

"Finished!" Alex exclaimed, pushing his notebooks back into his bag. "I'm going to the attic."

"Take your *Petit Quotidien*!" I said, and he grabbed the newspaper as he ran out of the room.

When Alex left, Eve turned to me. "I hope you don't mind," she said. "But I asked the children some questions about what they saw happening here."

"What kinds of questions?"

"It's important to understand how they see things. What their perspective is about what is happening between their parents. So I asked them. Alex has a very clear perspective of the situation. He understands that you and Nikolai are separating and that his father has been acting abnormal. He said you've been sad. It is your daughter who is confused."

"How so?"

"She told me that you don't want her to live in France," Eve said, looking disturbed. "That you asked her father to take her to Bulgaria. She said that you only want Alex."

"That's not true," I said. "Not at all."

"Of course not, but it's what she said," Eve told me.

Just then Nico ran up the stairs and began to gather her books and her pencil case. "Daddy says I have to do my homework with him," she said.

"But we already have everything set up here," I said.

"He doesn't want me to talk to . . ." She glanced at Eve, too shy to say her name.

"But why not?" Eve said. "We're having a nice time."

Nico furrowed her brow, looking embarrassed. "He says you're on Mama's side."

The phone rang again. Nico moved to grab it, but I intercepted. "Yes?"

It was Nikolai. "Send Nico down," he said, his voice flat and deep, without emotion.

I went to the window and saw him standing in the courtyard, his phone to his ear. "She's going to finish her homework upstairs."

"Don't tell me she's doing homework," Nikolai said. "I know that friend of yours is trying to influence her."

"Of course she's doing homework," I replied. It was true—their books were spread on the table among cherry pits and empty glasses of water.

"Do you think I'm stupid? Nico just told me that your friend is talking to her *about the divorce*."

"It's not such a strange topic," I said, still watching Nikolai. "Considering our present situation."

"I know what you're doing. I know you brought your friend here from Paris to help convince Nico to live with you. This is part of your brainwashing campaign, and I'm not going to let it happen. Keep that woman away from Nico."

Suddenly Eve appeared in the courtyard below. While I was speaking with Nikolai, she had taken the back staircase out into the courtyard, arriving at Nikolai's side just as he was speaking about her. He looked at Eve, surprised, then looked up at me, accusatory, as if I had sent her down there. Eve was smiling as she sat at the table and gestured for Nikolai to join her. He shifted his weight, uncertain of what to do. It was a surprise attack, and he was taken off guard. He adjusted his black hat. After giving me a final dark look, he dropped his phone on the table and sat down across from Eve. She poured him a glass of wine, then one for herself, and I realized suddenly that the emperor's mother was even stronger than I had imagined. She was not going to bother with small battles. She was going after the black king himself.

I helped Nico finish her homework, and when she was done, I went downstairs. Knowing that the first floor would be unoccupied, I went to the piano in the salon. I hadn't been in that room for weeks, and I missed it. The piano was glossy black, substantial. I sat on the cushioned bench and touched the keys, wishing I could play. I remembered the wonder I'd felt when Nikolai had first played the piano for me, the pleasure he gave to everyone at the piano shop in Iowa City. I remembered the way his long fingers skipped over the keys, the poise of his posture, his elegance. He was such a talented man. I had loved him for it. But this was the point where our paths would separate. There was no going back. Now it was time to move forward.

And of course we would. Our divorce would be finalized in September 2012. Within weeks of signing our custody agreement, Nikolai would leave Bulgaria with Nico and relocate to Providence, Rhode Island, where he would move in with a Bulgarian woman and her two children. Nikolai didn't tell me about his plans until after he'd bought the plane tickets, and he didn't tell me about the Bulgarian woman at all. Nico wasn't allowed to tell me about this arrangement, either, and so it became an elaborate secret. Nico was never good at lying, and I knew she was hiding something. Months later, when she finally told me the truth about her living situation, I filed a petition for custody in Providence Family Court. Nico was assigned a guardian ad litem, who represented her interests, and the custody arrangement we had signed in France was overturned, and primary placement of Nico was given to me. Soon after, my daughter came to live with me in New York City. She went to school in the West Village, and made new friends, and took ballet classes, and grew strong and smart and happy. Nikolai moved around for a few years with his girlfriend, then ended up back in Bulgaria. As of the writing of these pages, Nico, Alex, and I have not seen him for years. He disappeared from my life, as if he were no more than a dream.

In the aftermath of our separation, I was furious about how our marriage had ended. There were whole months when anger burned in me, making it impossible to even think of Nikolai, let alone forgive him. In fact, I didn't imagine that I could ever forgive him, not in this lifetime. Not in a hundred lifetimes. But a time came when the anger stopped or, rather, transformed. I remember the moment exactly. It was April 2014, and I was walking from our apartment on West Tenth Street through Washington Square Park, when I heard the quick, hummingbird heartbeat rhythm of Chopin's Prelude in B-flat minor, op. 28, no. 16. The song was coming from a grand piano set up near a fountain, below the Washington Square Arch. As the man played, his fingers flew over the keys in a way that was familiar. I stopped, not to listen, exactly, but to get my bearings. I felt disoriented, as if time were folding up around me. I felt myself return to the Iowa City piano shop in 2002, to the apartment in Izgreva in 2004, and to the courtyard of our old house in France, when Nikolai would get up, go to the piano, play for a few minutes, and then return to his chessboard. I stood for a moment, listening, inspired by the music. I put some money in the pianist's jar and walked away, feeling the layers of my life falling back into their proper order as I went.

I was almost out of the park when I began to cry. Not out of sadness but relief. It had been such a heavy burden, all that anger. Such a brutal weight could have pulled me down with it, if I had let it. I glanced at the pianist one last time, seeing him from a distance, then hurried away, the sound of Chopin at my back. As I walked, I remembered who I'd been the first time I heard that song. I remembered the young woman who had given her heart fearlessly, wholly. I remembered the magic I'd felt, and the scale of my dreams. It had been flawed, my love, but it had been beautiful, too.

An hour later I went up to the homework table and found everything as I'd left it—the conjugations and math papers, the bowl of cherries— only the kids were gone. I walked down the hall and up to the attic playroom, where Nico and Alex were at the computer, playing games.

"Where's Eve?" I asked.

"With Dad," Alex said.

"Still?"

"They're in the courtyard," Nico said. "Talking. Daddy told me to stay up here."

I went to the window and looked into the courtyard. It was true: Nikolai and Eve were still talking. A second bottle of wine had been opened and some cheese and crackers set on the table. *Had Eve made a cheese plate for my husband?* I tried to understand what they could be talking about. Nikolai was speaking with what appeared, from that distance, to be great feeling, while Eve sat, a glass of wine in her hand, listening attentively, nodding, as if in sympathy.

I leaned against the window frame, watching in disbelief as my lover's mother carried on what was clearly an intimate conversation with my estranged husband. I didn't like it. It felt wrong. I didn't want it to continue. That kind of thing was not supposed to happen. Eve was supposed to be my Trojan horse. She was supposed to sweep in, invite me to Paris with the kids for the weekend in a way that Nikolai couldn't refuse, and we were supposed to be off, Ariadne free from the Minotaur. And instead there she was, befriending my husband over a bottle of red wine.

But then, I thought, maybe Eve knew exactly what she was doing. Maybe, I realized as I looked out the window at their tête-à-tête, she had convinced Nikolai that she was on *his* side. They really seemed to be getting along well. He was talking a lot, gesturing and standing, lighting a cigarette for Eve—she was smoking with him!—before sitting down again. I had yet to see Eve say a word. Instead she left Nikolai spinning in a manic monologue, punctuated by jerky gestures—he put his hat on and took it off, he stood up and walked around the courtyard, then sat again. He was talking, and she was listening. She was gathering intelligence, making our escape easier. Not only had Eve entered the enemy camp, but from the look of it she was well on her way to full infiltration.

Nikolai and Eve remained in the courtyard while the kids and I ate dinner—reheated spinach-and-goat-cheese quiche, french fries, and chocolate pudding—and they remained in the courtyard while I put the kids to bed. Nikolai and Eve talked while I took a bath and put on my pajamas. Finally, three hours after they sat down together, Eve came upstairs. She was as white as a sheet, trembling, rubbing her arms as if reviving herself from frostbite. There was something wounded in her look, as if she'd walked out of a boxing ring. The strong, capable woman I'd picked up at the train station had been reduced to a shadow.

"What happened down there?" I whispered, letting her enter through to the Paris-Lyon glass door and locking it again.

"We were talking," she said, pursing her lips. "He had a lot to say."

"I saw that," I said. I touched her shoulder. She was trembling.

We walked to the living room and sat on the couch. Color was coming back to her cheeks. I learned later that Nikolai had told her all the things he'd been saying about me for months, but he had also spoken negatively of Hadrien, and this had shaken her.

"Are you okay?"

She shook her head. "No," she said. "It is clear to me that this man does not want to just end your marriage. He wants to destroy you, and even himself, before that happens." She took a deep breath and smiled. "I'm sorry. I'll be okay in a minute. I'm not sure I've ever been in the proximity of someone so . . . disturbed."

"He's really mad," I said.

She gave me a long, hard look. "Yes, that's true. But I don't think the anger comes from you, exactly. What I mean to say is—*yes,* he's angry about the divorce. He's furious about it. But the source of this anger, the real wound in his soul, is not from you. That comes from another place."

I took this in, remembering all the years I'd been with Nikolai, the years spent trying to understand and help him, and I knew she was right. I remembered one of his Christmas letters from 2003. He'd written that he was scared by his past, and that he couldn't erase the pain of his memories without me. I never knew what had happened to so disturb him. I never understood the cause or the depth of his wounds. He would never allow me to know this part of him. It had been walled up inside him, fortified, unreachable. It had kept me, who'd tried so hard to reach him, away.

"Pack a suitcase for you and one for the children. Tomorrow we'll go to Paris."

"Does he know?"

"You'll tell him in the morning. But we need to go right away tomorrow, on the first train. You can't stay here another day. I am not going to *allow* you to stay here another day."

And although I was ready to leave, I felt suddenly hesitant to walk out the door. It would be the beginning of a new story, and I was not sure how to live it. Our tale had been filled with romance and adventure, quests, treasure hunts, magic spells, ghosts and demons, devotion and betrayal and torture, and love. But the end had come. The gate was open. I only had to walk through it. And with that knowledge I packed two suitcases—one for me and one for the kids—and the next morning, our stubby guardian Fly in tow, we left for Paris.

Epilogue

Everything changed when I left the fortress. From Paris, I took charge of my situation. I solidified my legal position and got a handle on my finances. I saw a doctor, learned that I was anemic, and began taking iron tablets. I rented a small apartment in Aigues Vives, a village ten minutes from Aubais, where I would live until Nikolai left France. I took the first steps toward a new life.

After he was gone, I went back to the fortress. Nico and Alex were with me then, but soon Nico would leave for Bulgaria and Alex and Fly would go to the States. I planned to sell La Commanderie and needed to clean things up.

It was a mess. The day he'd moved out of the fortress, Nikolai collected cinders from the fireplace and spread them over the floors, dumped ash in the piano and on the windowsills. I later learned that this was a kind of departure ritual, a magic rite, although I never understood its purpose, other than making a mess. I could hardly face the house after all that had happened there. Thankfully, my mom flew to France to assist with the cleanup. With her help I felt better equipped for the job. We swept up the ashes and vacuumed the piano keys and sanded down the mantra carved in the door.

We cleaned out the empty wine bottles from the courtyard and the trash from Nikolai's office. And when it was done, the house was ready for the next owners, the ones who would inherit La Commanderie's treasures and ghosts after our departure.

As I was packing my closet, I pulled down a box of photos. I'd been throwing pictures into this box for years without organizing them, telling myself that someday I would put them into an album. As I sorted through the box, I saw hundreds of the moments my family had lived together. I saw Alex after his stitches from running into a pole; I saw newborn Nico at Maichin Dom; I saw the four of us at my parents' house in Wisconsin, standing before drifts of snow. There was our last Christmas in Aubais, the gifts and the food and the enormous tree, and the kids walking together on the beach at La Grande-Mott, Fly at Alex's heels. There was a picture taken in the courtyard of the fortress, the four of us together, surrounded by the protective wall, the one that had not, in the end, been strong enough to keep us together.

As I was packing up these photos, I found a letter in a sealed envelope. It was dated May 2010, but there it was at the back of the closet in 2012, waiting like a time capsule for me to open. It was a final love letter, one filled with all the talk of destiny and magic that had marked our relation-ship from the beginning. Our love, Nikolai wrote, had been like a journey, an escape into a dark forest, a place in which we hid from the ghosts of our past. He'd cast a spell on me the day we met, he wrote, but that spell had grown weaker as time passed. Magic wears off ghosts find other people to haunt, and past lives die. He hoped that we would find our way back to each other, but his magic had turned dark. Love, like miracles, could live on nothing but purity.

I folded the letter and put it into the box of photos. I wanted to keep it, just as I wanted to keep the pictures. They were a testament, a record of the life I'd lived and left behind, and I didn't want to forget them. I felt a rush of tenderness for the young woman I had once been, the woman willing to ride off into a dark forest with a sorcerer, the one who needed to believe in fairy tales. I had chased a big, beautiful dream, and while that dream had failed, I'd gained some-thing precious in the effort.

I closed the box and packed it away, knowing that someday I would want to open it again. Someday I would read his letter and see my family photos and remember the woman I used to be, once upon a time, the woman who lived in a fortress.

Acknowledgments

Thank you to Eric Simonoff, my kind and brilliant agent, for championing this book and being there every step of the way. Thank you to Lynn Grady, visionary editor and publisher, and to the whole team at Dey Street/HarperCollins for the extraordinary professionalism and sensitivity with which they brought this book into the world. At Random House Canada, I'd like to thank Zoe Maslow for weighing in. Thank you, too, to Nita Pronovost, whose early insights kept me on track. I'm deeply grateful to Sharyn Rosenblum, Shelby Meizlik, and Michael Barrs at HarperCollins, and Kimberly Burns at Broadside PR, for singing my praises. Thank you to Lucinda Treat, Kimberly Cutter, Donna Brodie, Michele Mitchell, Lisa Smith, and Bob Harris for reading early drafts and steering me clear of pitfalls. I will be forever grateful to The Writers Room in New York City, the sanctuary where I wrote (and rewrote) this book. Thank you to Ryan Evans for his wisdom. Thanks to Eric Zohn, Trina Hunn, and Michael Ruddell for acute legal advice. *Merci mille fois* to Nicolas and Yveline Postel-Vinay for giving me sanctuary. Thanks to Evan Bell and Liza DeLeon for keeping me afloat. I am the luckiest writer in the world to have all of you behind me.

I am particularly grateful to friends and family who were there during the events described in *The Fortress*, especially my parents, who came to France numerous times to help. Most of all, I am grateful to Hadrien and Eve. Without you, who knows how the story would have ended.

Center Point Large Print
600 Brooks Road / PO Box 1
Thorndike, ME 04986-0001 USA

(207) 568-3717

US & Canada:
1 800 929-9108
www.centerpointlargeprint.com